The Politics of Intellectual Property Rights and Access to Medicines

International Political Economy Series

General Editor: **Timothy M. Shaw**, Professor and Director, Institute of International Relations, The University of the West Indies, Trinidad & Tobago

Titles include:

Timothy Cadman
QUALITY AND LEGITIMACY OF GLOBAL GOVERNANCE
Case Lessons from Forestry

Andrew F. Cooper and Timothy W. Shaw (*editors*)
THE DIPLOMACIES OF SMALL STATES
Between Vulnerability and Resilience

Anthony Leysens
THE CRITICAL THEORY OF ROBERT W. COX
Fugitive or Guru?

Valbona Muzaka
THE POLITICS OF INTELLECTUAL PROPERTY RIGHTS AND
ACCESS TO MEDICINES

Mireya Solís, Barbara Stallings and Saori N. Katada (*editors*)
COMPETITIVE REGIONALISM
FTA Diffusion in the Pacific Rim

Peter Utting and José Carlos Marques (*editors*)
CORPORATE SOCIAL RESPONSIBILITY AND REGULATORY GOVERNANCE
Towards Inclusive Development?

International Political Economy Series
Series Standing Order ISBN 978–0–333–71708–0 hardcover
Series Standing Order ISBN 978–0–333–71110–1 paperback
(*outside North America only*)

You can receive future titles in this series as they are published by placing a standing order. Please contact your bookseller or, in case of difficulty, write to us at the address below with your name and address, the title of the series and one of the ISBNs quoted above.

Customer Services Department, Macmillan Distribution Ltd, Houndmills, Basingstoke, Hampshire RG21 6XS, England

The Politics of Intellectual Property Rights and Access to Medicines

Valbona Muzaka

Lecturer in Global Politics, Department of Politics and International Relations, University of Southampton, UK

palgrave
macmillan

First published 2011 by
PALGRAVE MACMILLAN

Palgrave Macmillan in the UK is an imprint of Macmillan Publishers Limited, registered in England, company number 785998, of Houndmills, Basingstoke, Hampshire RG21 6XS.

Palgrave Macmillan in the US is a division of St Martin's Press LLC, 175 Fifth Avenue, New York, NY 10010.

Palgrave Macmillan is the global academic imprint of the above companies and has companies and representatives throughout the world.

Palgrave® and Macmillan® are registered trademarks in the United States, the United Kingdom, Europe and other countries.

ISBN: 978–0–230–23529–8 hardback

This book is printed on paper suitable for recycling and made from fully managed and sustained forest sources. Logging, pulping and manufacturing processes are expected to conform to the environmental regulations of the country of origin.

A catalogue record for this book is available from the British Library.

A catalog record for this book is available from the Library of Congress.

10 9 8 7 6 5 4 3 2 1
20 19 18 17 16 15 14 13 12 11

Printed and bound in the United States of America

Contents

v

Abbreviations

AB	Appellate Body
ACTN	Advisory Committee on Trade Negotiations
ASEAN	Association of Southeast Asian Nations
CBD	Convention on Biological Diversity
CESC	UN Covenant on Economic, Social and Cultural Rights
CPTech	Consumer Project in Technology
EC	European Commission
EEC	European Economic Community
EFPIA	European Federation of Pharmaceutical Industries and Associations
EFTA	The European Free Trade Association
EU	European Union
FAO	UN Food and Agriculture Organisation
FDI	Foreign Direct Investment
FTAA	Free Trade Area of the Americas
FTAs	Free Trade Agreements
GATT	General Agreement on Tariffs and Trade
GI	Geographical Indicators
GPE	Global Political Economy
GSP	Generalised System of Preferences
HAI	Health Action International
IFPMA	International Federation of Pharmaceutical Manufacturers and Associations
IIPA	International Intellectual Property Alliance
IMF	International Monetary Fund
IP	Intellectual Property
IPC	Intellectual Property Committee
IPE	International Political Economy
IPRs	Intellectual Property Rights
IR	International Relations
M&A	Mergers and Acquistions
MSF	Médecins sans Frontières
NAFTA	North American Free Trade Agreement
NGOs	Non-Governmental Organisations
OECD	Organisation for Economic Cooperation and Development
PGRs	Plant Genetic Resources for Food and Agriculture

PhRMA	Pharmaceutical Research and Manufacturers of America
PLT	Patent Law Treaty
R&D	Research and Development
SPLT	Substantive Patent Law Treaty
TABD	Transatlantic Business Dialogue
TRIPs	Trade-Related Aspects of Intellectual Property Rights
UNCTAD	United Nations Conference on Trade and Development
UNDP	United Nations Development Programme
UNESCO	United Nations Educational, Scientific and Cultural Organisation
UNICE	Union of Industrial and Employers' Confederations of Europe
UNIDO	United Nations Industrial Development Organization
UPOV	International Union for the Protection of New Varieties of Plants Convention
USTR	United States Trade Representative
WHA	World Health Assembly
WHO	World Health Organisation
WIPO	World Intellectual Property Organisation
WTO	World Trade Organisation

Acknowledgements

One argument I make in this book is that intellectual products are best seen as social products rather than solely the result of individual efforts. The book itself lends support to this argument, for it would have been simply impossible to have completed this work without the intellectual and emotional support of so many people over the years. I should like to thank them all for their help and contribution. In particular, I would like to thank Professor Tony Payne for his enduring support and wise counsel and Dr. Tony Heron at the University of Sheffield, UK. I would also like to thank members of the Department of Politics, University of Sheffield, and of the Politics and International Relations Divisions at the University of Southampton, UK, for providing a great intellectual environment where I could discuss some of the ideas presented here. Gratitude, too, goes to the interviewees who generously gave their time to discuss some of the themes of this book with me. The usual caveats regarding remaining shortcomings apply. Professor Tim Shaw, Dr. Owain Williams, and Alexandra Webster and Renée Takken of Palgrave Macmillan have been immensely helpful in converting these ideas into final book form. My special thanks are also due to many friends and dear people who have generously given their time, love and support throughout the years. They are too many to mention here, but I should particularly like to thank my two wonderful sisters, Anila and Rovena, and brothers, Plarent and Alban, for being an unwavering source of love and kindness. I dedicate this book to the memory of my mother, Lefteria Prifti, who instilled in me the desire to learn and explore from very early on.

1
The Politics of Intellectual Property Rights and Access to Medicines: Some Empirical and Theoretical Issues

Unlike democracy, justice, human rights or climate change, intellectual property rights are often seen as legal and technical issues that are the purview of lawyers and a handful of regulators and need not concern others. But intellectual property rights (IPRs) are present and embodied in a multitude of 'things' that we use and have (or do not have because they are not available for our use or we cannot afford them). This book, for instance, is protected by intellectual property rights which you or your library are bound to respect, while my publisher, employer and I also share an agreement about how this property is managed. The music we play on our digital audio players is protected by intellectual rights and so are the films, artwork and shows we go to see. Integrated circuit designs and computer software, formulae for fertilisers and other chemical substances, new seed varieties, industrial designs, new environmentally friendly technologies, drugs used to treat all sorts of medical conditions, clinical tests, brands, trade secrets, internet domain names and most of the wines and cheeses on the supermarket shelves are all protected by some form of intellectual property rights or another. Intellectual property rights, then, are not simply legal entitlements filed away in legal texts; they empower and limit the way we live, learn, communicate, consume, create, innovate and develop. As such, how and what intellectual property rights are granted, to whom and with what consequences should be the concern of us all.

The institution of IPRs has developed over time and today represents a particular arrangement for resolving issues of control over intellectual 'goods', that is, knowledge, innovation, creativity, and the goods and services that embody them. Like the institution of property itself, that of intellectual property is complex and political. IPRs tell us who can own, control and make use of what type of knowledge and who cannot; for this reason, they are political and contested. Knowledge and innovation are a fundamental part of human history and the struggle for control over them has taken different forms through time. The current arrangement that governs intellectual property, or what is referred to here as the IPRs regime, is one particular manifestation of this historical struggle, and one which is bound to change. The current IPRs regime, that is, its principles, norms and rules, delineates the way in which knowledge is created, owned, controlled and diffused, domestically and globally. It is not difficult to make the case in the twenty-first century that knowledge is seen as wealth and as capital, the 'new capital', often deemed more important than labour, natural resources or even finance. IP laws, then, govern how this 'new capital' – knowledge – is created, appropriated and protected. With knowledge- and information-based sectors constituting the largest share of key advanced economies, how this 'new capital' is managed is obviously not insignificant to these economies, or to those aspiring towards them. However, knowledge is also a public good. It is a public good in the sense that it is inappropriable and non-rivalrous in nature. Unlike tangible property, which can be appropriated individually and thus visibly separated from the 'commons', knowledge and information are not appropriable in this way: once in the marketplace, knowledge can be used by anybody. It is also non-rivalrous, because its consumption leaves the same quantity and quality of knowledge to be consumed and enjoyed by others. Knowledge is also a public good in the sense that it impinges on the provision of other public goods such as health, education, food and the environment, to mention a few. It is precisely this dual nature of knowledge both as capital and as a public good that lies at the heart of any IP regime, whether domestic or global, and of contests over it. It captures the unavoidable and persistent tension permeating IP laws between those who seek to privately appropriate knowledge and those who seek its dissemination into the 'intangible commons', or public domain, for public use.

Intellectual property rights have been contested since their beginnings, but today we are no closer to settling controversial IP issues than before. If anything, contests over IP have become more intense and widespread over the past 25 years or so. Amongst other factors, the shift of some advanced economies from industry-based to knowledge-based economies from the early 1980s onwards, simultaneously enabled and accompanied by rapid technological developments and important ideological shifts, created the appropriate conditions for IP issues to be placed at the top of the agendas of businesses, politicians, state representatives, non-governmental organisations (NGOs) and scholars. These developments culminated in the negotiation and coming into force of the TRIPs (Trade-related Aspects of Intellectual Property Rights) Agreement at the World Trade Organization (WTO) in 1994. The TRIPs agreement is, without doubt, one of the most significant developments in the governance of IPRs. Before it came into force, there existed a number of agreements and conventions that attracted different membership and regulated different types of IP, patents, copyright, trademarks, plant varieties and the like. TRIPs did not override these specific agreements, but it introduced high standards of protection and enforcement for a great number of IPRs across most of the world. The shift was substantial: the majority of countries in the world now grant and protect similar types of IPRs regardless of their specific politico-socio-economic context, and are legally bound to do so, thanks to the WTO's ultra-binding dispute mechanism.

Amongst other things, TRIPs set in motion a global IPRs regime that largely governs knowledge as capital, and pays insufficient attention to how this arrangement affects the provision of the many public goods that rely on knowledge and innovation. It signals the premature emergence of a global regime which leaves unresolved the many complex tensions inherent in governing IPRs. As we shall see later, the TRIPs agreement treats IP protection as a trade matter, marginalising the many other issue-areas upon which IPRs impinge, such as health, innovation, education, technology transfer, biodiversity and human rights. And, by virtue of launching a far-reaching and globally enforceable but profoundly unbalanced IPRs regime, the TRIPs agreement has not only left the many tensions inherent in IP protection unresolved, but has helped make them more problematic, obvious and acute.

It is for these reasons that for a while now we have been witnessing increased tensions and conflicts between actors over several issues within the current IPRs regime. A legal regime for IP can function only to the extent that, as Bourdieu has suggested for law in general, '[it] attains recognition, that is, to the extent that the element of arbitrariness at its heart...remains unrecognised' (1987: 838). For reasons that will become clear in due course, the arbitrariness at the heart of the current IPRs regime – governing IPRs as a commercial matter – is both recognised and contested by many. Hence, the relatively short post-TRIPs period has been characterised by numerous contests over IPRs involving many groups and unfolding in various fora. Since TRIPs came into force, new IP rules have been negotiated, existing ones reinterpreted, and declarations, reports, recommendations and statements about IPRs issued, often simultaneously and in dissonance, in various organisations: the World Intellectual Property Organization (WIPO), regional or bilateral free trade agreements (FTAs), the WTO, the World Health Organisation (WHO), the UN Industrial Development Organisation (UNIDO), the UN Food and Agriculture Organisation (FAO), the World Bank, the Convention on Biodiversity (CDB), the UN Educational, Scientific and Cultural Organisation (UNESCO), various human rights commissions (ECOSOC, CHR), the UN Development Programme (UNDP), the G8, the World Customs Organisation (WCO) and so on.

This study seeks to offer a better understanding of some of these developments, but it focuses primarily on contestations over intellectual property rights and access to affordable medicines. The intersection of IPRs as protected by TRIPs and access to medicines is multifaceted, but is essentially underpinned by the tension that characterises all IPRs: private control over knowledge and innovation versus public access to it. More specifically, the conflict is between business actors who see IPRs as the indispensable capital which ensures they have a stream of new medicines to bring to the market and, ultimately, patients who have no access to those medicines due to the high prices enjoyed by patented medicines. This is one (important) way in which the core tension at the heart of IPRs manifests itself, but it is by no means the only one. Conflicts exist between protecting copyrights and ensuring access to education, or providing IP protection for plant varieties and food security. As it happens, concerns about the latter cluster of issues, and more generally over 'life-patenting', were raised immediately after TRIPs came into force in 1995. Nevertheless, as this study demonstrates, it was IPRs and their impact on access to medicines that took precedence over other concerns in the late 1990s.

In retrospect, there are several reasons for this order of events. For one, public health issues, especially epidemics such as HIV/AIDS, had been attracting considerable concern and attention at the global level throughout the 1990s. Secondly, a formidable global network of civil society groups working on the broad area of health came together and played a crucial role in raising the profile of the impact of IPRs on access to medicines in the late 1990s. Thirdly, their efforts found fertile ground, not only because of heightened concern over global health issues, but also due to increased awareness about the real scale of TRIPs obligations. This was particularly the case for developing countries, many of which shoulder a higher burden of public health crises and are required by TRIPs to ratchet up their IP protection to new and excessive heights. Just as important, access to lifesaving medicines is a visibly more emotive issue than access to education, for instance, which is partly why the IPRs-access to medicines debate became so politicised then and remains so today. As a result, considerable human capital and political will was to be exhausted over this issue alone from the late 1990s onwards – and with some effect, because certain provisions of the TRIPs agreement were amended by 2005. Notwithstanding such amendments, contests over IPRs and public health are far from resolved, and new ones have additionally come to the fore. I point to some of them in Chapter 7, in the hope that future research may enhance our understanding of the complex regime that governs IPRs.

So important did the IPRs-access to medicines issue become by the late 1990s that any observer of global affairs would have come across it or events related to it, such as the court case against the South African government by a group of pharmaceutical companies in the late 1990s, or the Doha Declaration on the TRIPs Agreement and Public Health in 2001. Considerably fewer would know the origins, course and outcomes of the complex contests that these specific events are part of. This study tries to address this gap by seeking to understand *how* and *why* the contests over IPRs and access to medicines emerged, unfolded and have been resolved so far. In other words, it is a study of the politics of the IPRs-access to medicines debate, seeking to uncover how and why a particular arrangement comes into being and not another, whose interests are advanced and marginalised by it, what conflicts are embodied in it and how they get resolved (or not). More broadly, by offering a comprehensive analysis of the IPRs-access to medicines contests, it builds a platform from which other contests over IPRs can be further studied and analysed. Ultimately, we can neither fully understand contests over IPRs governance, nor participate in them here and now, without a sound knowledge of the issues contested and of the actors involved in them. This explains in large part why I have undertaken this study, as well as the way it is organised and presented.

Contests over IPRs cannot be understood in isolation or independently of broader developments occurring elsewhere. This reasoning has obviously shaped my approach and, as I shall explain shortly, the structure of the chapters that follow. Importantly, this study is based on a specific understanding of regimes and global governance which sees them as essentially contested processes. It is driven by a search for a concept that is better at capturing what has been happening within the IPRs and trade regimes, whilst rectifying some of the gaps and constraints in the more mainstream interpretations of regimes. The result is a more complex conceptualisation of regimes which provides insights that may be relevant to observers and scholars of global governance in general, as well as those preoccupied specifically with IPRs, trade rules or access to medicines. That we live in an interconnected world is now an uncontentious assertion, but how issues interconnect and impact upon each other in practice is not yet fully explored or understood. Clearly, by mainly focusing on only three issue-areas – trade, IPRs and public health – this study makes only a partial contribution, but an important one. This contribution is both empirical and theoretical, even though the thrust of the book may at first sight appear empirical in nature. The ontological basis of this study is that facts are not somewhere out there in the world waiting to be discovered. Rather, they are constructed by both the social actors involved in social phenomena and their observers. In order to understand and participate in these social phenomena, both groups use frames and theoretical constructs which are often hidden or implicit, but present nevertheless. I briefly expound my own theoretical tools below, while the rest of the book instantiates and develops them further.

1.1 Some theoretical arguments on the nature of regimes and global governance

Repeated references so far to concepts such as *regimes* and *contests* necessitate an explanation of the theoretical framework which sustains them. The choice of the regime concept may appear unwise at first sight, with many in the field of International Relations maintaining that it has lost some of the charm it possessed in its earlier days. Today it is academically fashionable to use the concept of global governance, seen by most as one of the most promising and central themes for the study of global affairs in the post-Cold War period. In a widely held view, global governance refers to the set of formal and informal institutions, mechanisms, relationships, and processes between states, citizens and organisations through which collective interests are articulated, differences are mediated and common problems resolved (Weiss and Thakur 2010). What is at issue here is neither the existence nor the importance of global governance, which are well accepted. But its mainstream conceptualisation is disputed, insofar as it conceals the many conflicts, tensions and contestations that global governance embodies in practice. One could object to the concept of regimes on similar grounds, that is, that regimes are also often seen as collaborative arrangements where state actors come together to solve common problems. But this functionalist, positivist regime concept is not the one I intend to use here. Generally speaking, concepts do not have objective applications and meanings independent of the theoretical framework within which they are embedded, and the concept that informs this study does not sit easily with positivist approaches to the analysis of socio-political phenomena.

Years of debate between various nuances of neoliberal institutionalism, neorealism and constructivism over the nature of international regimes during the 1970s and 1980s have thankfully provided a useful definition. 'Regimes' are generally defined as a set of implicit or explicit principles (beliefs in facts, causation and rectitude), norms (standards of behaviour defined in terms of rights and obligations), rules (specific prescriptions for action) and decision-making procedures (prevailing practices for making and implementing collective choices) around which actors' expectations converge in a given area of international relations (Krasner 1982: 185). Despite this consensual definition, scholars belonging to different schools are still likely to stress different aspects of international regimes. For their part, constructivists, who were amongst the first to develop the concept and later present the most formidable criticism to mainstream regime theories, tend to stress regimes' norms and principles. This approach is broadly in line with their conceptualisation of international regimes as intersubjective and dialogical in character (Kratochwil and Ruggie 1986; Ruggie 1998). My understanding of regimes is located in the latter approach, and is in part driven by the need to question the kind of 'convergence of expectations' regimes are supposed to reflect, as well as the kind of actors who must share these expectations. Obviously regimes operate on shared understandings that make their existence possible in the first place, but how much convergence must there be in a regime? In other words, must all actors unreservedly agree on the interpretation and application of the principles, norms and rules governing an issue-area for there to be a regime? If so, it is likely that no regime has ever existed. In my view, rather than viewing regimes as benign, orderly and cooperative arrangements among (rational) state actors, or as fixed arrangements held together by bonds of coercion or ties of temporarily converging interests, regimes are better understood as evolving, dynamic and contested processes (Keeley 1990).

This understanding of regimes as dynamic and contested processes builds upon certain neo-Gramscian and Foucauldian insights used in regime studies elsewhere (Keely 1990; Gale 1998; Levy and Newell 2005). I have infused these and other theoretical insights with my observations of the developments within the trade and IPRs regimes that are the focus of this study. In a broad sense, regimes are concerned with governing an issue-area, that is, with the principles, norms, rules and procedures that govern an area, say, IPRs. This area in itself comprises several issues which are widely seen as substantively closely related and bundled together for regulatory purposes (Haas 1980; Leebron 2002). However, what issues are placed into or outside the remit of the regime, what the relationship between issues is understood to be, how they are or ought to be regulated, by whom and towards what ends, are matters of disagreement, tension and contestations. Their resolution does not follow logics outside regime actors' understanding and construction of them. It is precisely because actors have different understandings, normative concerns and interests on each one of these issues that regimes are better conceptualised as the loci of greater or lesser, but inevitable, tension between actors. As we shall see, contests over IPRs and access to medicines continue to occur precisely because regime actors do not have a shared understanding that IPRs are and should be governed as a trade issue, and many of these actors have normative and material interests that are not served by this formulation.

So regimes are contested processes and these processes have material and normative dimensions. That said, not all regimes are contested at all times. The intensity of conflict varies between regimes and within regimes over time; indeed, sometimes a regime may appear to be rather stable and ordered. In this case, conflicts and contradictions are largely hidden from view because a particular group of actors has been successful in legitimising its discourse and absorbing competing ones held by other actors (Howse 2002; Lang 2006). Whether currently stable or contested, regimes embody the outcomes of previous contestations among actors over a multitude of issues brought within the regime throughout time. Hence, at a given point in time, regimes are both the sites of current contests and tensions, and the outcome of previous contestations. Depending on the history and longevity of a particular regime, some of these outcomes may be deeply entrenched, widely accepted and currently non-contestable. Others may be less entrenched or more recent in nature, and hence more susceptible to further challenges and tensions. IPRs were earlier on seen as *privileges*, but today we unproblematically refer to IPRs as *rights*. Framing IPRs as rights is now a well entrenched understanding of IP protection that is very rarely questioned or challenged. But, as we shall see, recent developments that seek to frame IPRs as a trade issue (TRIPs) are fiercely contested. One can then think of regimes as consisting of overlapping layers with different properties: some are deeply entrenched layers and hence are difficult to change, while others are less entrenched and more susceptible to challenges and changes at a certain point in time (Bieler and Morton 2001).

Changes are bound to occur within a regime. They occur because new issues emerge or are brought into the regime remit continuously, old ones are often reframed, new actors enter the regime, regime actors' interests change, broader material or ideological shifts take place outside the regime, new knowledge emerges or the distribution of power amongst actors changes within the regime (Levy et al. 1995; Hasenclever et al. 1997 and 2000; Young 1991; Haggard and Simmons 1987). Regime actors initiate or respond to these changes, constrained or enabled by the context in which they find themselves, attempting to shape the regime and its content in ways which best address their understandings, concerns and interests. Obviously, the more regime actors there are, and the more varied their normative stance and material interests, the more likely it is that the regime will be characterised by tension and conflict.

With respect to actors, all mainstream regime theories, and the vast majority of constructivist ones, have maintained an unhealthy concern with states as the key actors in regimes. In practice, states, while central, are not the only group of actors involved in regime processes, although they have remained, at least until now, the only actors with the political authority to agree on *public* regime rules. But, as suggested by the regime definition earlier, agreeing on specific, technical rules is only a part of what goes on in a regime. The substance of the principles, norms and rules that make-up a regime embodies values, relationships and processes developed through time at many levels and among a multitude of state and non-state actors. Indeed, it would make little sense to discuss IPRs while focusing solely on the state. The history of IPRs is one which is shaped by both state and non-state actors; in fact, especially by the latter, that is to say, IP owners, holders, users and lawyers. Hence, regime actors need not be limited to states – all state and non-state actors (businesses, academics, experts, NGOs and so on) who *actively* participate in and shape, to a greater or lesser degree, the outcomes of contests over the principles, norms and rules that govern an issue-area must be considered regime actors (Levy and Newell 2005).

So, regimes are dynamic and contested processes involving state and non-state actors. The aim of regime actors and actors' coalitions partaking in these processes depends on their position within the regime and the particular issues being contested at a given moment in time. Some actors may be keen on maintaining the status quo and hence aim to absorb and reconcile the challenges made by other actors; others keen on bringing about change of a particular nature will aim to convince other actors about the importance and necessity of accepting such change. More broadly, there are two broader arguments to make about regime actors. Firstly, all agency is driven by both normative and instrumental motives. These categories are often separated for analytical purposes but in practice they are inseparable; behind every idea there is an interest and interests are shaped by normative ideas (Hall 1986). As we shall see in the course of this study, business actors, usually seen as being motivated by material concerns, justified their position during the course of the contestations using sophisticated normative arguments about the role of IPRs. Despite passionate language on patients' rights and the worth of human life, the Campaign NGOs we meet in the course of this study were likewise not devoid of material interests, either on their own account or on that of their constituents.

The second argument is that participating in regime processes does not occur along pluralistic or democratic lines. Rather, the opposite is true. Some actors are better positioned and have better resources at their disposal that give them better leverage over regime contests. The distinction between weaker and stronger regime actors in terms of material and structural power is real, and has important consequences over regime contests. However, the mere existence of such power does not necessarily guarantee success. The aim of regime contest is ultimately that of defining, ordering, normalising and stabilising particular meanings, principles and norms about how a particular issue or issue-area within the regime is or should be regulated, to the expense and marginalisation of others. To the extent that contests are about securing consent and actors holding other views and interests are not convinced or inclined to accept a particular discourse, the success of stronger (from a material point of view) actors in regime contests is not guaranteed a priori. For this reason, regime contests are better understood as dynamic, fluid and somewhat indeterminate.

Even when a group of actors succeeds in resolving regime contests over a particular issue in a manner favoured by them and secures the consent of other actors, such an arrangement is likely to be unstable. This is because the material and ideological realms evolve continuously, generating tensions and contradictions which often transform the terrain within a regime into a dynamic system, with actors both bringing about change and being changed by regime structures and processes (Levy and Egan 2003). Moreover, regimes do not function like boxes closed off from broader developments and structures. Rather, they are meso-level structures sitting, figuratively speaking, somewhere between the domestic and global in the continuum of human affairs (Levy et al. 1995). What this means in practice is that how regimes operate and how regime contests unfold and get resolved cannot be understood by looking only within a particular regime, but also by observing what goes on 'below' and 'above' it, so to speak. Furthermore, as this study demonstrates, developments within a regime are closely related and affected by what goes on 'next door' in other regimes, the more so now that human affairs have become increasingly interdependent.

I opt for this conceptualisation of regimes as dynamic, contested and essentially political processes because a narrow, technical focus on regimes as benign and fixed arrangements says very little about what goes on *inside* a regime, what shapes the behaviour and interest of regime actors, what the contests are about, how they unfold and get resolved and how they interplay with developments in other regimes and beyond. These shortcomings are not negligible, given that this study has the aim of understanding how and why contests over IPRs and access to medicines came about and how they have unfolded and been resolved so far. Moreover, I use this conceptualisation of regimes to intentionally politicise the concept of global governance itself. Global governance encompasses – at the very least – all regimes as understood here, formal and informal, public and private, and obviously many more. By extension, global governance itself emerges as a dynamic, conflictual and contested process. As with regimes, this process involves a large number of state and non-state actors with diverse normative concerns, understandings and interests, all attempting to shape the global governance edifice accordingly in a multitude of issue-areas. Global governance, then, is an arena of conflict, a contested process which favours certain actors and solutions over others. This is a more politicised concept but one that is closer to what we seek to understand, compared to merely conceptualising it as the locus where the (unproblematic) resolution of common problems can be found.

1.2   Some organisational and methodological issues

The conceptual tools and framework laid out in the previous section underpin the chapters that follow and will be revisited at the end of this study. Because of the complex nature of contests over IPRs and access to medicines, the book starts with perhaps a less thrilling but nevertheless crucial explanation of the concrete issues that lie at the heart of these contests. For it is one thing to say that there is a tension between knowledge as capital and knowledge as public good, and another to understand how this tension manifests itself in the area of pharmaceuticals. Chapter 2 seeks to explain how pharmaceutical IPRs impact upon access to medicines by first invoking the somewhat forgotten justifications of the institution of IPRs itself. As was indicated at the start, this institution is contested and political, but its *raison d'être* is ultimately that of ensuring public access to the knowledge goods whose creation it is set up to encourage. The language of IPRs as rights and the historical encroachment of private rights into the public domain have conveniently pushed the issue of access into the background, only for it to return with a vengeance in specific contests such as those over access to medicines. Arguments about IPRs in general in the first part of this chapter are then located in the pharmaceutical IP model. This model is essentially failing on two accounts: firstly, it fails to develop medicines for patients with low or no purchasing power who, incidentally, constitute the largest proportion of patients worldwide, and secondly, when it manages to generate medicines for certain health needs, it still prices out many patients who are not in a position to pay for expensive patented medicines. Understandably, patients with low or no purchasing power, especially in low and middle-income countries, have the right to question the grounds on which their governments justify IPRs obligations such as those undertaken in TRIPs.

But, as Chapter 3 shows, the TRIPs agreement did not manifestly garner the support of all trade regime members. Indeed, many developing countries initially opposed the idea of including IPRs into the trade regime during the 1980s, but key developed members and certain IP-reliant business actors had other plans. This chapter focuses on how the link between IPRs and trade was formulated outside the trade regime by certain business actors, and how it came to form the basis of a landmark agreement such as TRIPs. Generalisations of this kind are not to be made without caution, but it can be said that there would have been no TRIPs agreement had it not been for the political agency of the high-tech, luxury goods and entertainment business actors that we follow in this chapter. Not surprisingly, then, TRIPs emerged as unbalanced, framing IPRs as a trade issue and paying little attention to issues of access. In this respect, it resembles numerous other trade agreements that focus primarily on regulation and harmonisation with the aim of enhancing trade, but without fully considering the social consequences of such undertakings.

This imbalance at the heart of TRIPs, and the way in which it was negotiated, helps us understand why it was that contests over TRIPs emerged soon after it came into force in 1995. Chapter 4 follows developments as they unfolded in the immediate post-TRIPs period, focusing specifically over contests that emerged over IP protection and access to medicines, the actors involved therein and how these contests played out until the WTO Doha Declaration on the TRIPs Agreement and Public Health in 2001. One of the most striking features of the post-TRIPs contests that are the focus of this chapter has been the entry of new actors that were almost absent during TRIPs negotiations. Indeed, the emergence of the IP-public health link that is explored at length in this chapter is attributable to health NGOs which, just as business actors had linked IP to free and fair trade before them, linked IP protection for pharmaceuticals to lack of access to medicines and, more broadly, public health. As it happened, they were rather successful in securing the Declaration in 2001, thus providing an example of weaker regime members scoring a victory against the odds and providing support for the argument that the result of regime contests are not always predetermined, but rather dynamic and fluid.

Just as the TRIPs agreement brought with it the seeds of future contestations, the Doha Declaration added another layer which continued to be contested, challenged and opposed. Chapter 5 follows some of these contests, focusing primarily on developments on the issue of access to medicines within the trade regime. State and non-state actors have engaged in many contests over issues such as biodiversity, traditional knowledge, human rights and food security in the post-TRIPs and post-Declaration period but, given our focus on IPRs and access to medicines, this chapter focuses primarily on these developments, a focus also necessitated by their complex nature. After the Doha Declaration of 2001, IP-access to medicines issues were largely reduced to the issue of compulsory licensing for pharmaceuticals for countries that had no manufacturing capacities in the pharmaceutical sector. Efforts towards finding a solution for this single issue required the commitment of considerable resources on the part of both state and non-state actors until certain TRIPs provisions dealing with compulsory licensing were amended just days before the Hong Kong Ministerial Conference in 2005. This chapter seeks to explain how and why the same actors that secured the 2001 Declaration lost ground on these consequent developments. Pressure, coercion, fault lines, difference in interest and negotiation fatigue all played a role, but another interesting reason relates to IPRs contests having intensified and simultaneously expanded in various fora and regimes.

This trend towards multi-fora, multi-regime contests had been visible since the late 1990s and intensified further from then on. Chapter 6 deals with these developments, arguing that not only have contests over IPRs and access to medicines continued since the amendment in 2005, but they have become an important part of wider contests within the current IPRs regime. These other contests are essentially fuelled by issue-areas that, like access to medicines, were marginalised by governing IPRs as a trade issue. One outcome of such developments has been the drawing of regimes that deal with these other issue-areas, such as human rights and biodiversity, into the IPRs regime, creating what Raustiala and Victor (2004) call 'a regime complex'. Rules, reports, statements and studies on IPRs routinely emanate from various regimes and fora, including various human right bodies and the G8. Amongst other things, this state of affairs demonstrates that framing IPRs as a competitiveness and trade issue is not a view widely shared by other regime actors, although it is gaining more ground in practice through various coercive means. Should this particular way of governing global (pharmaceutical) IPRs emerge unchanged from these contestations, the impact on access to medicines for the majority of people with insufficient purchasing power is undoubtedly going to be negative. Ultimately, the ongoing encroachment of private IP rights into the public domain will probably have negative consequences, not only on the issue of public health, but for the future of the institution of intellectual property rights itself.

The concluding chapter does not speculate about the future, but points out the real risk of this scenario coming about unless the IP-trade frame is reshaped to more fully take into account the many issue-areas upon which IPRs impinge. This chapter brings together the main themes and arguments highlighted throughout the study, fusing them with the theoretical insights into the nature of regimes presented earlier on. One of the key arguments of this study is that, with few notable exceptions, the governance of IPRs has so far been geared towards securing wealth for some rather than health for all. Contests over IP and access to medicines continue, but their resolution requires a broader rethink of the social purpose of enforcing IPRs on the part of all the actors involved. Leaving such resolution to complex, prolonged and unequal contests unfolding in multiple regimes and fora does not bode well for a balanced solution, at least for as long as stronger actors continue to see heightened pharmaceutical IP protection solely in terms of improving their competitive position.

1.3   Sources

Ultimately, this book testifies to the fact that intellectual goods are collaborative in nature, for it would not have been possible without *access* to a considerable body of intellectual work and ideas developed by scholars and observers who have considered some of the issues touched upon here. I have made use of these works and have accordingly referenced them throughout. For the developments in IP-access to medicines issues, I have relied mainly on primary resources of two types. By far the most important were the interviews with representatives of some of the main state and non-state actors involved in them; these fundamentally shaped my understanding of these developments and of the issues raised therein. That said, the analysis of primary sources, such as official negotiating submissions and communications at the WTO TRIPs Council, minutes of the Council meetings, statements, letters and press releases from industry, health NGOs actors and IP experts, and information in mass media outlets has also been crucial in better analysing and understanding these developments. These sources are relatively easily accessible, which is why the interviews I carried out with state and non-state representatives were informal and anonymous, with a view to gaining insights and knowledge from the actors involved that were not publicly available. Because the aim of the interviews was to get a fuller understanding of events and actors' role in them, I opted for off-the-record, semi-structured interviews so as to remove any constraints that interviewees might have felt in this respect. Hence, all interviewees were assured of the confidentiality of the interview material and I have made use of such material with this promise in mind. As a result, there are no quotes in the text from these interviewees and when official sources for points raised by them have been found, I have used the latter instead. Similarly, the interview material is not attributed to named individuals; each interview is given a number (I1, I20 etc), and an indication of the interviewees' position and affiliation is provided in the bibliography.

I carried out over 40 interviews in the course of this study and sought to talk to members of all the groups involved: representatives from pharmaceutical industry companies and associations, trade negotiators from developing and developed countries' missions to the WTO, officials from international organisations such as WTO, WHO and WIPO, and representatives from some health NGOs. I found individual pharmaceutical companies' representatives less willing than other actors to discuss their involvement in these events with me. That said, industry associations' representatives were very approachable and quite candid about their substantial role and involvement in the governance of IPRs. I approached individuals who had been personally involved in the contests that unfolded from 1995 onwards with the aim of understanding their personal and official position, normative stance and interests during the contests. This group constitutes the great majority of the interviewees, but I also spoke to a small number of people who, although they had not participated personally, possessed a great deal of knowledge of the intricacies of these developments as part of the 'institutional history' passed down to them by those who had participated but had moved on to other positions. I found that *personal* dedication to 'the cause' was often a good explanation of the position taken in the negotiations at most, though not all, critical junctures during IPRs-access to medicines contests. This was especially true for representatives of developing country members and NGOs, that is, for the Campaign group. In many cases, initial positions were prepared not by distant officials in capital cities, but put together in close collaboration with like-minded officials and representatives in Geneva. However, official positions were also critical in many cases, especially during the WTO Ministerials where decisions are generally taken by higher-level government officials, or when pressure was placed on the governments whose representatives in Geneva were especially 'obstructive' during negotiations at the WTO TRIPs Council meetings.

I found plenty of examples of differences in positions within and between representatives' groups, be they state representatives or those of business and NGOs. This insight raises questions about the idea of unitary actors used in most political analysis. It is well accepted here that the 'actor' category is a frustrating but necessary analytical tool that can be further deconstructed. In this study, I have tried to reflect some of these nuances in Chapters 5 and 6, as and when they are important, but some differences had to be left out of the text due to space limitations and the lengthy and complex nature of the developments covered in this study. In addition, I found that *all* interviewees understood their involvement in contests over IPRs on normative and material terms simultaneously, although the latter were less explicitly or candidly exposed by NGOs.

As in all social and political affairs, actors occupying different positions in the IP-access to medicines contests not only had different normative concerns and interests, but sometimes different and conflicting understandings of what was going on at any point in time. This in itself is a useful insight. I sought to clarify some of these issues through cross-checking information in subsequent interviews, but when they represented real differences in understandings and affected developments in practice, I have reflected this in my analysis of the events, especially in Chapters 5 and 6. I have obviously not been an objective observer of these developments, if such a thing was ever possible. What I present here is ultimately how I understand these contests, the issues they seek to resolve, the actors involved in them and their outcomes. I have sought to make my ontological and theoretical position clear in this chapter. Finally, it is necessary to add that from a normative point of view, although I do not advocate the abolition of IPRs altogether, I am convinced that the current IPRs regime ought to be reformed or new IP protection forms devised which provide enough incentives for creativity and innovation and, importantly, allow *access* to and enrichment of the public domain. In other words, I do not think the current IP arrangement is normatively the best, or even a very good, way of governing IPRs and am encouraged by challenges such as those made from public health and other perspectives that seek to redress the imbalance at the heart of the current IPRs regime. I will have more to say on this in the last part of the book, after dealing with the origins and course of IP-access to medicines contests, to which we now turn.

2
Intellectual Property Rights and Pharmaceuticals

Despite the fact that we refer to *property* quite unproblematically in everyday parlance, the institution of property is complex, contested and highly political, and that of *intellectual* property is perhaps even more so. Property is not an object or a thing; rather, it is an entitlement, an artifice which has developed over time to help regulate and resolve contests over objects that people need or want (Drahos 1996). Because these objects are finite and human wants infinite, property rights aim, in principle, to resolve interpersonal conflict by allocating exclusive ownership to specified individuals or groups. Property rights, then, by virtue of determining who gets what and how, and excluding others altogether, are the quintessential contested political institution. Intellectual property rights (IPRs) are even more contested and political because not only do they determine how and where the borders between the 'haves' and 'have-nots' are set, but also because what is to be owned, that is, ideas, knowledge and other products of the human intellect, are not scarce and are intrinsically inappropriable. Indeed, knowledge is the classic textbook case of a public good, being both inappropriable and non-rivalrous in nature. Unlike tangible goods and objects, which can be appropriated individually and thus visibly separated from the commons, knowledge and intellectual products are intangible and not appropriable in this way; once created, knowledge can be used by anybody. Such use is non-rivalrous because the 'consumption' of intangible goods would leave the same quantity and quality of such goods to be consumed and enjoyed by others (Hughes 1997). That this is not the reality we experience today is testimony to the institution of IPRs itself, which, essentially, deliberately *creates* scarcity when none existed before, so as to enable the commodification and appropriation of otherwise plentiful, non-rivalrous intellectual goods (Kinsella 2001; May 2000).

18

With beginnings as far back as the fifteenth century, the IPRs regime has a relatively long history which, unsurprisingly, has been characterised by continuous and conflictual political contests between IP creators, owners, users and regulators (May and Sell 2006). Although the language used seems dispassionate, the shape and content of IP rules embodies the outcome of contests fought over time and in different historical, material and ideological contexts. IPRs are dynamic and continuously evolving, often because ideological, socio-economic and technological changes bring forth new actors, interests, demands and pressures for the rearrangement of IP norms and rules. It is within this broader terrain we need to place the ongoing contests over IPRs and access to medicines which concern this study and those over IPRs more generally. As the next chapter demonstrates, TRIPs itself entered the scene in 1995 as a result of complex changes which, amongst other things, empowered a particular group of actors to successfully embed their preferred way of governing IPRs in the TRIPs agreement. But, far from being the last development in the history of IPRs, TRIPs is but one juncture, albeit a crucially important one. By laying bare the historically unresolved and complex tensions embodied in IPRs at the global level, TRIPs helped usher in a period of heightened contestations in the history of IPRs. These contests are too complex to be covered here, but at their roots lies the persistent tension between those who seek to commodify and appropriate more intellectual goods into the private realm and those who seek their dissemination into the 'intangible commons' for public use and the protection of the public domain more generally.

The contests over IPRs and access to medicines that we follow in this study are a concrete, but not the only, materialisation of this tension involving certain groups of actors and unfolding within a specific material and ideological context. In order to better understand how they emerged and developed over time, we need to engage first with the issues that underpin them, no matter how technical they may appear at first sight. We cannot fully understand the politics of IPRs and access to medicines without first understanding how medicines are developed, by whom and where, what intellectual property rights are involved in this arrangement and what consequences they have for access to the medicines thus developed. How these issues are understood and framed by the actors involved in regime contests plays directly into how the latter develop and get resolved (or not). For these reasons, this chapter seeks to uncover the issues at the heart of the IPRs-access to medicines debate that emerged in the late 1990s. It starts by exploring the justifications for the institution of IPRs, especially that of access to intellectual goods. The second section follows by focusing more concretely on the IPRs model that has developed around pharmaceuticals and on some of the consequences of this model. In doing so, it introduces the key business actors involved in the IPRs-access to medicines contests, and provides insights into their normative and material position.

2.1   The forgotten justifications of IPRs

Intellectual property is a fairly recent term that has come to denote a whole set of different rights, of which the most familiar are patents, copyrights and trademarks. Despite considerable differences between various rights, they all offer IP-holders some form of exclusivity, that is, the right to exclude others from certain resources, while IP-holders can claim rights to the economic value of those resources (Braithwaite and Drahos 2000).[1] Take the case of pharmaceutical patents. Currently, provided a new drug passes certain thresholds of novelty, inventiveness and utility, a pharmaceutical patent grants its holder exclusivity for a period of twenty years, during which only the patent-holder, or its licensees, have the right to produce, use or sell the drug under patent. As we can see, although we routinely refer to a pharmaceutical patent as a property right, patents and other IPRs are in essence monopolistic privileges. More generally, through granting and enforcing IPRs, governments grant control over valuable knowledge, processes and expressions to IP-holders and deny others the capacity to use them, unless the IP owners' consent has been obtained (Anawalt 2003; Kinsella 2001). As was argued above, such exclusion is not an unfortunate side-effect of IPRs; indeed, it is their very aim (Benkler 2001: 268).

Of course, such exclusion has had to be justified for the institution of IP to be stable. The commodification and appropriation of knowledge through IPRs developed over time, as did the overall discourse which helps to justify them. The two key elements of this discourse are philosophical and economic in nature. The two most important philosophical justifications for IPRs can be attributed to Locke and Hegel, although Locke did not specifically address IPRs (Drahos 1996). For Locke, people were naturally entitled to the fruits of their labour and furthermore, they deserved benefits from their labour insofar as the latter created or added social value (Hughes 1997; Hettinger 1997). These influential arguments were later used in conjunction with Hegel's personality theory of property, which justified property as a unique and particularly suitable mechanism for a person's self-actualisation, personal expression and recognition as an individual (Drahos 1996).

Hence, an idea or intellectual good belongs to its creator because it is a manifestation of the creator's personality or self. Recognising an individual's property rights, then, is an act of recognising the individual as a person, although this justification is inapplicable to ideas that do not contain clear elements of what might be recognised as personal expression (Hughes 1997), the pharmaceutical patent being a case in point.

The arguments of Locke and Hegel were especially powerful during the eighteenth and nineteenth centuries, a time during which IPRs laws were being moulded in their modern form, and they have remained obstinately influential in contemporary debates (Mossoff 2001). One observable impact of these arguments has been that thinking of intellectual matter as property that can be owned has come to be seen as natural and, more importantly, that its ownership is a natural right. Thanks to business actors' efforts, this remained the case even for corporations and businesses which, having been recognised as singular personalities in law by the nineteenth century, were subsequently granted IP rights for the work created collectively by their employees (Fisk 2003). Once in place, the language of rights helped perpetuate a romanticised view of the author and a heroic image of the inventor, and these are misleading (Aoki 1994). Creativity of all sorts is collaborative, rather than individual; indeed, creativity and innovation are better conceptualised as residing both in the individuals and in the social networks that connect them together, an aspect which current IPRs fail to recognise and reward. Ultimately, intellectual activity is not creation from nothing; intellectual products are better seen as social products, the result of human effort in general rather than of individual labour (Hettinger 1997; Kinsella 2001). The latter argument raises important issues about how IP laws can attribute a just reward to IP-holders for their individual contribution. Current IP laws relate that reward to the market value of the intellectual good, but, while the labourer has the natural right to own and personally use the fruit of his or her labour, it does not necessarily follow that s/he or the company has the natural right to receive whatever market value that product will garner. As Hettinger (1997: 23) has argued, market value is a socially created phenomenon which cannot be produced or controlled by an individual or company alone. It is clear that, far from being natural rights, the rights of IP-holders to receive all or most of the market value of their products are in fact socially created privileges and ought to be governed as such (Hettinger 1997; Drahos 1996; Boyle 1996).

We find some justification for society agreeing to grant these spectacular privileges to a minority in Locke's arguments about reward for labour that creates or adds social value. These arguments are strengthened by other economic and utilitarian arguments in which the issue of access becomes more visible. According to the latter arguments, IPRs are justifiable because they provide adequate incentives for the creation of socially valuable intellectual products which would not otherwise be produced (Kinsella 2001; May and Sell 2006). That is, granting IPRs provides an overall net benefit for the society, since the benefit of access to more intellectual products for use surpasses the cost of granting exclusive IPRs to their producers. Crucial here is the expectation that society would receive access to new knowledge and creativity and the intellectual goods that embody them. This 'bargain' is best exemplified by the paradox of patents, according to which 'by slowing down the diffusion of technical progress, patents ensure that there will be more progress to diffuse' (Robinson 1969: 87). The utilitarian argument is not concerned with efficiency per se; rather, it justifies the inefficiency in knowledge consumption that results from creating and maintaining excludability by the need to permit IP producers to receive a benefit for their efforts, regardless of the fact that this arrangement causes an underutilisation of knowledge (Arrow 1962). Hence, because societies want access to more and better intellectual goods, they should grant IPRs, as these create the necessary incentives to enable the production of such goods (Arrow 1996; Braga and Fink 1997).

The underlying assumption here is that human intellectual endeavours are motivated by individual reward, while the focus is on the benefits to users of intellectual goods, that is, to the society at large (Hettinger 1997). But innovation and creativity are driven by multiple economic and non-economic motives, not just by the potential reward granted by IPRs. Indeed, the desire to explore and create lies at the core of human nature, whether it is rewarded with property or not. Even if individuals and companies engaged in creative and research activities for economic returns alone, it is not at all clear whether IPRs are the indispensable incentives they are made out to be. In some cases, the market structure is a more important factor in the creation of intellectual goods. In the case of patents, IPRs may not be strong prerequisites for research and development in many industries; early market occupancy, the reputational and learning curve advantages of being a first mover are in many instances much more important (Scherer 2001). Hence, IPRs are not necessarily the only or even the most effective way of providing incentives for innovation and creativity. Indeed, they may actually stifle innovation by reducing the incentives for IPRs holders to progress and compete in the market though other means, by making knowledge more expensive for others to use, or by unnecessarily reducing the pace of progress in general.

Today IPRs are framed as indispensable rights that ensure that more intellectual goods are available for society. More worryingly, the current view is that the more IPRs are granted and the stronger they are, the more socially valuable intellectual goods would be available. But, as we have seen, IPRs are social privileges that need to find a careful balance between providing incentive for innovation, creativity and technological advancement on the one hand, and enhancing public utility, diffusion and access to knowledge goods on the other. We see this tension present in the very first patent statute enacted in 1474 in Venice, whereby patents were awarded on the authorities' assessment of *social* considerations and economic utility for the municipality, representing an early effort of balancing the public benefits of dissemination and private rewards to encourage intellectual activity (Braudel 1981). This tension between the private and public domain has remained at the heart of IPRs contests ever since. Although, regrettably, the story of these contests is one of further encroachment of private IPRs into the public domain (Boyle 2003), in the final analysis, the public domain remains the very cornerstone of the institution of intellectual property. Granting an individual or group of individuals the privilege of harnessing most or all of the market value for a particular IP good without guaranteeing that society at large has access to it on reasonable and affordable terms is philosophically, economically and morally unjustifiable.

2.2   Medicines and IPRs

The utilitarian arguments mentioned above have historically resonated well with the claims made by the proprietary pharmaceutical companies that useful medicines would not be developed in the absence of IP protection, especially patents. Pharmaceutical industry representatives have long defended IPRs in general and patents in particular as the 'lifeblood of our industry – we literally could not exist without them' (Sykes, in von Braun and Pugatch 2005: 604; also Mossinghoff and Bombelles 1996; Bale 1998). In a classic study on the importance of the patent system, Mansfield (1986) gave credence to this claim by arguing that the pharmaceutical and chemical industries were more reliant on the patent system than any other industrial sector. He estimated that around 60 per cent of inventions in the pharmaceutical industry (38 per cent for the chemical industry and 25 per cent for the next sector) would not have been introduced or developed in the absence of patents. Given the great importance the proprietary pharmaceutical sector places on patents, it is not surprising that it stands alone in its involvement with the patent system and has done much to ensure that the system meets its requirements (Macdonald 2002). As we shall see in the following chapters, alongside other business actors, it has played a crucial role in refashioning and strengthening IP protection for pharmaceuticals in the TRIPs agreement and beyond.

2.2.1   The peculiarities of the pharmaceutical R&D process

Proprietary pharmaceutical companies base their claim for strong IP protection largely on two characteristics of pharmaceutical innovation: first, the increasingly lengthy and costly nature of the research and development (R&D) process; and, second, the easily codifiable nature of pharmaceutical innovation, which means that competitors can produce the same drug through reverse engineering (Kuhlik 2004). An understanding of the pharmaceutical R&D process is crucial to industry's position regarding pharmaceutical IPRs. The R&D process can be divided into four main phases, stretching from drug discovery to its market approval and large-scale production (Table 2.1). A crucial moment in the R&D process is the application for an investigational new drug, which is distinct for the market approval process. Before allowing a company to initiate tests on people, the health regulatory authorities (the Food and Drug Administration (FDA) in the US, the European Agency for the Evaluation of Medicinal Products (EMEA) in the EU and other national health authorities in most countries) review an investigational new drug application submitted by the drug's developer to protect patients from unreasonable risks in clinical trials. It is when this authorisation is secured that clinical trials can begin and, if upon completion they satisfy the health authorities' standards of drug effectiveness and safety, the new drug is granted marketing approval.

But health authorities do not grant patents. Many pharmaceutical and biotech companies file patent applications on one or more components of a new molecular entity to patent offices well before they apply for investigational new drug approval to health authorities (Nogués 1990). This is a conscious strategy on the part of research-based pharmaceutical and biotech companies; firstly, patent offices grant patents on account of the compound's novelty, inventiveness and utility, rather than its safety or effectiveness; secondly, and perhaps more importantly, patents protect the company from competitors who consequently cannot develop, patent or produce the same drug (indeed, a strategically written patent will effectively protect against product infringement

Table 2.1 The pharmaceutical R&D process

Phase I Drug discovery	Phase II Pre-clinical testing	Phase III Clinical testing	Phase IV Market approval
Around 10,000 compounds screened	Around 250 compounds tested in vitro and in animals to assess the chemical, biological and toxicological properties of the compound	*Investigational New Drug Application* → Around 5 compounds enter clinical trials stage: **S1:** the drug is tested for safety, safe dose range and mechanism of action in 20 to 100 *healthy* volunteers **S2:** the drug is tested on 100 to 500 volunteer *patients* to establish that the drug effectively treats the disease. Researchers continue to evaluate the drug's safety, side effects, and optimal dose strength and schedule. **S3:** the drug is tested in large trials with 1,000 to 5,000 *patients* in hospitals and clinics to determine effectiveness, to identify long-term effects, toxicity etc.	Only 1 successful drug Market approval from health regulatory bodies
2 years	1–2 years	6–8 years	1–2 years

Source: PhRMA 2005; EFPIA 2004.

by other companies for a long time); and, thirdly, health authorities' review of clinical trials is usually accelerated for patented compounds. What this means in effect is that the patent(s) that protect a drug in the market would have usually started before clinical trials and hence would have an 'effective life' of around 10 to 12 years. The argument so far has focused on *product patents* that protect the compound and the composition of a new drug, but companies almost always also apply for and receive *process patents* that protect the method by which a new drug is produced. Although we speak of 'a patented medicine', it is worth noting that a new medicine reaching the market is normally protected by over 100 different patent families (EC 2009). Often referred to as 'patent thickets', many of these patents are pursued so as to exclude competition, rather than pursue innovative efforts.

Ironically, despite continuous technological advances and the existence of pharmaceutical IPRs, the pharmaceutical R&D process has lost its innovative edge. In total, the annual number of new molecular entities (NMEs)[2] reaching the world market during 1990–1999 was 44, down from 48 in the 1980s and about 93 introduced in the 1960s (Chew et al. 1985; Borrus 2002). In 2009, there were only 26 NMEs launched into the global market (CMR 2010). Some of the explanations put forward by companies include suggestions that the 'easier' medicines have already been discovered; that current medicines research is focused more on chronic, degenerative and previously incurable illnesses; and that regulatory requirements are far tougher with respect to the safety and efficacy of new medicines than before. While these claims may be true, the loss of pharmaceutical innovative edge precisely during a period of time when pharmaceutical IPRs have, if anything, become stronger runs counter to the mainstream logic of IPRs, according to which we should expect more innovative drugs to reach the market as we provide more and stronger IP protection to proprietary pharmaceutical companies.

Furthermore, the pharmaceutical R&D process has become not only less innovative, but also more lengthy and expensive (Table 2.2). Recent industry reports have put the cost of developing a new drug around the US$1 billion mark over a 12 year process (EFPIA 2009). But measuring the overall cost of developing a new drug from the moment of its discovery to its marketing is a difficult and controversial task. Most estimates have been presented or deduced from data offered by pharmaceutical companies, which have a clear interest in inflating costs. The most frequently cited research in this area has been that of DiMasi et al.

Table 2.2   The length and cost of R&D process

Period	Length of R&D process (years)	Average cost of new drug [million, in year 2000 Euros (in year 2000 US$)]
1960s	4.7	–
1970s	6.7	149 ($138)
1980s	8.5	344 ($318)
2001	12	868 ($802)
2007	12	*$1.059 (in year 2007 US$)*

Source: DiMasi et al. 2003; EFPIA 2009.

(1991 and 2003) which estimated the average cost for developing a new drug in 2001 at US$802 million (in 2000 US$). This figure has since then been used to represent the *de facto* cost of developing a new drug by both industry associations and governmental sources. But DiMasi's US$802 million estimate has been challenged on many accounts. The estimate is based on 68 self-originated (in-house) new molecular entities from ten pharmaceutical companies. This greatly limits the applicability of the estimate to the larger group of new medicines, given that the majority of the new approved medicines do not represent new molecular entities or even self-originated ones. Further objections are raised with regard to the method of calculation; for instance, half of DiMasi's 2001 estimate is accounted for by the opportunity cost of capital.[3] Critics have argued that R&D expenses are seen as deductibles rather than investment for tax purposes, and for this reason should not be capitalised (Goozner 2004; Angell 2004). Addressing some of the issues mentioned here, an independent inquiry in the US pegged the out-of-pocket, after-tax cost per new drug at US$71 million (year 2000 US$), a figure over ten times lower than that based solely on industry data (Public Citizen 2001).

Part of the disagreement over the cost of pharmaceutical R&D relates to the fact that estimates refer to self-originated medicines, thus ignoring the important role of public funding and academic research in pharmaceutical innovation. As is well known, none of the early developments in the pharmaceutical and chemical field would have been possible without the substantial contribution made by universities and academia and major support from governments. Indeed, nearly all inventions before the 1880s were introduced by academics and physicians, particularly French and German ones (Achilladelis 1999). The undisputable success of the German chemical and pharmaceutical companies during the nineteenth century and beyond was achieved to a large extent through close cooperation between academic institutions and industrial enterprises, as was the growth of the US pharmaceutical sector after World War II (Tweedy and Lesney 2000). This is a point worth stressing further, as it sets the proprietary pharmaceutical sector apart from other industries; in addition to enjoying favourable tax incentives for R&D, the riskiest and most expensive basic research (early R&D) has traditionally been funded largely by public money, with the industry only becoming involved when such research indicates promising results. For instance, a study by Massachusetts Institute of Technology (MIT) of the 21 most important medicines introduced between 1965 and 1992 found that publicly funded research played an important part in discovering and developing 14 of the 21 medicines (Public Citizen 2001). Although the industry does not completely deny the importance of publicly funded research, it estimates its involvement on a considerably smaller scale. The issue remains unresolved, pointing once again to the difficulty IPRs face in justifying generous private rewards to individual groups for intellectual goods that are intrinsically social and collaborative in nature.

Disagreements over the real cost of drug development matter insofar as proprietary companies maintain that strong intellectual property protection for pharmaceuticals is vital for providing incentives for expensive drug innovations. Pharmaceutical patents allow companies to recoup the cost of the R&D process over time by preventing other proprietary pharmaceutical and generic companies from making, manufacturing and selling the drug under patent for a period of twenty years. Some patented drugs generate exorbitant profits for their companies during the patent term. The most impressive performance of proprietary pharmaceutical companies in this respect was during the 1980s and 1990s when some companies derived as much as 50 per cent of their profits from a single drug (Achilladelis 1999). Often termed 'blockbuster' drugs, these were drugs that worked for the majority of the patients with a certain condition and achieved sales of around US$1 billion per year. Like IPRs, high prices for patented drugs are justified on account of the high and continuously increasing cost of pharmaceutical R&D.

It may be that the real cost of developing a new drug will remain unknown unless the pharmaceutical companies open their books for independent scrutiny. Some R&D trends are, however, clear. For instance, the major part of pharmaceutical R&D expenditure is located in the US and goes towards developing products acting on the central nervous system, cancers and metabolic diseases, and the cardiovascular system (26, 21 and 18 per cent respectively) (Borrus 2002). In terms of the pharmaceutical market, these three classes of disease account for almost half of the world market value (EFPIA 2004). While the majority of pharmaceutical R&D goes into developing medication for these profitable therapeutical markets, only a negligible part, less than 5 per cent of world pharmaceutical R&D, goes towards developing cures for diseases such as malaria or tuberculosis that are confined to patients with no purchasing power, living largely (but not exclusively) in the developing world (UK IPRs Commission 2002). A recent study which surveyed the world's eleven largest pharmaceutical companies found that of the 1,393 medicines introduced in the last 25 years, only 13 treated tropical diseases (less than 1 per cent) that are the biggest killers in the developing world (Goozner 2004). The development of such medicines has largely been left to charitable and public initiatives at the national and, more recently, global level. One major development in this respect has been the creation of several global private-public partnerships between public agencies and private NGOs. For instance, between 2000 and 2004 over 60 such projects existed worldwide, involving pharmaceutical companies such as GlaxoSmithKline, Novartis, Astra-Zeneca and Sanofi-Aventis and a number of NGOs and foundations, of which the most prominent has been the Gates Foundation. A reported 18 new products are now in clinical trials (Wogart 2006), but the outcome of these efforts remains to be seen.

It is clear from the discussion so far that the current pharmaceutical IPRs model is problematic. Its logic is such that companies will focus their R&D efforts where there is a potential market that will enable them to recoup investment and make profits, not necessarily where there is a genuine human health need. As Türmen and Clift (2006) have argued, the ability of IPRs to provide the necessary incentives for biomedical R&D in diseases affecting people with no or little purchasing power 'may be limited or non-existent...because the market demand is...small and uncertain'. And we have seen that diseases affecting the poor do not feature high on the R&D agenda of proprietary pharmaceutical companies. This is in contrast to two gradual but prominent trends in the pharmaceutical market. One is that of the 'medicalisation' of lifestyle disorders for which there is a market. This trend is particularly obvious in the developed world, where the realm of the 'normal' has become increasingly narrow and most lifestyle disorders such as obesity, depression and other conditions such as baldness and sexual dysfunction are now considered as illnesses and are therefore medicalised (Moynihan and Smith 2002). The second trend is one which has been on the rise especially since the 1980s and is the increasing number of 'me-too' drugs in the market. These are versions of successful (that is, profitable) existing drugs that claim patent protection on account of making incremental improvements on existing drugs, a patenting strategy also known as 'evergreening' (von Braun and Pugatch 2005). Although 'me-too' drugs are competitive vis-à-vis other similar drugs in terms of *usage*, they enter the market at the same or an even higher price level than their nearest therapeutic substitute already in the market (Lu and Comanor 1998), offering patients none of the benefits expected from competition. What is worse, because they usually go through all the

R&D stages discussed above, 'me-too' medicines utilise pharmaceutical R&D resources in a manner which is both uneconomic and unethical, as is the use of resources expended on fierce legal disputes over the merits of 'me-too' patents that have proliferated because of this trend.[4]

Looking beyond the pharmaceutical R&D process, it is worth noting that the largest proprietary pharmaceutical companies spend an average of 18.6 per cent of sales on R&D (see Table 2.3.) while, according to some studies, between 25 and 35 per cent of their annual sales is spent on promoting their brand-based medicines worldwide (Pugatch 2004a; EC 2009). According to a UNIDO study, marketing expenditure is not only higher than R&D expenditure as a percentage of sales, but has also been increasing faster: 24 per cent of annual sales in 1990, up from 16.5 per cent in 1975, compared to 13 per cent and 10 per cent respectively for R&D as a percentage of sales (Ballance et al. 1992). These figures raise important questions about the industry's claims that IPRs and high prices are necessary to cover high R&D costs and, indeed, whether the proprietary pharmaceutical sector is a research-intensive or, instead, a marketing-intensive sector. Such is the brand loyalty developed through years of patent protection and marketing efforts by proprietary pharmaceutical companies that it is not unusual for brand drug prices to remain at the same level after the generic entry (Scherer 2000). Indeed, one can argue that in some cases brand-name loyalty

Table 2.3   Top 12 pharmaceutical companies ranked by total revenues, 2009

Rank by revenues	Company	Total revenues (US$ million)	R&D as % of sales (2008 data)
1	Johnson & Johnson (US)	63,749	20.74
2	Pfizer (US)	48,296	17.99
3	GlaxoSmithKline (UK)	44,654	18.06
4	Roche (Switzerland)	44,267	21.98
5	Sanofi-Aventis (France)	42,179	16.60
6	Novartis (Switzerland)	41,459	18.84
7	Astra Zeneca (UK)	31,601	16.39
8	Abbot Laboratories (US)	29,527	16.09
9	Merck (US)	23,850	20.34
10	Wyeth (US)	22,833	16.42
11	Bristol-Myers Squibb (US)	21,366	20.24
12	Eli Lilly (US)	20,378	19.92

Source: Fortune 2009; SCRIPT 2009.

may be a more effective method of guaranteeing high returns than the patent system itself.

2.2.2 The peculiarities of the pharmaceutical market

In addition to its wasteful use of resources and gaps in health needs that it cannot address, the current IPRs model is also questionable in terms of access to the medicines that it actually manages to create. Issues of access to existing patented medicines are linked to a number of factors, such as price, insurance schemes, availability of medical staff and the state of public health infrastructure and spending, to mention a few. Of these, the price of patented medicines is directly linked to the pharmaceutical IPRs model and, as we shall see, has been at the core of the IP-access to medicines contests we follow in this study. The issue of the price of patented medicines is particularly relevant in the case of less developed and developing countries where public or private health insurance schemes offer only partial coverage or are non-existent. This is not generally the case in the developed world, where different price control schemes are in place for pharmaceuticals, which are often part of universal public healthcare systems or public insurance schemes (Danzon and Keuffel 2005). From a worldwide perspective, there is a weak relationship between per capita income levels and on-patent drug prices, which is why it is not unusual to find a patented drug priced at a considerably higher level in a developing or poor country compared to its average price in developed markets (Danzon and Towse 2003).

More broadly, the issue of patented drug prices is closely related to certain peculiar characteristics of the pharmaceutical market structure where the ordinary principles of demand and supply do not readily apply. This is not only because pharmaceutical IPRs are interventionist and monopolistic. Just as important, the demand for pharmaceuticals is largely oligopsonistic, that is, there are only a few purchasers for each drug, most notably hospitals and health insurance schemes in the developed world. Patients are not like customers in other markets, as they do not choose which medicine to purchase. This decision is taken for them by the physician and often (in developed countries) neither the physician nor the patient pays the (full) market price of the selected medicine. Patients' purchase of prescription medicines is often reimbursed in whole or in part by insurance, be that private, public or both. This is certainly true for the majority of developed countries, although it must be noted that reimbursement schemes vary widely. The US is perhaps the most notable exception, although the widespread (though not universal) establishment of private health insurance there essentially provides a secure market for pharmaceuticals. This type of demand structure may appear unfavourable at first sight, but it is this very structure that provides pharmaceutical companies with a substantial market and assured cash flow. Proprietary pharmaceutical companies, then, have a more or less guaranteed market for their products, thanks in large part to the emergence of socialised medicine in most developed countries in the post-World War II period (Ramirez and Tylecote 1999). This is another important dimension of the close relationship between governments and the pharmaceutical sector that extends beyond granting and enforcing IPRs, spending public funding for basic research and offering R&D tax reliefs. And because pharmaceutical markets in the developed world are well protected by public and private health insurance schemes which mitigate the adverse effects of unemployment and reduced income, the performance of pharmaceutical companies is relatively independent of business cycles (Jungmittag and Reger 2000).

Generally, it can be said that demand for medicines is relatively insensitive to price levels in most of the developed world, which, incidentally, constitutes the largest share of the world pharmaceutical market. As a UK study pointed out in 2002, less than 20% of the world pharmaceutical market, valued at a total of US$406 billion, was accounted for by developing and least developed countries, with Africa claiming only around 1 per cent of the total (UK IPR Commission 2002). Demand for pharmaceuticals is not insensitive to prices in this last quintile of the pharmaceutical market, which is by far the most populous. The IP-access to medicines contests we follow are essentially over access to medicines in this part of the market where on-patent drugs are well beyond patients' reach. Take for instance the case of antiretroviral (ARV) drugs. Even some of the older generation triple ARV therapies still cost around US$1 per person per day, at a time when 40 per cent of world's population lives on a meagre income of less than US$2 per day (World Bank 2008). Newer generation ARV drugs are priced well beyond this level. Beyond HIV/AIDS drugs, several studies have shown that patients in developing countries face drug prices that are not only higher than their average per capita income, but often higher than drug prices in developed countries, and in some cases even higher than US prices, which are amongst the highest in the developed world (Maskus 2000; Scherer and Watal 2001). The issue of access to on-patent drugs in the developing and less developed world, then, is one of both inappropriately high drug prices and low purchasing power on the part of patients. These facts raise substantial problems in terms of access to medicines, especially when we consider that private spending by households is today the principal source of pharmaceutical spending worldwide, and especially so in developing and less developed countries (WHO 2004). Indeed, on-patent drug prices are an issue for both individual and public healthcare programmes in developing countries, as the share of public healthcare expenditure spent by the latter on pharmaceutical procurement can be as much as 60 per cent of total health expenditure, compared to around 10–20 per cent in the developed countries (WHO 2004).

That said, it is worth noting that developed countries' healthcare budgets have also come under considerable pressure since the 1990s, when most governments sought to contain their ever-increasing healthcare costs, pharmaceuticals often being the hardest-hit component. These efforts have included stricter price controls, withdrawal of reimbursements from selected pharmaceuticals and increased use of generic medicines. The prices of generic drugs vary widely, but they tend to be considerably lower than the prices of original patented drugs, often around 60 to 80 per cent less (Grabowski and Vernon 1992). As a result of such measures on the part of governments everywhere, the world market share of generics has been increasing rapidly even in the US and the EU markets, although because of substantially lower prices, generics' share of the total pharmaceutical market value in the US and EU was still less than 18 per cent in the late 2000s (IMS 2009). Against the backdrop of less innovative but more expensive R&D, proprietary pharmaceutical companies responded by adopting a series of strategies, such as merging with other companies to strengthen their competitive position and improve their R&D output, as well as increasing their presence in the generic market itself (Achilladelis 1999). As a study in the US pharmaceutical market showed, about 80% of generic medicines in the late 1990s were actually manufactured by research-intensive companies themselves (Tarabusi and Vickery 1998), further blurring the distinction between the proprietary and generic sector.

Other major changes that swept the proprietary pharmaceutical sector in the 1990s include a series of horizontal mergers and acquisitions (M&A) between large research-intensive pharmaceutical companies, as a result of which the proprietary pharmaceutical sector has become more concentrated. For instance, the ten largest proprietary pharmaceutical companies accounted for 48% of global sales in 2000, up from only 12 per cent in 1987 (Danzon et al. 2003: 7). Table 2.3 lists the 12 largest pharmaceutical companies ranked by revenues, incidentally the key pharmaceutical business actors we follow in this study, most of which are the result of one or more M&A during the 1990s and 2000s. Concentration has become even more obvious within therapeutical fields (cardiovascular, central nervous system, etc) where it is not unusual for the top three products to account for 45–80 per cent of total sales in a particular therapeutical class (Tarabusi and Vickery 1998). We can see, then, that in addition to the monopolies granted by IPRs, the proprietary pharmaceutical market also enjoys an oligopolistic supply and demand structure which, basic economics tell us, does not bode well for competitive prices.

Looking at the pharmaceutical market from a geographical perspective, the most notable characteristic is that the bulk of pharmaceuticals are produced and consumed within OECD countries. According to industry data, almost 80 per cent of the global pharmaceutical market – which has recently reached a value of US$700 billion – is accounted for by the US, Canadian and European markets, the US market accounting for around 40–50 per cent of total world sales alone (EFPIA 2009). It is worth noting in passing that the US market has a special place in the proprietary pharmaceutical market, not only due to its size, but also due to its nature. Unlike other developed countries' markets, there are very few price or profit controls placed on proprietary pharmaceutical companies operating in the US. This makes it by far the most profitable pharmaceutical market in the world which, according to industry data, accounts for around 60 per cent of total proprietary pharmaceutical industry profits (EFPIA 2004).[5] Many of the M&As mentioned above were carried out with a view to increasing the penetration of the US market, an understandable strategy if one were to take into account other characteristics, such as the existence of deep and well developed capital markets and the unchallenged advantage in biotechnology the US enjoys (Borrus 2002; Ramirez and Tylecote 1999). The American proprietary pharmaceutical sector is therefore quite transnational. This characteristic, coupled with some traits of the US policymaking process that facilitate its capture by specific interests, goes some way to explaining the crucial role the US pharmaceutical industry and the US government have played in bringing about TRIPs.

The most notable, but not surprising, change in pharmaceutical IP protection introduced by TRIPs is in the field of pharmaceutical patents. The TRIPs agreement grants a twenty-year protection to the owner of a pharmaceutical patent that prevents anyone within the granting territory from exploiting the invention, that is, from using, making, or selling the new patented drug. Before TRIPS, patent duration was significantly shorter in many countries. For example, both developed and developing countries provided for patent terms ranging from 15 to 17 years, whilst in certain developing countries patents were granted for shorter terms of five to seven years (WHO 2005). Importantly, before the TRIPS agreement came into force, many countries provided only process, not product, patents. As mentioned earlier, product patents provide for protection of the product, whereas process patents provide protection for the process or method of manufacturing used. Essentially, process patents do not prevent the manufacture of patented products by a different process, such as reverse engineering, where a process or method different from that which was invented (and patented) is used. Developing countries that have substantial generic pharmaceutical sectors were able to support their development through national and international IP laws that allowed them the flexibility to protect pharmaceutical products and processes only partially, if at all. India provides perhaps the best example of a developing country designing an industrial and IP strategy in the 1970s aimed at supporting its generic pharmaceutical sector through, *inter alia*, providing only for pharmaceutical process but not product patents. As a result, the Indian generic industry became one of the most successful in the world, although its continued successful performance will no doubt be affected by the entry into force of TRIPs obligations for pharmaceuticals in India in 2005.

Today, the options for supporting or strengthening generic pharmaceutical sectors are rather limited for developing countries, this being one of the very goals of TRIPs. This is an important challenge in terms of improving access to affordable medicines in the developing world because although some large developing countries, such as Israel, Brazil and Thailand, have reasonably well developed generic sectors, they are capable only of producing medicines out of ready-made active pharmaceutical ingredients. Only a handful of developing countries, namely Argentina, Mexico, India, China and South Korea, have generic sectors capable of manufacturing a patented drug through reverse engineering (Kaplan and Laing 2005). In any case, the production of generic versions of on-patent drugs through reverse engineering is no longer an option, unless the pharmaceutical company has decided not to apply for patent protection (or its application has been unsuccessful) in these countries and those to which they may wish to export. One legal option for authorising the generic production of patented medicines is through compulsory licences,[6] but governments in developing and developed countries alike tend not to use this option lightly for fear of sending negative signals to foreign investors about their commitment to protecting private property and providing a business-friendly environment more generally. In any case, the TRIPs agreement, at the insistence of proprietary pharmaceutical business actors, laid out a series of procedural requirements for compulsory licenses, which effectively limit their use (but do not eliminate it). Such TRIPs obligations for pharmaceuticals essentially have the effect of limiting and delaying the use of generics and fencing off the markets of proprietary pharmaceutical companies that helped bring TRIPs about. But, as we have seen in this chapter, this strategy comes at a high cost, in that while proprietary pharmaceutical companies routinely top business ranking in terms of profitability (Scherer 1993; Public Citizen 2002), unmet health needs persist and many patients go without treatment altogether, even when medicines to treat their condition exist.

As we shall see, these concerns thrust the IP-access to medicines contests to the forefront of the IP regime in the late 1990s. At its core, as argued in this chapter, it is essentially a conflict between business actors, the proprietary pharmaceutical companies, who see knowledge as capital, and those who see it largely as a public good, or as facilitating the provision of public goods such as public health. The only case of proprietary pharmaceutical companies actively lobbying for weaker IP protection invoking public goods arguments occurred at the beginning of the twentieth century, when the American pharmaceutical industry found that its growth prospects were severely limited due to the patent protection enjoyed by the then dominant German companies. The American Pharmaceutical Association strongly appealed to moral arguments which highlighted the role of pharmaceutical IPRs as primarily aimed at enhancing public benefit (Dutfield 2003a). But, once the German pharmaceutical industry was stripped of its patents after World War I and the US pharmaceutical industry emerged as a key player in the world pharmaceutical market, the position of the US pharmaceutical industry came into line with the industry as a whole on the issue of public interest: new pharmaceuticals would not be available to address health needs in the absence of IP protection. Since the 1980s we have seen the strengthening and expansion of IP protection for pharmaceuticals, first in the developed world and, through TRIPs, across the world as a whole. But this extension of IP protection worldwide has not been balanced with improved, affordable access to medicines worldwide. As was argued earlier, the granting of IPRs which are not balanced with affordable access to the products invented and protected is economically, socially and morally unjustifiable. When unbalanced, they are even more unjustifiable in the case of pharmaceuticals because of their direct impact on human health and life.

3
Linking IPRs to Trade: The Making of TRIPs

When the GATT Uruguay Round was launched in 1986, its ambitious agenda included an item on IPRs that appeared almost as a footnote that some thought would not survive the end of the Round (Adede 2003). Seven years later, not only had the item survived, but it had resulted in an agreement, the TRIPs agreement, which eventually became one of the key pillars of the trade regime itself. What is most impressive about this turn of events is not so much the success of the regime actors pushing for IPRs in eventually securing an agreement, although this was no mean feat. The TRIPs agreement is, without doubt, *the* most important development in the governance of IPRs in the last 100 years or so, having set in motion a legally-binding 'one-size-fits-all' global IPRs regime which has visibly expanded and strengthened IP protection and enforcement across most of the world. But, rather more impressive was the success of these actors in launching a global IPRs regime that governs IPRs largely as a trade and competitiveness issue at the expense of much else. As we shall see, this new stage in the IPRs regime was brought about by these specific interests and was not based on any substantive analysis or discussion on how a global IPRs regime should balance the many interests and issue-areas affected by IPRs. Indeed, as TRIPs itself states, the primary purpose of enforcing IPRs is to promote free trade in goods and services that embody IP (Katzenberger and Kur 1996; May 2000; Anawalt 2003). That is, free trade, and not enhanced innovation and public access, the very cornerstone of the institution of IP, is at the core of the current IPRs regime.

Despite certain references to public interests in its preamble, then, TRIPs is not primarily concerned with how the (strong) IP protection it mandates affects innovation and access to knowledge, nor the provision of public goods such as healthcare. It is built on the assumption that strong IPRs are good and necessary for innovation and technological advancement. But, as we discussed in the previous chapter, IPRs are essentially contested and, despite the sophisticated analytical tools at our disposal, there is no agreement yet over what IPRs accomplish and whether we can do without them altogether (Machlup 1958; Abbott et al. 1999). A second assumption implicit in TRIPs is that the lack of strong IP protection is a barrier to free trade which needs to be eliminated. In a very basic sense, IPRs are indeed linked to trade; as we saw in the previous chapter, the very purpose of IPRs is to ensure that intangible (knowledge) goods are commodified and then traded (May 2000). But this was not what lay at the core of the IPRs–trade link; rather, the lack of IP protection in certain key and prospective markets was framed as 'theft' and 'piracy', that is, as a barrier to the 'legitimate' trade in goods embodying IPRs. Framed as a trade barrier, lack of worldwide IP protection became a legitimate issue to be regulated by the trade regime. The problem is, of course, that IPRs are hugely complex and many more issues than trade are implicit in them. Few would argue that IPRs do not have an impact on trade. But they also impact upon many other issue-areas, such as health, education, creativity, agriculture, competition, biodiversity, technological innovation and transfer, human rights, development and investment (Maskus and Reichman 2004). The links between these (and more) issue-areas and IPRs were marginalised by the IPRs–trade link established through TRIPs, only to emerge later on at the very core of IPRs contests, including those over access to medicines.

The claim that lack of IP protection is a barrier to free trade was used to legitimise TRIPs within the trade regime, but it is one that even free-trade supporters themselves do not accept wholeheartedly (Bhagwati 2002). Indeed, some of the most passionate defenders of free trade in the nineteenth century were in fact convinced that IPRs (especially patents) had a *constraining* effect on free trade, and were actually successful, albeit only for a while, in rolling back patent protection in several European countries in the late 1800s (Penrose 1951). The early trade regime appeared to have had internalised some of these concerns because, while it did not prevent its members from granting IPRs (GATT Article XX (d)), it only permitted IP protection on condition that it did not lead to arbitrary trade discrimination (Katzenberger and Kur 1996; Watal 2001). Less than 50 years later, a radical change of mind occurred as all trade regime members became legally bound to grant and enforce (similar) IPRs, and regime membership itself became predicated upon the acceptance of such obligations. This chapter follows the process through which this change of mind came about and, by doing so, it helps reveal why it was that TRIPs entered the scene carrying with it the seeds of the contestations that we follow in the coming chapters. Put simply, contests ensued because not all regime actors had a shared understanding of the necessity and merits of governing IPRs as a trade issue. The change of mind referred to earlier occurred primarily within a specific group of actors who (re)defined their interests as intrinsically linked to stronger, legally-binding IP protection worldwide. As this chapter shows, the remaining trade regime members were largely coerced into accepting this framing of IPRs. Acceptance of these terms was in part facilitated by certain characteristics of the trade regime during the 1980s that are briefly highlighted in the next section. The rest of the chapter follows with an analysis of the key regime actors that helped bring about TRIPs, with a special focus on pharmaceutical business actors and the broader concomitant changes that facilitated their success.

3.1   The trade regime of the 1980s

The TRIPs agreement cannot be understood simply as the successful outcome of strategic action on the part of certain actors, nor can it build its legitimacy on that basis alone. Its legitimacy was claimed on the basis of a specific framing of IPRs as a trade issue, whilst also invoking the role of IPRs in technology transfer, foreign investment and development, so as to appeal to and assuage other regime members' concerns. Just as importantly, the inclusion of IPRs into the trade regime was sought and eventually made possible due to a number of ideological and material changes that were taking place within the trade regime from the 1970s onwards. Regimes are dynamic processes, and changes occurring within the trade regime in the 1970s and 1980s were especially significant in facilitating the successful inclusion of IPRs into its remit. The 1970s was a tumultuous and complex period in the world economy that had significant repercussions within and beyond the trade regime but, for our purposes, one noteworthy change was the shift away from the 'ad hocery' of reciprocal tariff concessions that had characterised the early trade regime towards inside-the-border policies (Ostry 1997; 2000). It was during this period that a significant conceptual redefinition of what policy areas were trade-related and hence subject to regulation occurred, often including areas, such as IPRs, previously regarded as pertaining to the domain of domestic economic policymaking.

More broadly, this change was part of the unravelling of the embedded liberalism that had characterised the early trade regime, the compromise whereby the long-term expansion of open, multilateral trade relations was to be balanced with governments' responsibility for managing the economy in ways that ensured domestic stability (Ruggie 1982). In essence, this compromise allowed key regime members, most notably the US and some Western European countries, to selectively liberalise trade in certain sectors, fiercely protect others, and fulfil the political and social vision of the progressive interventionist state at the same time (Howse 2002). This worked reasonably well in the West during the boom years of the 1950s and 1960s, but the recession of the 1970s, combined with increasing competition from the East, resulted in the adoption of various sorts of protectionist measures at the insistence of the domestic industrial sectors affected. In fact, key regime members found that their economic make-up placed them under considerable pressure both to adopt protectionist measures for certain domestic sectors in decline, and to press for liberalisation measures multilaterally on behalf of other dynamic sectors, such as services and high-tech industries (Lipson 1982).

Perhaps no other government was experiencing these contradictory pulls during the 1970s more strongly than that of the US. And, incidentally, no other regime member's domestic exigencies had been able to influence the trade regime to the extent that those of the US have done until recently. Developments in the US political scene during the 1970s were complex, but it is noteworthy that its growing trade deficit was blamed not on overconsumption but on the existence of non-tariff trade barriers and 'unfair' competition from abroad (Destler 1992; Hudec 1991). Hence, against the backdrop of the deepening economic recession and rising protectionism of the 1970s, it was under great pressure from the US, and its use of bilateral retaliatory threats against 'unfair' and 'unjustifiable' foreign barriers which hindered American trade, that trade negotiations at the Tokyo Round were initiated and concluded (Destler 1992; Winham 1986). The Round (1973–79) concluded with a series of agreements on non-tariff trade barriers, such as safeguards, subsidies and government procurement, but this venturing inside the domestic regulatory domain, and the conceptual blurring between 'domestic – international' and 'trade – non trade' that it set in motion, was only a glimpse of what was to come in the following years.

Importantly, these developments were part of broader changes, of which the ascendance of the Washington Consensus was perhaps the most profound, as it questioned the very normative basis of embedded liberalism (Howse 2002). But while the compromise of embedded liberalism was thus unravelling in the western world, that process was never fully extended to developing countries. In fact, domestic stability was often purchased in industrialised countries partly by externalising the cost of adjustment to developing countries (Ruggie 1982; Lang 2006). Most such countries, differences in levels of development notwithstanding, had been largely marginalised within the early trade regime. In fact, their experience until the late 1970s had convinced them that the trade regime was either hostile or indifferent to their interests (Oyejide 2000; Srinivasan 1999). During the 1980s, however, the shift towards inside-the-border measures set in motion earlier was accompanied by a substantial change in the attitude of most developing countries towards the trade regime. Their economic policy had by then shifted away from import substitution towards export-oriented industrialisation strategies (Ford 2002). This change was partly facilitated by the gathering debt crisis, which exploded in full in the 1980s. Under the severe financial conditions that followed, the strategy of boosting trade competitiveness and market liberalisation in order to increase foreign exchange earnings had great appeal for some developing countries. For those that remained unconvinced, the IMF and World Bank structural adjustment policies, and the conditions of market reform and liberalisation contained therein, removed all remaining doubts as to the necessity of undertaking such steps.

Eventually, these changes, accompanied by evidence of high rates of growth in East Asia generally attributed to export-led strategies (Clement et al. 1999), caused developing countries to seek greater participation in, and influence over, the trade regime. Importantly, the new economic opportunities that some of the larger and more advanced developing members' markets offered to the major regime members made the case of incorporating them fully into the trade regime increasingly appealing (Payne 2006). Hence, both groups found in the late 1980s that their interests in the trade regime had become intertwined, although not necessarily compatible. Contests between regime members since then have been numerous, but it can generally be said that power differentials within the trade regime are such that developing members as a group have had little success, apart from blocking deals, in shaping the agenda or achieving outcomes that are clearly in their favour.

As we shall see shortly, it was the coming together of all these (and other) developments that facilitated the inclusion of TRIPs into the trade regime. Among other things, the economic recession of the 1970s in the developed world helped to thrust to the forefront of economic recovery the more promising and dynamic high-tech industries, most of which were reliant on IP protection. This change occurred at a time when the role of the state was being redefined from, broadly speaking, one of ensuring domestic stability to one of creating and maintaining a favourable policies and a regulatory environment able to attract and retain private investment. Essentially, this opened up space for the (IP) concerns of these business actors to come to the forefront of the political agendas in key developed countries, especially in the US and Europe. That they would soon go on to become an important item in multilateral trade negotiations was not improbable, given the advantageous bargaining position enjoyed by their home countries within the trade regime and the strides the latter was making into the domestic regulatory domain.

3.2   Bringing the IPRs–trade link into the trade regime

Ideas about linking trade to services and IPRs, probably the two most contentious issues which eventually became part of the Uruguay Round negotiating agenda in 1986, had been contemplated since the 1970s. Concerns about the lack of IPRs protection as constituting a barrier to trade were voiced during the late 1970s from all three sectors with the highest stakes in the IP regime: the copyright, brand-name goods, and research-intensive industries. But until the early 1980s their interests and strategies were not coordinated in any significant way. For instance, the copyright industry's vocal complaints about the growth of 'piracy' of copyrighted works prompted certain developed countries to attempt to revise and strengthen the Berne Convention (Matthews 2002a). Likewise, research-intensive industries were also voicing demands for a reform of the Paris Convention in the late 1970s. Pfizer, one of the major proprietary pharmaceutical companies, played a key role in these attempts as, having decided to aggressively market its products in developing countries, it was particularly concerned about any reverse engineering of its patented medicines abroad (Braithwaite and Drahos 2000). Indeed, armed with arguments about the need for minimum IP protection and enforcement standards, Pfizer's CEO Edmund Pratt,[1] alongside IBM's John Opel, took the initiative to WIPO himself in the late 1970s (Ryan 1998a). The brand-name goods industries had also mobilised during the late 1970s to protect trademarks in luxury and high-fashion goods; the International Anti-Counterfeiting Coalition had been successful in persuading both the US and the EEC to table an anti-counterfeit code in the latter stages of the GATT Tokyo Round (Adede 2003). These multilateral efforts were accompanied by efforts to strengthen IPRs protection through other mechanisms, such as through raising IPRs issues in bilateral talks and challenging IPRs infringement in national courts (Sell 2003; Matthews 2002a).

Nonetheless, these efforts did not bear much fruit: the GATT Anti-Counterfeit Code was presented too late in the Tokyo Round and attracted only a lukewarm response. At the same time, efforts towards reforming WIPO's Conventions were met not simply with resistance from developing countries, but with diametrically opposed demands from the latter to weaken IP protection worldwide as part of wider efforts to establish a New International Economic Order in the late 1970s. Apart from WIPO, contests over IP standards spilt over to UNESCO (through linking copyrights to education and other human rights) and UNCTAD (through linking patents to technology transfer and development). Nevertheless, these two other fora, and potential IP linkages, were effectively marginalised: some developed countries argued successfully that UNCTAD had no competence over IPRs (Drahos and Braithwaite 2002), while the US and UK withdrew from UNESCO altogether in the early 1980s. Thus, in the late 1970s and early 1980s, WIPO became the main stage for contests between the opposing interests of IP-reliant industries and developing countries. Ultimately, the revision of the Paris Convention regarding patents proved unsuccessful and broke down in 1984, only two years before the start of the Uruguay Round.

Contests at WIPO, and their outcome, had important implications for how the actors involved redefined their interests and strategies. The revision process seemed close to conclusion in 1982, when negotiations stalled mainly over the issues of compulsory licensing. Owing to this fact, developing countries were probably lulled into a certain complacency which blurred their judgment about the real changes taking place with regard to IP protection in the developed countries (Watal 2001). They continued to consider IPRs as an issue linked to development and were slow to come to terms with the fact that, as we shall see, their developed counterparts had come to see IP protection as a key competitiveness issue (May 2000). At the same time, contests over WIPO IP conventions convinced IP-reliant industries that WIPO was not the forum to be trusted with IP protection worldwide, or expected to deliver higher levels of such protection. In the words of Pfizer's General Counsel, 'our experience with WIPO was the last straw in our attempt to operate by persuasion' (Clemente, quoted in Santoro 1992: 8). With the failure of the last session of the revision process convened in Geneva in 1984, the position of developing and developed countries regarding IP protection could not have been further apart. Importantly, the IP–trade linkage had also been established by then. From this point in time until the completion of the TRIPs agreement, the developing countries moved into a defensive position on the IPRs front, while IP-reliant industries and their home countries emerged determined to ensure that IPRs protection was dealt with 'appropriately' elsewhere.

In retrospect, WIPO might not have been the ideal forum in which to deal 'appropriately' with IP protection from the perspective of IP-reliant industries. WIPO administered IP protection in an atomised fashion, wherein separate treaties with varying membership dealt with different IPRs, preoccupied primarily with their technical details, but with no enforcement or dispute mechanism[2] and no regard to the larger picture (Emmert 1990). Moreover, by the late 1970s, the larger picture had changed substantially. Changes in economic activities and organisation in some advanced industrialised countries had set in motion a clear shift of their economic make-up from industry-based to knowledge-based economies. In other words, high-technology, brand-name goods and entertainment industries emerged as key and promising industrial sectors capable of delivering in economic terms when most other traditional industrial sectors were in relative decline. Indeed, OECD figures confirm that the contribution of advanced technology industries to economic performance for most developed countries has increased substantially since 1970s (Dutfield 2003a). This shift was, and continues to be, enabled and accompanied by significant technological advances which both facilitate and threaten it, in that they increase the possibility of 'theft' and 'piracy' on an unprecedented scale at home and abroad (May and Sell 2006). Indeed, the language of 'theft' and 'piracy' abroad was used successfully to raise sentiments of unfairness regarding IP protection, but, in reality, those charges were not valid as long as intellectual property was not recognised as property by the laws of other countries (Henderson 1997). Furthermore, 'theft' and 'piracy' abroad was fuelled largely by the desire of (mainly developing) countries to catch up in the industrial process, much as today's advanced countries had done during their early developmental stages. However, once the latter came to perceive their further growth closely linked to growth in their knowledge- and information-based sectors, the protection of these sectors' assets, particularly IPRs, became a priority for both domestic and international economic policy.

Both the US and the EEC had been alerted by the concerns raised by US and European business about the need to improve international IP protection since the late 1970s.[3] However, it was the US which had both an absolute and a comparative advantage in the IP-reliant sectors mentioned above. In addition, it was the institutional changes within the US which enabled and facilitated the framing of IPRs protection as a trade issue, although the idea itself was perhaps first formulated by the UK Publisher's Association request in 1978 to the US Trade Representative (USTR) to take trade actions against infringements worldwide.[4] The USTR did not at that time appreciate the significance of UK publishing interests aiming to influence US public policy (Matthews 2002a), but the Association's proposed strategy was precisely what the USTR adopted not long thereafter. It was in the 1984 Trade Act that the US government officially linked IP protection and international trade, thus accepting and incorporating an approach to international IP protection developed and distilled in the private sector during the preceding years.

The separate efforts of different IP-reliant industries began to merge and gain momentum in the early 1980s. The International Anti-Counterfeiting Coalition, bringing together trademark interests pressing for a GATT code at the end of the Tokyo Round, was joined by the Copyright Alliance, pressing for changes in US trade policy, while patent-reliant industries were testifying before Congress in favour of patent, copyright and trademark interests as a whole (Sell 1999). The coalition of these sectors established in the early 1980s was formidable, but it would not have been as successful as it proved to be had it not been for certain macroeconomic and institutional changes taking place in the US during the same period. As is well known, the US growing trade deficit during the 1970s was mainly presented as a problem of 'unfair' trade which fuelled concerns that foreign markets were less open than America's, that US firms and workers were facing 'unfair' competition from abroad, and that the US was losing out in the marketplace (Hudec 1991; Destler 1992). Over time, the inability to remedy the trade deficit shifted the political focus to trade policy; the latter became the focus of US efforts to improve both its deficit and its competitiveness in the global market (Sell 2003). In turn, the US preoccupation with competitiveness strengthened the hand of business in shaping its trade policies (Strange 1993).

Not surprisingly, in 1974 the US Congress undertook the major revision of the 1930 Tariff Act which included an amendment of Section 337. This amendment was aimed at offering remedies to domestic industries deemed to be subject to 'unfair' practices of foreign companies, including measures to combat infringements of domestic IPRs. It also incorporated the infamous Section 301, which allowed the President to initiate, upon his initiative or private complaint, retaliatory trade actions against countries that maintained 'unjustifiable' and 'unreasonable' barriers that burdened American trade (Destler 1992). No retaliatory acts were taken under Section 301 in its early years and the amended Section 337 provided no relief for IP infringements *abroad* (Matthews 2002a). Due to industry pressure about these issues, Congress later sought to strengthen Section 301 provisions in the 1979 amendments, as well as to increase the private sector's input into (international) trade policy through the Advisory Committee on Trade Negotiations (ACTN) already established by the 1974 Act, thus offering the US private sector access to government to a degree unheard of in the EU and other countries.

By this time, private sector interests regarding strengthened IP protection abroad had started to come together and once Pfizer's CEO, Ed Pratt, became chair of the ACTN in 1981, the stage for linking IPRs to trade policy in the US was set. At this point in time, no coherent formulation linking the two areas existed within the private sector, but some successful bilateral consultations initiated in 1982 at the behest of various US private interests between US trade officials and Korea, Mexico, Singapore and Taiwan on their IP laws had already demonstrated to both the US government and IP-reliant industries that exploiting the IP and trade linkage was fruitful (Enyart 1990). From then on, Ed Pratt and John Opel, both members of the ACTN, embarked upon efforts to convince other companies that infringements of their IPRs abroad were unacceptable (Drahos 1995) and that improvement on IP standards worldwide was possible through a trade link (Matthews 2002a). For their part, US copyright interests had identified that their problems lay not with IP standards, but with their enforcement. Indeed, the Motion Picture Association was successful in securing a provision in the Caribbean Basin Economic Recovery Act of 1983 which excluded countries pirating US copyrighted products from Generalised System of Preferences (GSP) benefits (Ryan 1998a). This small victory had significant implications. Importantly, it found expression in the 1984 Trade Act amendments, which not only made GSP status and benefits dependant upon satisfactory IP protection, but also strengthened Section 301 still further, both by giving the USTR authority to initiate cases on its own and by explicitly stating that the failure of other countries to protect IP adequately would be actionable (Sell 1995).

These changes incorporated in the 1984 Act were the direct result of mounting pressure from high-tech and copyright industries, which laid the blame for the growing trade deficit abroad on lack of IP protection; they promoted themselves as viable and vibrant industries capable of improving US competitiveness, but especially if their IP assets were protected abroad so as to ensure free and fair trade. Hence, as Sell (1999: 180) argued, by laying the blame for the economic malaise elsewhere and offering an attractive alternative that resonated with the long-standing free-trade ethos of the US, the ideas formulated by these industries captured the attention of US policy-makers as both feasible and politically desirable. The link between trade and IP protection abroad was thus established in the US by 1984, but bringing this link into the GATT regime was not a *fait accompli*. However, it may be argued that given (i) the strong resistance by developing countries to rising IP protection standards at WIPO, (ii) the rearrangement of US trade policy objectives to include the protection of US-owned IPRs abroad by means that included coercion; and (iii) its enormous leverage as a GATT member, seeking to bring the IP issue into the trade regime was the obvious next step. Once global IP protection entered the US trade policy stream, it was very likely that it would go on to become a GATT issue.

Indeed, in 1984, the USTR requested private sector input on the issue of including IP in the upcoming GATT; a year latter, Jacques Gorlin, a consultant to the ACTN, presented a report[5] which synthesised the business sector's thinking on IPRs up to that point and outlined the contours of a possible multilateral agreement for the GATT (Sell 1999). According to Gorlin, the advantages of incorporating IP into the multilateral trade regime included: (i) the availability of a dispute settlement mechanism; (ii) the possibility of linking progress on IPRs to other issues in the Round (a precedent for which was set during the Tokyo Round); and (iii) the greater political leverage of trade officials (compared to IP regulators) in domestic settings. Presented with impressive figures of losses due to 'piracy' in various countries by business interests in the mid 1980s, the USRT initiated a Section 301 investigation against Korea and Brazil which carried the implicit threat of trade sanctions if negotiations failed (Ryan 1998a). Korea acquiesced one year later, establishing 'better' IP protection laws and thus offering a clear example of what could be accomplished using trade instruments to achieve IP objectives (Mossinghoff 1991). The talks with Brazil continued for nearly three years and, although there was no agreement, the impact of this pressure to get Brazil to agree to the Uruguay Round agenda was not negligible. These developments set a precedent for the bilateral pressure that was soon to fall upon other developing countries designed to break their opposition to the IP agenda in the upcoming Uruguay Round.

At the beginning of 1986, the USTR Clayton Yeutter asked Pratt and Opel of the ACTN for their assistance in putting IP on the Uruguay Round agenda, pointing out that this was dependent on support from the EU, Japan and Canada (Sell 2003).[6] By this point, the USTR had already convinced the reluctant US copyright industries to join the multilateral efforts by pointing out that the inclusion of IP in a GATT multilateral agreement offered both wide international coverage and enforcement mechanisms to deal with infringement of IPRs worldwide (Braithwaite and Drahos 2000).[7] The next step was getting the other Quad members on board. As we noted before, the EEC was already aware of business concerns about weak IP protection abroad, but its members differed both in their support for overall enhanced IP protection and in their attitudes to it being negotiated at the GATT (Drahos and Braithwaite 2002). Nonetheless, the EEC amended its trade law in the same year as the US to accommodate IP issues amongst obstacles to trade adopted or maintained by third countries.[8] In addition, as early as 1987, it also took measures against South Korea (as the US had done one year earlier) for alleged IP-related offences, withdrawing GSP benefits for certain Korean goods imported into Europe (Dutfield 2003a). Not long afterwards, it moved against Indonesia and Thailand for record piracy (Drahos and Braithwaite 2002). For its part, Japan initially favoured the more modest approach of a code on counterfeiting, although it generally found itself siding with the US and the EEC on the IP issue at the GATT (Matsushita 1992).

Upon calls for help from the USTR, Opel and Pratt created the Intellectual Property Committee (IPC) in March 1986 which included several proprietary pharmaceutical companies.[9] From that point on, the IPC made it its mission not simply to bring European and Japanese business on board, but to see to it that the IP issue was included in the Uruguay Round agenda and was concluded satisfactorily therein. In the few months between its creation and the GATT meeting at Punta del Este in September 1986, the IPC was remarkably successful in convincing its European and Japanese counterparts (UNICE and Keidanren) to increase pressure on their governments to put IP on the trade agenda, mainly by appealing to the common interest of ensuring the protection of these industries' intangible assets worldwide (Sell 1999; 2003). Both UNICE and Keidanren were concerned that IP was too new a subject to become part of the GATT and that, anticipating the complex Uruguay agenda and the opposition of developing countries to incorporating IP into the GATT, felt initially that IP was ill-suited to the Round (Ostry 1990). Eventually all agreed that the issue of IP protection was too important to leave to governments and that business needed to come together with a course of action, if it was to safeguard their future prosperity. UNICE and Keidanren eventually wholeheartedly adopted the trade-based approach formulated by IPC and were successful in putting pressure on their governments to do so too.

Meanwhile at the GATT, developing countries' representatives, who had paid little attention to such developments and were already of the view that the existing international IP regime was tilted in favour of developed countries, argued that WIPO rather than GATT had competence over IP issues and that IP protection levels ought to remain a sovereign choice. From the 1982 GATT Ministerial meeting, when only a limited agreement was reached about considering a potential anti-counterfeit code due to opposition from some developing countries, until well into 1985, the latter vehemently opposed the inclusion of IPRs on the trade agenda. At the GATT Preparatory Committee established in 1985 to identify the next Round's agenda issues, some key developing countries, particularly India and Brazil, continued to oppose the inclusion of both IPRs and services, focusing, mistakenly as it turned out, much more energy on the latter (Watal 2001). Given that no effective counterproposals were offered by these opponents, apart from the argument on GATT's incompetence on IP issues, a proposal emerged from the Preparatory Committee on July 1986 setting out a compromise between those insisting on the inclusion of IPRs and those questioning GATT's competence (Matthews 2002a). This proposal, although it did not receive unanimous support, formed the basis for the inclusion of IPRs at the Punta del Este Ministerial Declaration on 1986, which stated that the aim of negotiations on IPRs was to 'clarify GATT provisions and elaborate as appropriate new rules and disciplines' as well as to 'develop a multilateral framework of principles, rules and disciplines dealing with international trade in counterfeit goods, taking into account work already undertaken at the GATT and without prejudices to ... initiatives ... by the WIPO or elsewhere' (GATT 1986: 25–26). IPRs were thus officially part of the GATT agenda, but, as we shall see in the next section, opposition to the IPRs–trade link was to continue well into the Round.

3.3   Negotiating TRIPs (1986–1993)

As we saw, the inclusion of IPRs into the GATT rested only on some vague instructions to 'elaborate as appropriate new rules and disciplines', but interpretations varied amongst actors. In its description of the Declaration, the IPC argued that it included 'a strong negotiating mandate for intellectual property in the new round' (Drahos and Braithwaite 2002: 120); for its part, the USTR was keen to see the inclusion of all IPRs in the GATT (Matthews 2002a), while the EEC had not yet decided whether the GATT should set minimum standards on IPRs (Watal 2001). Most developing countries adopted a rather restrictive interpretation of the Punta del Este mandate on IPRs as mainly related to counterfeit goods and other strictly trade-related issues, maintaining that WIPO was the organisation with competence over IPRs standards (Adede 2003). From early 1987, when formal negotiations for the Round began, until the mid-term review in April 1989, when developing countries accepted the inclusion of *substantive* IPRs standards into the GATT, negotiations on IPRs did not venture beyond defining the mandate of negotiations on IPRs. However, the longer it took to shape the IPRs agenda at the GATT, the weaker the developing countries' opposition became, the more established the IPRs–trade link, and the more hardline and extensive the position of some developed countries and their IP-reliant industries.

Ideas and proposals about how an agreement on IPRs could be brought into the GATT were still fluid, both within the TRIPs negotiating group and within business circles at the beginning of the Round. This said, the essential elements of what was to become TRIPs were present in the very first proposals submitted by the US, the EEC, Japan and Switzerland. It is noteworthy that, while the US position at this point was that negotiations ought to include patents, trade secrets, copyright, trademarks and so on, the EEC proposal lacked statements concerning substantive standards, focusing instead on issues related to enforcement provisions (Matthews 2002a). This difference in position appears to have been the main sticking point between the US and the EEC until mid 1988, at which point the EEC agreed on GATT's competence on substantive IPRs standards, perhaps as part of an agreement reached among developed countries to include geographical indicators as IP matter, for which the EEC had come under pressure from European wine and spirit producers (Watal 2001). Importantly, the rapprochement of the EEC to the US position, which by mid 1988 had expanded and solidified even further, was closely linked to certain developments taking place within business sector thinking on the IPRs–GATT issue.

We noted earlier that the IPC was created only months before the launch of the new Round and that it played a crucial role in bringing the IP item onto the Round's agenda. Once this initial aim was achieved, the IPC shifted its focus towards developing a consensual model of a

GATT IP agreement in conjunction with UNICE and Keidanren. During two years of intensive work stretching over three continents, a set of principles was developed and presented in the 1988 'Basic Framework on GATT Provisions on Intellectual Property: Statement of Views of the European, Japanese and United States Business Community' (the Framework), with the aim of providing a multilateral blueprint for trade negotiations at the GATT (Sell 1999; 2003). In reality, the Framework was not a modest collection of views; it prescribed a set of basic principles on dealing with IPRs if countries wished to see the benefits of high-technology entrepreneurialism within their borders. Hence, precisely as TRIPs was to mandate five years later: (i) minimum standards of IPRs would have to be set (on all IPRs of interest to industries involved in the drafting of the Framework); (ii) infringement of IP would have to be criminalised; (iii) states had to put limits on public interest exceptions to IP protection; and, (iv) states themselves would have to agree to become subject to dispute settlement procedures if they failed to comply with their obligations on IP protection (Drahos and Braithwaite 2002).

Being a consensus document, the Framework also included some compromises; importantly, one related to compulsory licensing, which the US pharmaceutical companies strongly opposed but conceded to, in order to keep the European and Japanese industries on board. Another related to transition periods for developing countries, and was included in order to induce the broadest possible participation in an IP agreement; this was likewise urged by European business (Sell 2003). Once consensus was achieved, the IPC, UNICE and Keidanren presented their Framework to their governments, other industries and the GATT Secretariat in order to use the principles and norms it contained as the basis for the GATT IP agreement. This turned out to be much easier for the IPC which, having already been urged by the USTR to help in developing the official US negotiating position in 1987, received requests for 100–150 copies of the 1988 Framework by the US government, which then sent it out as reflecting its own views (Sell 1999). In addition to synthesising fundamental principles for dealing with IP protection at the GATT in the Framework and cooperating closely with their respective governments, the IPC, UNICE and Keidanren also worked closely with the GATT Secretariat and other governments, most notably with those of the Friends of Intellectual Property Group, formed around the time of Punta del Este to help bring about the trade-IP agenda.[10] Such efforts were welcome, as neither trade officials of these (and other) governments nor the GATT Secretariat had much competence in or knowledge of IPRs issues.

While as a direct result of the principles and ideas developed in the private sector the developed countries' proposals at the GATT negotiating table were converging by 1988, developing countries had not moved much from their initial position. In the TRIPs negotiating group, India and Brazil continued to lead the opposition of other developing countries to the discussion of substantive issues on IPRs. Their argument was on much the same lines as early on: the WIPO was to deal with IPRs standards, while GATT should have competence only over trade in counterfeit goods. Moreover, they argued that IP protection should be subjected to other technological and developmental priorities. Both the EEC and US submissions during 1987 and 1988 countered this claim by arguing, as business interests had done in the Framework, that adequate protection and enforcement of IPRs was crucial to economic development, although empirical evidence is not conclusive on such a link, and their own economic development route certainly does not support it. It is noteworthy, however, that developing countries' opposition was not united; throughout 1988, countries belonging to the Association of Southeast Asian Nations (ASEAN) abstained from openly attacking developed countries' positions (Watal 2001), probably due to the bilateral pressure that was brought to bear on them. Indeed, it was under such pressure that, only two months after a bold submission to the TRIPs negotiating group in October 1988, Brazil also visibly weakened its opposition.

Brazil, alongside Argentina and Korea, again became the focus of US section 301 investigation at the end of 1988 following complaints from certain US IP-reliant companies, including pharmaceutical patent protection.[11] As we noted earlier, Brazil had been targeted since 1985; it amended its copyright law in 1987, but that same year the US Pharmaceutical Manufacturers' Association filed a complaint to the USTR on the absence of effective patent protection for pharmaceuticals. Faced with reluctance from Brazil to amend its patent law, the US government increased tariffs to 100 per cent on several Brazilian goods, affecting trade worth US$39 million, in the very same month that Brazil made its submission at the GATT (October 1988) (Ryan 1998a). The Brazil case was used strategically by the US government to weaken developing countries' opposition at the GATT negotiating table and, given that sanctions are expensive even to the country setting them, it was also a clear display of the level of the US and US business actors' commitment to the IP cause (Drahos and Braithwaite 2002).

Indeed, the US business actors had kept up the momentum on the IP front at home, even though the IP mandate was now part of the

GATT negotiating agenda. Following the request of the USTR in 1987 to develop quantitative estimates of the distortions in US trade caused by inadequate IP protection abroad, the US International Trade Commission (ITC) presented its comprehensive study in February 1988, which estimated overall losses to be between US$43–61 billion (Emmert 1990: 1327). Incidentally, an independent (and more limited) study undertaken by Gadbaw and Richards (1988) estimated losses in revenues due to piracy abroad around the US$3.4 billion mark. As expected, ITC figures had a formidable effect on policy-makers who, under increased pressure for a trade remedy for America's economic woes, amended the Trade Act again in August 1988.

The 1988 Omnibus Trade and Competitiveness Act, achieved under sustained pressure from private sector groups to use Section 301 more vigorously, gave a definite boost to the trade-based approach to IP protection. Amongst other measures, the 1988 Act transferred authority from the US President to the USTR to identify *and* take action under Section 301 against IP-violating countries within strict time-limits. In addition, it mandated an annual list (the so-called Special 301 provision) identifying priority offending countries based on information provided by the private sectors affected (Sell 2003).[12] The 1989 inaugural list included Korea, Brazil, India, Mexico, Thailand, China, Saudi Arabia and Taiwan and was published, incidentally, just as the scheduled GATT meeting in Geneva was to take place with the aim of resolving differences on TRIPs (and agriculture and textiles). With the opposition of developing countries effectively damped down through bilateral pressure, negotiators agreed in April 1989 that negotiations on IPRs would encompass substantive IP protection standards, as well as the issue of dispute settlement on IPRs (Adede 2003).[13] So weak had the developing countries' position become that they were not able to extract any sort of concession from developed countries at this point in exchange for conceding to the demands of the latter (Watal 2001).

It was thus through pressure and coercion that resistance to bringing IPRs within the GATT was stifled and the trade-relatedness (or 'GATTability') of IPRs was established. Given the nature of arguments raised by developing countries on IPRs at the GATT and WIPO, and the fact that even after changing their IP laws under bilateral pressure IPRs enforcement did not improve dramatically (Sell 1995), it can be argued that the discourse of *strong* IP protection as a prerequisite to free trade and economic development was one which developing countries did not fully accept. This discourse originated within the private sector, with high stakes on IP protection in the developed countries that were able to reformulate their narrow interests on strong IPRs using the language of competitiveness, free trade and economic growth. Cast in these terms, such a formulation resonated well with certain broader structural, ideological and material changes taking place during the same period, thus effecting the prioritisation of this discourse over other potential ones. But, while developed countries with substantive IP-reliant sectors redefined their IP interests, thereby endorsing this discourse, developing countries were drawn into doing so both through coercion and strategic use of the institutional mechanisms of the GATT. By being confined to the IP–trade linkage within the trade regime, developing countries were already starting from a weaker bargaining position insofar as: (i) their trade dependency on the markets of developed countries made them susceptible to bilateral pressure either through Section 301-type action or through the GSP status route; (ii) their increased interest in international trade (as part of a broader trade-led development strategy) obliged them to make concessions and trade-offs during trade negotiations (the IP issue being one of them); and (iii) the nature of power-relations and decision-making at the GATT meant that they would be unable to conclude a GATT agreement on IPRs that reflected their interests, unless a strong ally could be found within the Quad members.

As we have observed, no such ally was to be found on the issue of the 'GATTability' of IPRs. Moreover, when the developing countries realised that the choice was between 'the GATT and USTR, not the GATT and WIPO' (Ryan 1998b: 566), and the green light was given to negotiations on substantive standards relating to IPRs in early 1989, the position of key developed members about how such a linkage should be made was already well entrenched. Developing countries' negotiators were joining the negotiations rather late; the EEC proposal submitted in March 1990, bearing a strong resemblance to the 1988 Framework authored by business actors (Cottier 1991), was to all intents and purposes a *draft agreement*. Only one month later, the main elements of the EEC proposal appeared again in the US submission, suggesting that the text was the result of coordinated effort between the two, while also reflecting the consensus achieved within the private sector (Matthew 2002a; Drahos and Braithwaite 2002).[14] Thereafter, a group of 14 developing countries[15] did try to work together towards a detailed common text which would effectively counter these proposals. It eventually materialised in May 1990 but, rather than offering an effective negotiating position, it actually revealed not only fissures in their ranks but their reluctance to adopt a hard-line position due to persistent bilateral pressure. As Watal (2001: 31) has suggested, interested developing countries missed another opportunity to accept many of the more reasonable demands made by the developed countries in exchange for limitations on IPRs, reasonable transition periods and the moderation of more extreme demands.

In fact, bilateral pressure continued unabated alongside multilateral negotiations and was successful in undermining further resistance at the GATT. Countries such as Argentina, Colombia, Chile, Brazil, Malaysia, Egypt, India, China, Korea and Thailand made regular appearances in the Section 301 'priority watch list' during the late 1980s and 1990s and saw their IP laws repeatedly targeted in bilateral negotiations. Such relentless pressure had a strong negative impact on the nature of participation of developing countries in the GATT IP negotiations. In addition, developing countries' trade negotiators often found themselves pitted against the much larger, more skilled negotiating teams of developed countries (Drahos 1995; Watal 2001). For their part, throughout the negotiations, the latter had the advantage of drawing on abundant advice and expertise from private sector groups (namely the IPC, UNICE and Keidanren). The latter had not only extensive experience on dealing with international IP protection issues, but also vital interests in ensuring that the agreement's provisions deviated as little as possible from their preferred mode of dealing with such issues.

Given such disparity in bargaining power, it is not surprising that the negotiations at the TRIPs group proceeded largely in ways conducive to the interests of key developed countries and their IP-reliant industries. But this is not to say that the developing countries involved in the negotiations were completely unable to shape the content of the agreement. Indeed, some concessions were made during the negotiations, but they were limited either to non-operational provisions or provisions covering issues on which key developed countries had divergent views. Due to differences on domestic IP laws, certain disagreements between the US, EEC and Japan persisted, especially over patent rules, performers' neighbouring rights, moral rights and rental rights under copyright and geographical indicators, in addition to disagreements between them and developing countries on the terms of patent protection, compulsory licensing and the patentability of plants and animals (Matthews 2002a). The draft sent to the Brussels Ministerial in December 1990 thus contained a range of unresolved issues to be tacked by ministers.

Most of the pending issues were resolved and the draft of the TRIPs was essentially drawn up during the second half of 1990, including work in the Brussels Ministerial, and the second half of 1991, thanks not least to two vital procedural innovations from the GATT Secretariat.

One such procedure was introduced in the second part of 1990 whereby a '10 plus 10' (ten developed and ten developing countries)[16] group of key negotiators met informally with the aim of speeding up the negotiations, alongside other informal meetings, thus effectively driving the TRIPs negotiations 'underground' (Gorlin 1999). The second procedural innovation was the introduction during 1991 of a process whereby the Chairman of the TRIPs negotiating group and the GATT Secretariat cooperated in drafting negotiating texts based on their *judgement* of what would be acceptable to participants; thus the language in these texts was no longer that expressed by negotiators. This new procedure had the effect of simultaneously taking much of the heat out of the highly politicised arguments presented by negotiators, and of shifting power from national delegations to the GATT Secretariat and the TRIPs group Chairman (Matthews 2002a; Watal 2001). When the GATT Director-General Arthur Dunkel presented his draft in December 1991 with the aim of achieving progress towards the overall conclusion of the Uruguay Round, the draft TRIPs agreement presented an arbitrated resolution, for which Dunkel was responsible, of issues undecided by the negotiations (Sell 2003). For instance, the issue of moral rights was resolved to the satisfaction of the US (by not being included); the EEC lost on moral rights but gained on geographical indicators; and the issue of scope of patentability was resolved again to the satisfaction of the US (by extending patents to all fields), although some exceptions to patentability were allowed, largely on the insistence of the EEC and developing countries (Drahos and Braithwaite 2002).

With regard to developing countries' demands, the Dunkel Draft also included transition periods (of five, ten and fifteen years) before they undertook the implementation of the TRIPs agreement; on the scope of patentability, certain exclusions were obtained largely due to the EEC's opposition to patenting life forms; on the compulsory licensing issue, language more permissive than the narrow conditions preferred by the US was adopted, largely due to the similar position taken by the EEC and Canada; and, on the issue of parallel trade (ironically a strictly trade-related issue), the pre-existing flexibilities on differing national policies was retained, thanks to the initiative of New Zealand and Australia to exclude the subject from TRIPs altogether (Gorlin 1999; Watal 2001; Sell 2003). Of these small victories, it was mainly for the transitional periods and provisions over compulsory licenses that the Dunkel Draft came under heavy criticism from US business actors, particularly in the pharmaceutical sector, criticism that obscured how much it had won otherwise (Weissman 1996). Related to transitional periods, the

US pharmaceutical business actors also objected to the absence of 'pipeline' protection for patented drugs awaiting marketing approval from the draft (Sell 2003).[17] Hence, taking over the complaints coming from the pharmaceutical industry, the US proposed again at the end of 1992 the inclusion of 'pipeline' protection in the agreement, alongside requests to substantially shorten the transitional periods (Drahos and Braithwaite 2002). The proposal for pharmaceutical 'pipeline' protection was along the lines of agreements already achieved through bilateral pressure with Korea in 1986, Mexico in 1990 and China in 1991 (Watal 2001). In the end, the original transitional periods and the more limited protection afforded to pharmaceuticals through the 'mailbox' provisions[18] already in the Dunkel Draft remained untouched, much to the consternation of the US pharmaceutical business actors. On the final day, apart from a few changes, it was the draft TRIPs agreement contained in the Dunkel Draft that was accepted in December 1993 and adopted formally at Marrakesh in April 1994.

Thus, in just over a decade, the fragile link between IP protection and trade had not only been consolidated, but also transformed into binding law; indeed, it could be said that it solidified into one of the three pillars on which the trade regime now rests. As Braithwaite and Drahos (2000: 203) have argued, it is an implausible achievement to persuade a regime concerned primarily with liberalising trade and enhancing competition to extend monopoly rights to private right-holders. And all this in addition to 'persuading' the majority of its membership, who incidentally are net importers of IPRs, to sign an agreement which, if nothing else, will dramatically increase the cost of their IP imports. As we saw, the IP–trade linkage was formulated outside the regime and brought into the trade regime by a group of business actors who, operating as 'entrepreneurs of ideas', were able to enrol the support of some major trade regime members to eventually transform these ideas into concrete and binding obligations and commitments for the rest of the regime's membership. There would not have been a WTO TRIPs agreement, had the support of the key trade regime members, particularly the US, not been enrolled; likewise, it would have been unlikely that these key members would have made mandatory international IP protection a priority in the Uruguay Round had it not been for the successful organisation of private sector groups, both domestically and internationally, with the sole purpose of achieving this specific objective at the GATT/WTO. The success of business actors was best captured by Gorlin, one of the key architects of the private sector's strategies, when he declared that 'we got 95% of what we wanted' (quoted in Sell 2003: 160). No matter how

TRIPs is justified, then, there should be no doubts that it essentially protects and enforces *private* rights. It is a remarkably imbalanced arrangement, which advances the competitive advantage of business actors and certain developed countries that have sizeable IP-reliant sectors. It advances the questionable view that strong, enforceable IP protection is essential to trade, innovation and development, whilst saying nothing about how the other side of the IP bargain – *access* – is to be ensured. For these reasons, far from being the end, a new set of contestations was set in motion soon after TRIPs came into force, this time involving many more actors and competing interests, many of which are still playing out today.

4
Contestations Post-TRIPs and the Emergence of the IP–Access to Medicines Debate

The principles, norms and rules governing IPRs have always been contested. Given the territorial nature of most IP law-making since IPRs came into existence, such contestations among state and non-state actors have largely, although by no means solely, been confined to the domestic level. Until TRIPs entered the scene in 1995, international IP agreements allowed national governments significant policy space in which to design their own IP laws, thus allowing domestic IP laws to be embedded, at least to some extent, in the corresponding domestic socio-ethical-economic context that makes these norms possible in the first place (Murumba 1998). TRIPs interferes overtly with this process because, by imposing a certain form of IP protection developed elsewhere, it precludes the possibility of legal norms being contested and developed domestically. In other words, TRIPs turns the traditional national-international paradigm upside down, requiring that the domestic deliberations which traditionally have produced legal norms and procedures be renegotiated in light of TRIPs obligations rather than domestic exigencies (Okediji 2003).

Hence, by de-contextualising and launching already contested IP norms and rules on the global level, TRIPs set in motion a considerably more complex set of contestations and interactions. These contestations have been provoked in part by the contentious nature of IP protection, in part by the way TRIPs was negotiated and in part by the way it deals with IPRs. As we saw in the previous chapter, TRIPs embodies a strategic linkage that was articulated and promoted by a limited group of IP-reliant transnational business actors in the (post-) industrialised countries with a view to protecting their competitive advantage in worldwide production and distribution of knowledge goods. But TRIPs has implications beyond the industries in which these actors operate; indeed, it has important implications for entire industrial sectors, societies, countries and the global economy and welfare overall. This is because TRIPs, and the national IPRs laws it mandates, ultimately delineate the way in which knowledge, both as capital and public good, is created, owned, controlled and diffused, domestically and globally. Paradoxically, TRIPs was not driven by a common concern and consensus about creating a *balanced* IP regime that reconciles the interests of knowledge developers, owners, users and the public at large, whether at the domestic or global level (Maskus and Reichman 2004). Indeed, whether TRIPs and subsequent developments have struck the right balance between providing global IP protection to private right-holders and encouraging real innovation, knowledge creation and, ultimately, diffusion and access is still very much open to question.

Balancing these competing interests and demands is a complex task at any level, and more so at the global one. They raise difficult challenges which cannot and should not be addressed simply as trade or commercial matters, which is what TRIPs does. Clearly, this is not the way in which TRIPs was legitimised by its promoters. As we saw in the previous chapter, as IPRs negotiations were extended beyond trade in counterfeit goods, a discourse of IPRs as a benefit to trade and development became necessary to support and justify their inclusion in the trade regime (I1 and I2, 2006). This discourse had both an instrumentalist component that saw TRIPs as part of the WTO package deal and a normative component. Normatively, it was argued that all regime members, especially the developing members that were resistant to the expansionary IP agenda, would benefit from the TRIPs agreement insofar as the stronger IP protection it mandated would stimulate more foreign direct investment (FDI), more transfers of better technology, and more R&D and innovation than before (Rapp and Rozek 1990; Gould and Gruben 1996; Vandoren and Martins 2006). Not surprisingly, several reports that defended this view were funded and circulated by interested business actors during the negotiations.[1]

However, the assumption that IPRs are a handmaiden for economic development is generally accepted as an article of faith, rather than being based on sound evidence (Blakeney 2006: 19). Indeed, there is wide acceptance amongst economists and IP scholars today that our collective understanding of the role IPRs can or should play in the economic development process is substantially incomplete (Abbott 1998: 502). Historical evidence suggests that the role of IPRs in economic development is context-sensitive, depending on the technological capacities and the social and economic structures in a specific country at a certain point in time (Abbott 1998; UK IPR Commission 2002). What can be said with some degree of certainty is that strong IP protection as mandated by TRIPs precludes imitation as a legitimate tool of technological 'catch-up' on the part of developing countries. In any case, one cannot realistically expect the technological gap between the developed and developing countries to be closed by virtue of stronger IPRs mandated by TRIPs. The latter were negotiated precisely with the aim of establishing and protecting the competitive advantage of certain high-tech industries and thus clearly have the aim of preventing the narrowing of the technology gap which would, in effect, diminish such competitive advantage (May 2000).

In the meantime, the long-term impact of TRIPs on developing countries as a group and on the world economy as a whole remains unclear and impossible to calculate with any certainty (Hoekman and Kosteci 1995; Dutfield 2003b; Hindley 2006). Several studies suggest that, at least in the short term, TRIPs will have a negative impact for developing countries as a group (Abbott 1998; McCalman 2001). A World Bank study, for instance, estimated that industry in developed countries will receive annual transfers of more than US$20 billion in royalties and improved market share when TRIPs is fully implemented (World Bank 2002). These predictions make it all the more pertinent to recall that developing countries accepted such an disadvantageous agreement partially under pressure from key regime members keen to protect their competitive advantage in IP-reliant sectors, and partially as an exchange for 'gains' offered in other areas, such as agriculture and textile trade. These were not concessions in the usual GATT sense as, in fact, developing countries were exchanging trade concessions for non-trade concessions (IPRs), in addition to giving away concessions on the industries of tomorrow for concessions on the industries of the past.

As it turned out, gains in agriculture mainly took the form of *commitments* to consider future liberalisation (Watal 2001; Maskus 2004); as for textile trade, key developed members were, in effect, simply giving up protectionism in an area which at that point had outlived its purpose (Martin and Winters 1996). But, unlike the textile agreement(s), TRIPs has implications that are both difficult to measure and bound to materialise in more than just one industrial sector or a limited group of countries and peoples. Indeed, IP laws impinge upon many industrial sectors, as well as on the provision of public goods such as health, education, scientific research, agriculture and the environment. As was noted in an earlier chapter, designing domestic IP laws that balance such private and public interests is difficult enough and highly contested; importantly, when these unresolved tensions are transferred from their territorial base to the global level, they become far more acute (Maskus and Reichman 2004: 293). In sum, then, TRIPs is contestable at its very core because of the nature of the subject-matter it covers, as well as the way in which it deals with it. It tilts the balance clearly in favour of private IP right-holders, with implications for entire countries and peoples. For these reasons, TRIPs was ripe for contestations since the outset. And, not surprisingly, the few years since TRIPs entered into force have seen an 'explosion' of contests over IP issues in a broad array of international fora, including those dealing with health, food and agriculture, genetic resources, human rights and trade.

While each of these sets of contests and the existing groupings of actors and issues involved is worthy of further analysis, the focus of this chapter is on those that emerged over IP protection and public health, the actors involved in those contests and how they played out and were 'resolved' within the trade regime. One interim 'solution' was the amendment of the TRIPs agreement in 2005, marking the first time in the admittedly short life of the WTO when deliberations between state and non-state actors, and more specifically over issues raised by developing members and civil society groups, resulted in a 'hard law' solution in the form of amending a WTO agreement. The amendment process will be considered at length in the following chapter; here, the focus is primarily on the post-TRIPs contests, on the emergence of the IP–public health linkage formulated and promulgated initially by a group of NGOs and on the adoption of the 2001 Doha Declaration on the TRIPs Agreement and Public Health ('the Declaration'). The emergence of the IP-access to medicines issue was in part the result of IP-reliant business actors' agenda of further expanding IP protection beyond the levels provided by TRIPs. Developments in the post-TRIPs period are complex, but the following section necessarily focuses on those that more directly impacted upon the emergence of the IP-access to medicines contests. The second section then deals with the way in which the IP–public health linkage was formulated by certain non-state actors, initially outside the trade regime and then brought into it. Organising these events in this way helps us to more clearly expose the differences between various actor groups and their positions; in reality, of course, the strategies of state and non-state actors that we follow were closely interrelated and together constitute part of the overall developments taking place during the post-TRIPs period. The chapter concludes with a section on the Doha Declaration of 2001 which, as we shall see in the following chapter, marked an important juncture but not the end of contests over IP and access to medicines.

4.1   Implementing TRIPs: narrowing down exceptions and broadening private rights

The extent to which the more pessimistic predictions of the impact of TRIPs on individual countries and global welfare will materialise was always bound to depend largely on the way in which TRIPs was implemented domestically. It is true that the 'minimum' IP standards it mandated were quite high and subject to enforcement and dispute settlement mechanisms. Nonetheless, together they establish the minimum level of IP protection above which countries are *not* obliged to legislate, although they are free to do so. Furthermore, in all multilateral agreements the objectives of the stronger actors are diluted, to a larger or lesser extent, by the necessity of avoiding contentious issues or allowing national discretion over others, in order to have all actors on board. Likewise, TRIPs offers enough ambiguous language and 'wiggle room' for manoeuvring with the design and implementation of IP laws domestically (Reichman 1997a; 2000). In practice, this means that, as with many complex international agreements, many of the unresolved conflicts in TRIPs are expected to be 'sorted out' in one way or another during the implementation phase and beyond. In this respect, the two key issues that emerge are deciding what constitutes the bare minimum set of obligations mandated by TRIPs and what flexibilities are allowed by TRIPs to domestic policymakers in designing and implementing IP protection laws. The way these two issues were to be dealt with at the domestic and global level had the potential to counter some of the most negative impacts of TRIPs and enable countries to capitalise on some of the opportunities it may offer them.

Defining the rules and flexibilities contained in a multilateral trade agreement is not simply a legal task. Legal discourse, the legal interpretation of a treaty language, is an important form of communicative practice which helps to shape intersubjective understandings about the objectives and values embodied in that particular agreement, as well as in the regime more generally (Lang 2006). In other words, important ideas are communicated through legal discursive processes with regard to the 'appropriate' way a responsible member of the regime, and the international economic community more broadly, should deal with IP protection and, consequently, how it should design and implement its IP laws. Hence, given the particularly contested nature of IPRs, it is important to ask *who* dominates these discourses, that is, who decides how TRIPs standards and flexibilities are to be interpreted and implemented in practice?

Within the trade regime, legal discourses and interpretative processes occur both during the course of trade negotiations and through the operations of the newly-established WTO Trade Policy Review and Dispute Settlement Mechanisms, all of which interrelate with each other and with developments occurring at the domestic and regional level through a complex web of channels and actors. These two important mechanisms were both captured by IP-reliant business and state actors that implemented TRIPs soon after it came into force. These actors entered the post-TRIPs scene in an advantageous position insofar as their favoured discourse on IP protection as a trade and competitiveness issue was well-entrenched and dominant, not to mention their strategic positioning within the trade regime, which already afforded them considerable leverage over other regime actors. But, having 'suffered' the dead weight losses associated with multilateralism, these actors were keen on ensuring that higher IP protection standards, better enforcement and faster implementation than those offered by TRIPs were achieved worldwide (Okediji 2004; Dutfield and Suthersanen 2004). These being their goals, they focused their efforts at the WTO through the TRIPs Council and the WTO dispute mechanism, and outside it through resorting to unilateral pressure and bilateral free trade agreements (FTAs).

Members' compliance with TRIPs obligations has been monitored through a review process in which members of the TRIPs Council identify and discuss differences in interpretation and deficiencies in implementation. The main aim of this surveillance process continues to be that of ensuring that members take their TRIPs commitments seriously by implementing them 'properly' and on time, thereby also serving as an important means of dispute prevention (Otten 1998; Vandoren 1999). The process thus provided a crucial venue through which actors could strategically formulate and promulgate their preferred interpretative stance over TRIPs provisions in the early post-TRIPs period. The dominant actors have been the US and the EU, both of which, as was the case with TRIPs negotiations, relied heavily on IP-reliant business actors for implementation and enforcement information and views (Vandoren 2001; Sell 2003). The review process in the early post-TRIPs years, focused mainly on the implementation process in *developed* countries, was used strategically by these actors to serve a two-pronged purpose: first, through vigilant scrutiny of their counterparts' legislation, to show that lax implementation and enforcement of TRIPs obligations by any member was not going to be tolerated, and, second, to 'teach' and provide a 'template' for the implementation of TRIPs provisions in developing countries.

Indeed, both business actors and the USTR have openly accepted that the review process provided an excellent opportunity to 'educate' developing country members as to how TRIPs provisions must be implemented in their laws (Smith 1996; USTR 1998). For their part, the business actors that came together before the Uruguay Round with the aim of securing global enforceable IP protection maintained the momentum post-TRIPs, simultaneously assuming two new roles; that of TRIPs guardians and 'TRIPs plus'[2] advocates. Various business reports in the early post-TRIPs period clearly indicate the commitment of these actors to a timely, indeed an accelerated, and rigorous implementation of TRIPs, particularly in developing countries.[3] Of these reports, perhaps the two most important were the TABD Chicago Declaration of 1996 and the joint IPC-UNICE Statement of 1998, both of which encouraged developed countries to put pressure on their developing counterparts with respect to implementation and enforcement issues in the TRIPs Council meetings (Matthews 2002b). In addition to these official channels, they continued their own surveillance and 'mentoring' exercises in developing countries of particular interest to them.

Overall, then, geared towards locking in and enhancing the competitive advantage of certain IP-reliant business actors and their respective countries, the interpretation of TRIPs provisions in the early TRIPs Council review meetings was not concerned at all with finding ways in which developing countries could make use of TRIPs flexibilities in designing IP laws appropriate for their stage of development. On the contrary, the aim was that of highlighting TRIPs obligations through construing rights granted to private right-holders as broadly, and flexibilities and margins as narrowly as possible (I4 and I2, 2006). This was particularly the case not so much with the review process but with the technical assistance that provided a rather more effective avenue through which dominant actors could translate their preferred interpretation of TRIPs provisions into concrete IP laws throughout the developing world. Indeed, technical support to these countries, mandated by TRIPs Article 67 and offered mainly by the WTO and WIPO,[4] was primarily forthcoming in the shape of model, ready-made IP laws that paid little consideration to the diverse economic and social structures of different countries or the question of how these countries could use TRIPs flexibilities to serve their interests (Musungu and Dutfield 2003; Blakeney 2006). In this regard, WIPO was particularly inclined to provide 'pre-emptive' technical assistance by advising and designing IP laws that incorporated 'TRIPs plus' provisions so as to avoid developing countries becoming involved in WTO dispute resolutions (Drahos 2002: 777).[5]

However, this 'Trojan Horse' approach to technical assistance provided by WTO and WIPO was only one channel through which a restrictive interpretation of TRIPs was being promulgated across developing countries. Another channel was the *bilateral* assistance offered by both the US and EU, which generally emphasised IP protection and enforcement as priority areas and downgraded the need to make effective use of TRIPs flexibilities. This was particularly the case with US bilateral technical assistance in which business actors, including proprietary pharmaceutical companies, featured prominently; by comparison, EU bilateral assistance was arguably more varied and balanced but, similarly, paid minimal attention to the needs of developing countries (Matthews and Munoz-Tellez 2006). Institutional and bilateral technical assistance in combination have gradually resulted in many developing countries adopting IP laws incorporating 'TRIPs plus' provisions, with only a few, mainly the large and well-resourced such as India, Brazil and China, taking advantage of TRIPs flexibilities in designing more balanced IPRs laws (I2, I5 and I6, 2006).

4.1.1 WTO dispute cases relating to IPRs and pharmaceuticals

It turned out that even when some developing countries took advantage of the vagueness and flexibilities of TRIPs to tailor IP laws according to their socio-economic make-up, they found themselves either facing a WTO dispute panel or subject to bilateral pressure, or both. This was particularly the case with IPRs that, from some business actors' perspective, had not been dealt with satisfactorily in TRIPs, or for certain developing countries which, having reached a certain level of economic development, constituted significant markets for business interests. For their part, business actors made every effort to ensure that WTO litigation was used strategically by bringing cases which had good chances of success, as well as cases that would set powerful examples and eventually develop the necessary body of precedent.[6] Clearly, business actors cannot officially be part of WTO disputes but, ultimately, it is infringement of their IPRs that prompts governments to bring cases of inadequate IP protection in other countries before WTO dispute settlement panels. This is not to say that governments bring a case to the

WTO every time complaints are made by business actors; rather, when a TRIPs complaint is brought at the WTO, official positions are based on close consultations with the affected business which, in turn, is both keen and well-placed to provide specialist knowledge and expertise on the IP issues being deliberated.

It is worth recalling that the need to attain global *enforcement* of IPRs was one of the main reasons for bringing IP protection within the trade regime. Indeed, 'appropriate' IP laws may be in place, but they will not serve their purpose if not enforced. It is for this reason that ensuring enforcement of TRIPs provisions through the WTO dispute settlement mechanism (DSM) becomes important, although the latter was not designed with complex IP protection and enforcement issues in mind (Reichman 1997b; Dreyfuss and Lowenfeld 1997). In addition to having to deal with IP matters that by their nature are difficult to adjudicate, the DSM has to adjudicate in the absence of a body of precedent in IP litigation at the *international* level. The degree to which panels make use of GATT jurisprudence and national IP jurisprudence in their decisions is difficult to determine, but the US and the EU emerge undisputedly as the main actors with litigation expertise in both venues.[7] Unsurprisingly, then, that of the 24 TRIPs-related disputes brought before the WTO dispute settlement procedure by 2001, either the US or the EU (or both) initiated 22 of them, with the remaining two constituting *symbolic* claims filed by Canada and Brazil in response to complaints brought against them (Williams 2002; Shaffer 2004). Of particular importance for the IP-access to medicines contests were the cases brought against India, Pakistan, Canada, Argentina and Brazil, all filed by either the US or the EC (or both) on behalf of complaints raised by their pharmaceutical business actors. Of these, the Indian and Canadian cases were the only two to go through the WTO dispute settlement procedure, including the Appellate Body in the Indian case, with the rest being settled bilaterally.

In the cases brought against India and Pakistan (in July and April 1996 respectively) the US was acting on complaints from the proprietary pharmaceutical industry about losses in these countries due to inappropriate protection for pharmaceuticals under the mailbox and exclusive marketing rights requirements of TRIPs (Article 70.8 and 70.9).[8] The Pakistan case was dropped when the country introduced the requested legislation in 1997,[9] while in relation to the Indian case, the US was subsequently joined by the EU which filed a separate complaint in 1997, also acting on behalf of its research-based pharmaceutical industry (EFPIA) (Sell 2003). It is worth recalling that India has a vibrant and competitive generic pharmaceutical sector. Hence, given the importance of the Indian case to the pharmaceutical industry, it chose to adopt a dual strategy, enrolling the support of both the US (through PhRMA) and the EC (through EFPIA), in addition to coordinating its surveillance and information-gathering activities globally through INTERPAT[10] and the India International Task Force. The latter was established by pharmaceutical business actors with the sole purpose of feeding information and expertise into the WTO dispute deliberations (Matthews 2002a). Although the Indian patent office was accepting patent applications under an *administrative* (mailbox) mechanism, from the perspective of pharmaceutical business actors the absence of legal provisions that ensured the priority of such applications introduced considerable commercial *uncertainty*. Indeed, both the Panel and the Appellate Body found that such administrative measures did not amount to an adequate fulfilment of the object and purpose of the relevant TRIPs articles,[11] thus concurring with the interpretation of such articles made by business actors and developed countries (Reichman 1998: 594). Although the Appellate Body overturned the Panel's findings with regard to 'non-violation' complaints, it failed to recognise India's administrative route to fulfilling 'mailbox' provisions as an acceptable method. In doing so, it sent mixed messages about the degree to which WTO TRIPs jurists would display deference to local methods of implementing TRIPs. On the other hand, given the great lengths to which pharmaceutical business actors went to organise internationally and enrol the support of both the US and the EU, the Indian case served as a clear display of their determination to ensure that their IPRs were protected fully and without delay (Matthews 2002a).

Although the US pharmaceutical industry stood to benefit more than its European counterpart from a favourable WTO Panel ruling, it was the EC that filed a complained against Canada in 1997 related to the so-called Bolar provisions in Canadian law that permitted both access to proprietary data for experimental use by generic drug companies and the manufacturing and storage ('stockpiling') of generic versions of patented drugs before the expiry of the patent term. These pro-competitive provisions were aimed at, *inter alia*, ensuring that generic versions of patented drugs were introduced in the market immediately after the expiry of the 20-year patent protection term. The proprietary pharmaceutical business actors, through the coordinating mechanism of INTERPAT, chose the EC route because the US Hatch-Waxman Act of 1984, containing similar provisions on experimental use (but not 'stockpiling'), made it nearly impossible for the USTR to file such a complaint (Matthews 2002a; Pugatch 2004a).

After long deliberations, the Panel concluded in 2000 that Canada's provisions related to testing for marketing approval of generic drugs constituted an exception consistent with TRIPs provisions (Article 30 on 'limited exceptions'), while those related to 'stockpiling' amounted to serious breaches of TRIPs provisions (Article 28 on 'rights conferred' and Article 30).[12] Arguably, this interpretation of Articles 28 and 30 of TRIPs by the Panel construed private rights broadly and exceptions to such rights narrowly, because it unreasonably included benefits accruing to patent-holders from the extension of market exclusivity beyond the patent term due to regulatory requirements as part of the 'normal exploitation' of patents.[13] At the same time, the Panel paid little attention to third parties' interests, including those explicitly recognised by TRIPs itself, such as health and social and economic welfare, when interpreting exceptions to such rights. The latter point is important in that, while in a developed country generic companies can bring their versions of off-patented drugs to market within a few months in the absence of 'stockpiling' provisions, this period is substantially longer in developing countries, precisely where delay in the introduction of affordable generic versions can have the most significant health consequences (Berger 2002; Trebilcock and Howse 2005: ch.13).

Hence, by outlawing 'stockpiling' provisions, the Panel failed to show full deference to national IP laws and the various methods national authorities may wish to adopt to balance competing social-economic goals. The Panel's interpretation of TRIPs Article 30 came close to that preferred by the pharmaceutical industry,[14] as well as by the US and EC which, during the period when the Panel was scrutinising Canadian patent legislation, were simultaneously engaged in diplomatic 'consultations' with Israel over *draft* Bolar-type provisions that aimed to emulate those found in Canadian legislation. Israel, like India, has a well-developed globally-orientated generic industry, hence any relaxation of protection for pharmaceutical IP rights had the potential of diminishing the competitive advantage of proprietary pharmaceutical companies. As a result of pressure by these actors, the 1998 amendment to Israel's Patent Act afforded generic companies only access to proprietary data for marketing approval, but prohibited any other undertakings, including stockpiling activities, before the expiry of the patent term (Cohen 1998).

Determined to guard and enhance the protection of their IPRs worldwide post-TRIPs, both the Argentine and Brazilian WTO cases (in 1999 and 2000 respectively) were also brought forward following complaints by the (US) pharmaceutical industry. These related to the failure of Argentine patent law to provide TRIPs-mandated protection as related to exclusive marketing rights and protection of pharmaceutical test data (amongst other issues added in 2000), and about the local working requirements and parallel import provisions retained in Brazil's patent law (Shanker 2002; Sell 2003; Drahos 2004). Of the two cases, the case against Brazil attracted most controversy because such provisions were aimed at, *inter alia*, ensuring the sustainability and continuity of its highly successful, publicly funded HIV/AIDS programme, in addition to the fact that subsequently Brazil strategically challenged potentially TRIPs-inconsistent local working requirements in the US laws by filing a complaint at the WTO in early 2001 (I3 2006).[15] The Brazilian case was eventually withdrawn from the WTO and 'transferred' to bilateral consultations in June 2001, in which the US obtained (unjustifiable) guarantees from the Brazilian government to provide it with advance notice before utilising such provisions (USTR 2001a). The Argentine case was settled in 2002, after a mutually-agreed solution between the two countries dealt 'satisfactorily' with patent and test data protection for pharmaceuticals (WTO 2007).

4.1.2 Bilateral pressure and FTAs

Presumably, the mutual settlement of disputes between members is preferable to resorting to full-blown WTO dispute procedures, but not if side-stepping the latter means that (weaker) members are *obliged* to take on more burdensome obligations than would have been the case otherwise. Indeed, the benefits of the WTO settlement mechanism for developing members rest partly on it providing a means that can alleviate bilateral pressure put on them by the major regime members. Nevertheless, at least as regards IP protection, bilateral pressure did not reduce significantly during the post-TRIPs period. In fact, only one year after TRIPs came into force in the developed countries (1996), the number of trading partners coming under pressure under the US Section 301 mechanism increased by 25 per cent (USTR 1998). A review of the USTR categorisation of countries under Special 301 into the 'priority watch list' and 'watch list' from 1996 until 2000 indicates that countries such as Canada, Brazil, Chile, Colombia, Costa Rica, Pakistan, the Philippines and Thailand made regular appearances in the 'watch list' each year, while countries such as Argentina, India, Turkey and Israel saw their IP laws secure them appearances in the higher profile 'priority watch list' each year during the same period.[16] Amongst other countries, *all* those mentioned above found their IP laws targeted by the USTR due to, *inter alia*, inadequate and ineffective IP protection for pharmaceuticals from the perspective of proprietary pharmaceutical business actors. Although trade sanctions under Section 301 have not been used routinely by the USTR, the effectiveness of the Special 301 process relies on it 'keeping up the heat' on the IP protection and enforcement front abroad, by pressuring weaker partners to adopt US-like or 'TRIPs plus' IP laws so as to avoid further action under the 301 process. Indeed, the Deputy USTR himself marvelled at its effectiveness: 'one fascinating aspect...occurs just before we make our annual determinations...IP laws are suddenly passed or amended and enforcement activities increase significantly' (Fisher 1999: 3).

In addition to this relentless pressure to 'improve' IP protection standards (including IPRs for pharmaceuticals), an effective way to drive IP protection standards upwards and ensure the developing countries' swift integration into the global IP regime has been through bilateral and regional free trade agreements (FTAs) involving either the EC or the US (which has used this route most aggressively) and a weaker state or group of states. This mechanism started to be used assertively by the US, and more recently by the EC, particularly as resistance to their expansionist IP agenda increased both within and outside the trade regime from the late 1990s onwards. Far from giving up unilateralism on trade and IP issues, from 1995 until 2000 the US signed four FTAs with developing countries and initiated many more, most of which have demanded the implementation of 'TRIPs plus' standards in exchange for the seemingly more immediate advantage of access to the lucrative US market (Drahos 2001; 2003; Okediji 2004). Hence, as with TRIPs, market access and trade liberalisation in general continued to be linked and exchanged for increased IP protection standards. Alongside other strategies, such as technical assistance, TRIPs Council meetings, WTO Dispute Settlement Procedures and unilateral pressure, the signing of these early FTAs was used by certain business and state actors to 'fill the gaps' in TRIPs standards in the immediate post-TRIPs period. One of the consequences of this strategy has been the undermining of the policy space and discretion afforded to governments by the TRIPs agreement itself and, more specifically, the roll-back of whatever gains developing countries had secured during its negotiation. Overall, then, whether within the WTO or outside it, these post-TRIPs strategies adopted by certain IP-reliant business actors, the pharmaceutical industry featuring most prominently, and the US and EC demonstrate their collective determination both to ensure an implementation of TRIPs that concurred with their interests and the achievement of concrete results in areas dealt with ambiguously or not covered by TRIPs.

4.2 Establishing new linkages: the emergence of the IP-access to medicines debate

The TRIPs agreement was, in many ways, unfinished business. Not only its interpretation, implementation and enforcement, but also the built-in agenda mandated by the agreement itself meant that TRIPs would engage both its proponents and opponents in complex and persistent contestations for some time to come. As noted in the previous chapter, developing countries' stance on the IP protection front at the WTO was defensive during the TRIPs negotiations. This continued until the preparations for the WTO Seattle Ministerial in 1999, whereupon their opposition to the TRIPs agenda became both stronger and more strategic (I7 and I2, 2006). Meanwhile, in the intermediate Ministerials, TRIPs-related issues did not make it to the top of the developing countries' list of concerns. Indeed, during the Singapore Ministerial in 1996, there were only a few references to IP protection, complemented by a few additional concerns raised during the Geneva Ministerial in 1998 by some developing countries about the potential costs associated with TRIPs implementation (I7 2006).[17] The Seattle Ministerial saw a significant change in the position of developing countries towards TRIPs, in that they emerged armed with stronger criticism and concrete demands and proposals on certain TRIPs-related issues. It must be noted that this change of attitude was part of wider changes in developing countries' participation in the trade regime during the post-Uruguay period. Their experience during the Uruguay Round had taught them that greater participation did not automatically translate into influence, as well as emphasising the importance of defining resistance around a positive and progressive agenda (Tussie and Lengyel 2002). Developing countries' resistance to TRIPs at the WTO is better understood, then, as part of a larger and more complex picture emerging in the post-Uruguay period, which includes an array of issues being contested between trade regime members in addition to IP protection. On the IP front, this change in developing countries' position occurred in the Seattle Ministerial partly because the true nature and extent of TRIPs obligations, costs and implications had not been *fully* appreciated during the preceding years. In addition, while the approaching deadline for its implementation by developing countries helped to reveal the complexity of TRIPs, the strategies followed by business and state actors dealt with in the previous section had the inadvertent effect of further fuelling developing countries' dissatisfaction with the agreement.

The scheduled 1999 built-in TRIPs agenda included three issues: review of provisions on the protection of plant and animal inventions ('life-patenting') (Article 27.3b); work on geographical indicators (GI) (Article 23.4 and 24.2); and review of the 'non-violation' dispute moratorium (Article 64.3). The fault lines in the latter two issues cannot be drawn in simple North–South lines; most developing and developed countries were keen to see the moratorium on 'non-violation' complains extended beyond 2000, with the most notable exception of the US;[18] on the GI issue, the EC and some developing countries were keen to see their scope expanded, while some other developing countries and the US were less than enthusiastic in considering such enhanced protectionism.[19] Nevertheless, it was the controversial debate over 'life-patenting' in which developing countries' positions went well beyond resistance to include certain concrete proposals and demands that were diametrically opposed to the interests of biotech and pharmaceutical business actors. Proposals put forward included those for the establishment of new IPRs for traditional knowledge, the amendment of TRIPs to oblige patent applicants to disclose origins of genetic material and share benefits with the respective communities when relevant, to expand the definition of products and processes that can be excluded from patentability, to clarify the relationship between TRIPs provisions and those found in the UN Convention on Biological Diversity (CBD) and the International Union for the Protection of New Varieties of Plants (UPOV) Convention.[20]

For their part, the US and the EC continued to broadly reflect the position of their IP-reliant industries during the built-in review process. On the issue of 'life-patenting', for instance, the US requested the elimination of exclusions from patentability of plants and animals as well as the incorporation of UPOV provisions for plant variety protection; more generally, its priorities lay with the timely implementation of TRIPs obligations in developing countries and opposition to any demands to weaken such obligations by the latter.[21] Similar positions were held by both the EC and Japan which continued to insist that TRIPs was the basis for further improvements and that there was no question of lowering IPRs protection standards.[22] This unified position, or at least language, was strikingly similar to that presented by business actors during preparations for the Seattle Ministerial; the IPC in the US, UNICE in the EU, the transatlantic TABD and pharmaceutical associations such as PhRMA and EFPIA had worked together during this period to ensure that downgrading of the IP protection level during the Seattle Ministerial was to be prevented at all costs (Pugatch 2004a). Indeed, in addition to making their position clear to the US, EC, WTO and WIPO officials in a series of meetings pre-Seattle, pharmaceutical business actors also insisted on the US and EC putting forward proposals for unrealistically tougher IP demands as a counter-strategy to dampen developing countries' demands and proposals (Pugatch 2004a).

The Seattle Ministerial collapsed, but the many issues raised during the built-in review process continued to fuel debates at the WTO TRIPs Council, with some developing countries becoming more assertive thereafter.[23] This continued to be the case especially with issues related to traditional knowledge and 'life-patenting' which, from the perspective of a majority of developing countries, remain intrinsically linked to food security, agricultural sustainability, the rights of indigenous peoples and protection of traditional knowledge. In addition, many of these IP-related issues had already spread and 'shifted' to other regimes. In fact, contestations over IP protection within the trade regime are best understood not only as part of a more complex set of contestations over several other issue-areas within this particular regime, but also as part of wider and interrelated contestations over IP protection in *other* regimes. Importantly, just as certain business actors and their home countries have used 'forum-shifting' to achieve their preferred ends, developing countries and certain NGOs have also been active in the post-TRIPs period in shifting IP protection issues into other regimes (Helfer 2004). For instance, contests at the TRIPs Council over 'life-patenting' were (and continue to be) closely linked with contests in two other regimes, one governing biodiversity and the other plant genetic resources (PGRs) for food and agriculture, run by the CBD and the UN Food and Agriculture Organisation (FAO) respectively. Some counter-norms have emerged from these deliberations, such as the recognition (but not the enforcement) of farmer rights,[24] protection of indigenous knowledge, disclosure and benefit sharing of genetic resources, and so on. These other fora have been used strategically by some developing countries and NGOs to, *inter alia*, redress certain imbalances of the TRIPs agreement, especially those related to biodiversity and 'life-patenting' (Helfer 2004).

Deliberations over biodiversity and 'life-patenting' issues continued at the WTO but only two years later, at the 2001 WTO Doha Ministerial, they had taken a back seat to the highly controversial debate over IP protection and access to medicines. Interestingly, as with the trade–IPRs linkage, the IP–access to medicines linkage was also formulated outside the trade regime by a network of NGOs during the latter part of the 1990s. Just as business actors had earlier linked IP protection to the advancement of free trade, this NGO network linked strong IP protection for pharmaceuticals and high prices for prescription drugs, particularly in the developing countries, with restricted access to medicines and unnecessary loss of human health and life. While business actors had argued that strong IPRs = free trade, these NGOs were arguing that strong IPRs = expensive drugs = loss of health/life. This formulation resonated particularly well with growing concerns about the unfolding HIV/AIDS crisis which, from its small-scale start in the early 1980s, had reached appalling proportions by the mid 1990s, as had the prices of first line, patented antiretroviral drugs. Although the access to medicines linkage started off as access to HIV/AIDS drugs, it gradually expanded to include access to (essential) medicines and public health more broadly.

The domestic origins of this NGO network lie with the NGOs' mobilisation during the US public health debate of the early 1990s (including Hillary Clinton's healthcare reform proposal); with the conclusion of TRIPs, Ralph Nader and Jamie Love's group (Consumer Project on Technology, hereafter CPTech) emerged as the most prominent critic of US trade policy as it related to IP protection, health care issues and TRIPs in general. For instance, as early as 1995, Nader and Love protested against the narrow focus of the USTR on protecting US pharmaceutical interests in a letter directed to the then USTR, Mickey Kantor (Sell 2002). Soon afterwards, Health Action International (HAI, based in the Netherlands), initially focused on certain pharmaceutical companies' practices, began to get interested in IP issues and joined CPTech on the TRIPs and IP protection for pharmaceuticals front in 1996. From these beginnings, the network consolidated and grew to include, importantly, two heavyweight humanitarian NGOs: *Médicins sans Frontières* (MSF), a non-partisan NGO involved with delivering healthcare services in the developing countries, joined the network in 1998, while Oxfam, working primarily on poverty and development issues, also joined what became known as the Access Campaign in 2000 (I8 and I9, 2006).[25]

Early meetings involving various NGOs on TRIPs and healthcare issues had been organised by HAI and CPTech since 1996, but it was the unfolding of the South African lawsuit in the late 1990s that perhaps more than any other event helped strengthen the network's cause and internationally raise the profile of the IP–access to medicines debate. Having passed the Medicines Act in 1997, South Africa became a target of pharmaceutical business actors because certain provisions of the

Act, authorising parallel importing and compulsory licensing as means to deal with public health challenges (particularly HIV/AIDS) were considered by these actors to be inconsistent with TRIPs. As part of their strategy to ensure a timely and 'proper' implementation of TRIPs, 39 pharmaceutical companies sued the South African government in February 1998 on the basis that the Medicines Act was unconstitutional and in breach of South Africa's international commitments.[26] From this point in time until the case eventually reached the courtroom in 2000, a growing number of NGOs mobilised and made increasing use of media coverage and campaigning activities to reframe what was being cast as a technical legal matter into 'patents versus patients' terms. This formulation had a particularly strong standing insofar as South Africa had (and continues to have) one of the worst AIDS epidemics in the world (UNAIDS 2008). For their part, pharmaceutical companies continued to frame the issue as a matter of upholding their legitimate rights, and were successful in obtaining the initial support of both the USTR and the EC Trade Commissioner; the latter put pressure on the South African vice-president in a letter in early 1998 to repeal the offending legislation (t'Hoen 2002), while in the US, at the behest of PhRMA, the USTR placed South Africa on the 1998 'watch list' and suspended its GSP benefits, with further pressure coming from the US Presidential office and even the US Congress (Ostergard 1999; Kongolo 2001). Through naming and shaming these policies and organising demonstrations in major cities worldwide, the NGO network managed to put considerable pressure on governments and pharmaceutical companies to withdraw the case. In particular, CPTech, joined by the US-based NGO ACT UP, made strategic use of Al Gore's electoral campaign in the summer of 1999 to raise awareness of the South African lawsuit and the US executive's stance through continuingly disrupting campaign appearances; the public impact was such that within a matter of weeks Bill Clinton's Administration withdrew objections to the Medicines Act and removed South Africa from the 'watch list' (Sell 2002).

Further, and most crucially, there were three other routes which the network used strategically to channel its concerns over the impact of TRIPs on access to medicines at the international level: (i) in the public health regime, through the WHO Revised Drug Strategy of 1998; (ii) in the trade regime, through the WTO Seattle Ministerial in 1999; and (iii), in the human rights regime, through certain resolutions from 2000 onwards. The controversial involvement of the WHO with pharmaceutical IPRs occurred only *after* TRIPs came into force, initially through advisory work undertaken since 1996, which encouraged its member states to make full use of TRIPs flexibilities to achieve their national health goals. In particular, the process for the scheduled 1998 Revised Drug Strategy was captured by the Access Campaign and some developing countries, such as Brazil, South Africa and Zimbabwe, to ensure that the Strategy advocated TRIPs flexibilities and highlighted the importance of placing access to medicines and public health above commercial concerns (I10 2006). Such recommendations also appeared in a WHO-sponsored guide to the public health consequences of TRIPs in 1998 whereupon the US and the EC, viewing the guide as a threat, sought to suppress its publication (I10 2006). Indeed, the European DG Trade, referring explicitly to considerable concern amongst pharmaceutical business actors (IFPMA and EFPIA), stated clearly to the WHO in 1998 that no priority should be given to health over IP considerations and that no evidence of conflict between the two existed.[27] Despite such resistance, the World Health Assembly (WHA) unanimously passed a (slightly watered down) resolution in May 1999 which encouraged member states to ensure equitable access to essential drugs and review options under international agreements to safeguard such access.[28] Following a slow change of heart on the part of the US and the EC in 2000 and 2001 over the competence of the WHO on IP issues in the face of the growing HIV/AIDS crisis and NGOs' campaign activities, the WHA further strengthened the WHO's involvement with IP issues in two subsequent resolutions in 2001.[29]

Maintaining the momentum generated at the WHO, the Access Campaign wrote a letter to all WTO members in November 1999, urging them to make public health their highest priority when implementing TRIPs provisions (MSF, HAI and CPT 1999a). This also signalled the moment when the IP–access to medicines debate was brought within the trade regime. In addition, by this time, the United Nations Development Programme (UNDP), UNCTAD and the World Bank had also become involved with analysing the potentially negative impacts of TRIPs upon developing countries (I2 2006). In preparation for the Seattle Ministerial in November 1999, the Access Campaign consolidated its agenda in its Amsterdam Conference just before the Ministerial. The Conference resulted in the Amsterdam Statement which was addressed to all WTO members and firmly requested for the WTO to establish a working group on access to medicines, allow exceptions to patent rights under Article 30, endorse the use of compulsory licenses as permitted by Article 31, and avoid an overly restrictive interpretation of Article 39 as it related to pharmaceutical data protection (MSF, HAI and CPTech 1999b). Recall that these issues were at the heart of pharmaceutical business actors' demands for IP protection during TRIPs negotiations, and 'TRIPs plus' demands after TRIPs came into force.

As was noted above, the intense contestations during the Seattle Ministerial, including those over TRIPs, resulted in the collapse of the Ministerial, but, far from signalling the premature end of the IP–access to medicines linkage within the trade regime, the Seattle crisis opened up opportunities for its further development, both within the trade regime and elsewhere. Within the WTO, the Seattle crisis caused developed members to approach the forthcoming Doha Ministerial with a more flexible attitude towards the demands of their developing counterparts; indeed, the whole new Round set off in Doha was named the Doha Development Round. These demands included those related to TRIPs which, in Doha, were overtaken by the IP–public health debate. With regard to the latter, a significant start was set in motion in Seattle when President Clinton announced that the application of US trade law would remain sufficiently flexible to respond to legitimate public health crises.[30] This crucial signal was further enforced by Clinton's Executive Order of May 2000 which prohibited the USTR from pressuring sub-Saharan African countries for strategies aimed at ensuring access to affordable HIV/AIDS drugs.[31]

Clearly, this change of heart in the US and the EC with regard to access to medicines in the context of the HIV/AIDS epidemic was brought about by the growing public pressure from the Access Campaign, but only in part. The organisation and discursive strategies of the Campaign group were successful in this regard not least because of the ongoing redefinition of the national interest on the part of the developed countries which, at this point in time, concurred with the case being made by the Campaign. More specifically, since the end of the Cold War, the concept of national security has been expanded to include a variety of threats, *inter alia*, those emanating from global infectious diseases. Indeed, such epidemics, and poor health in developing countries in general, has gradually come to be understood as posing a dual threat to such countries: an immediate, direct threat that results from the spread of the diseases, and an indirect threat to international security posed by the projection of domestic political and economic instability associated with poor health in these countries at the international level (Fidler 2004). The UN Security Council itself recognised in its first session on health in July 2000 that the HIV/AIDS pandemic, 'if unchecked, may pose risk to stability and security'.[32] Indeed, public health concerns, particularly as they related to HIV/AIDs and other pandemics, attracted increased attention at the international level during the 1990s; for instance, a series of UN conferences during the 1990s resulted in the adoption of the UN Millennium Development Goals in 2000, which included targets for improving public health in developing countries,[33] whilst proposals to address HIV/AIDS and other pandemics more effectively at the global level resulted in the creation of the Global Fund against AIDS, Malaria and TB in 2002.[34]

Apart from the fact that developed countries have an interest in containing and dealing with serious health challenges in the developing world, access to medicines had the advantage of providing an easier target than the more demanding 'health for all' goal established by the WHO and the UN Covenant on Economic, Social and Cultural Rights (CESC) (Hein and Kohlmorgen 2007). In fact, enjoyment of the highest attainable standards of health is framed as a human right. Not surprisingly, NGOs within the Access Campaign deliberately used the human rights regime as another venue in which to achieve their goals. For instance, in response to a statement of some NGOS that challenged the compatibility of TRIPs with human rights obligations, the Human Rights Sub-Commission adopted a resolution on 'Intellectual Property Rights and Human Rights' in August 2000 which stated, *inter alia*, that conflicts in many issue-areas, including public health, existed between TRIPs provisions and those of CESC.[35] In addition, it set out an ambitious new agenda built upon the principle of placing human right obligations above economic agreements, an agenda which the UN human right bodies took to heart only too readily, generating considerable recommendations and reports, including resolutions on access to medicines and public health issues which established access to essential medicines as a basic human right.[36] Most notably, much of this body of work raised trenchant critiques of TRIPs; indeed, of all the fora mentioned so far, the human rights regime has taken the most antagonistic approach to TRIPs.

Faced with growing pressure from both civil society actors and international organisations, and in an attempt to improve their declining reputation, pharmaceutical business actors adopted a strategy of price-cutting for several patented HIV/AIDS drugs. The first round of price cuts happened in May 2000, just as Clinton passed his Executive Order, and took the form of the Accelerated Access Initiative in collaboration with the UN.[37] A second round of price cuts followed in March 2001, just before a scheduled court hearing of the South African lawsuit, again largely in response to pressure from Access Campaign actors who criticised the Initiative for being non-transparent and for not ensuring meaningful price cuts.[38] Importantly, through providing much-needed price reductions, pharmaceutical business actors were upholding their rights to IP protection, in that the ability to control prices is part and parcel of the monopoly rights provided by IP protection. In other words, pharmaceutical business actors were willing to negotiate price cuts, but not reductions on IP protection standards. Recall that, at this point, Brazil's patent law was being challenged at the WTO and the South African court case was ongoing. However, both eventually came to an abrupt end amidst immense and growing public pressure. By 2001 the chorus of criticism, often cast in terms of 'medical apartheid', coming from civil society groups, international organisations and governments, including at this point the US Congress and the EU Parliament, eventually had its effect and the companies decided to withdraw their case in April 2001.[39] This retreat was also influenced by the emergence of evidence that the most contentious section of the offending legislation was based on a WIPO Committee of Experts draft text (Sidley 2001), which weakened many of the companies' legal arguments. In addition, their claims of property rights over their products were damaged by evidence, uncovered and disseminated by CPTech, that many of the HIV/AIDs drugs (which could become subject to parallel importing or compulsory licensing in South Africa) had been developed with substantial input from publicly funded research.[40] Less than two months after the pharmaceutical companies withdrew their case, the US also officially withdrew its WTO case against Brazil. In the same month that the companies withdrew from the lawsuit, the WTO TRIPs Council accepted a request from Zimbabwe to hold a special Council Session on TRIPs and access to medicines.[41] The IP–access to medicines linkage had entered officially into the trade regime. And it did so with a vengeance, for the issue of TRIPs and public health became a key subject during the Doha Ministerial.

4.3   The 2001 Doha Declaration on the TRIPs Agreement and public health

Encouraged by the withdrawal of the South African and Brazilian legal challenges and by the huge public pressure on the IP–access to medicines issue, in the first ever TRIPs Council devoted to access to medicines in June 2001, Zimbabwe proposed on behalf of the African Group that a declaration be issued affirming that nothing in TRIPs should prevent members from adopting measures to protect public health.[42] Certain developed members, such as the US and Switzerland, were opposed to the idea of a ministerial declaration in the first place, insisting that IP protection did not constitute a barrier to access to medicines (I11 2006). For its part, the US floated an informal proposal for a moratorium on TRIPs-related WTO dispute cases for sub-Saharan African countries on measures taken to address the AIDS pandemic, as well as for an extension of transition periods for the least developed members.[43] These measures were considered by developing countries to be an effort to limit the debate to a few pandemics rather than public health measures in general, as well as an attempt to undermine developing countries' solidarity during the negotiations (I12 2006).

For their part, developing countries, led by India, Brazil and the African Group, worked together and alongside the Access Campaign group to forge a joint position on the IP–access to medicines issue in the run-up to the Doha Ministerial, and were able to maintain their solidarity on this issue before and during the Ministerial (I1, I12 and I12, 2006). In addition, two further developments helped to shape the outcome of contests at the Ministerial. One related to a 'propaganda war' unfolding in the few months before the Ministerial, initiated by pharmaceutical business actors who widely circulated two studies on the interplay between patent protection and the AIDS crisis in Africa.[44] Both studies concluded that poverty and limited spending on healthcare, and not patents, were the most important barriers to access, an argument which was used repeatedly by the US and Switzerland in the TRIPs Council preparatory meetings in the run-up to Doha (I14 2006). CPTech, Oxfam and other NGOs from the Campaign responded immediately by rebutting all claims set forth and by arguing that issues such as poverty or spending should not deflect attention from the impact patent protection had on access to medicines (CPTech et al. 2001). In addition to TRIPs Council meetings being caught in between this 'propaganda war', another development which shaped the deliberations on the IP–access to medicines debate was the anthrax scare following the 9/11 attacks in the US, when the government seriously contemplated the use of compulsory licensing for Ciproflaxin in order to cope with a potential public health crisis (Correa 2002; Sell 2005). As it turned out, no compulsory licensing was issued, but the event substantially weakened US resistance to the Declaration in the TRIPs Council meetings.

Nevertheless, such developments did not result in smooth negotiations at the Doha Ministerial. The language to be used in the Declaration had been the subject of heated debates in the run-up to the Ministerial, not least because of fears of some developed countries that too permissive a language would weaken the commitment to patent protection and TRIPs obligations in general (I1, I12 and I15, 2006).

A comprehensive draft declaration text was proposed by the African Group and nineteen other developing countries in a TRIPs Council session held in October 2001; at the same meeting the US, Japan and Switzerland, supported by some other developed members, circulated another draft which stressed the importance of IP protection for crucial medical R&D and adopted a language that more restrained than that of the African Group's text.[45] The submission by the developing countries was bold and assertive, stating that, on the basis of access to medicines and public health being a basic human right, and the unprecedented public health challenges, governments had the freedom to override TRIPs provisions when taking measures to deal with public health, including compulsory licensing, parallel importing and speeding up the entry of generic medicines into the market. Campaign NGOs fully supported the language and the measures proposed in the text (MSF 2001a). On the other hand, the proposal of the developed countries made a feeble reference to the appropriateness of using TRIPs flexibilities to address pandemics, while focusing more on the role of pharmaceutical IPRs and TRIPs in contributing to the development and availability of medicines and hence contributing to public health globally. This position was in line with that of the pharmaceutical industry, which insisted that TRIPs contained enough flexibility for governments to respond to public health concerns (I16 2006). For its part, the EC tried to play the role of 'honest broker' during the negotiations, although its approach clearly sided with that of the pharmaceutical industry in Europe (t'Hoen 2002; Pugatch 2004a).

In a continuing effort to divide developing countries, just before the Ministerial officially began, the USTR Robert Zoellick tried to persuade African ministers of the merits of the developed countries' option by presenting the developing countries' joint submission as nothing but a ploy by India and Brazil to advance the interests of their generic pharmaceutical industries, rather than to promote the cause of public health *per se* (Jawara and Kwa 2004). In the end, the developing countries' text provided the basis for the Doha Declaration, although the original language of the proposal was substantially watered down in a series of infamous green room meetings for which public records do not exist (I1 and I12, 2006). Negotiations over the Declaration were part of the WTO Doha Ministerial Conference in November 2001, where the launch of another WTO Round with a liberalising agenda in new issue-areas demanded by some developed members continued to meet with resistance from developing countries. Unlike Seattle, however, the Doha Ministerial was successful in launching the new Round as well as finalising the Doha Declaration on the TRIPs Agreement and Public Health.

While not introducing new obligations or rights, the Declaration first reiterated members' commitment to TRIPs obligations and it recognised that the latter was not in conflict with members' right to protect public health. Second, the Declaration recognised the flexibilities provided in the TRIPs Agreement and the right of regime members to use them, stating that these flexibilities should be interpreted in a way supportive of public health. Importantly, the Declaration specifically reinforced the right of the members to grant compulsory licenses, the freedom to determine the grounds upon which licences are granted and the freedom to establish the regime of exhaustion of IPRs (an issue closely related to parallel importing). Most notably, the Declaration covered measures to deal with healthcare concerns in general rather than simply the issue of access to essential medicines. Such reaffirmation of the flexibilities available to governments to undertake measure to promote public health ran directly against the restrictive interpretation given to the respective provisions until then, as the first part of this chapter showed.

Broadly speaking, the Declaration was a victory for developing countries and civil society actors in that, being endorsed by *all* the trade regime members, it explicitly recognised the flexibilities afforded in TRIPs and the right of these members to use them to address public health concerns. In addition, it provided some ordering of norms by suggesting that protecting public health warranted the temporary weakening of IP protection, although this interpretation of the Declaration was not shared by all the actors involved. True, the Declaration did not challenge any aspects of TRIPs, but the IP–access to medicines debate was not about rolling back TRIPs obligations. Rather, it was about advocating the use of flexibilities already in TRIPs, and this the Declaration did. In any case, just like TRIPs itself, the Declaration was not the last word on the subject for it remained open to interpretation, and depended on the willingness of the members to use it, and whether or not certain regime members and business actors would attempt to 'claim' back whatever was 'lost' in the Declaration through other means and in other venues. Indeed, just as TRIPs brought with it the seeds for future contestations within the trade regime and outside it, the Declaration, as we shall see shortly, continued to be contested, challenged and opposed.

5
TRIPs Revisited

The Doha Declaration was widely perceived as a victory for the developing countries and Access Campaign network insofar as all WTO members agreed to a flexible interpretation of TRIPs provisions for measures taken to deal with public health concerns. The main proposition of the IP–public health debate had been not so much that IP protection *per se* ran counter to ensuring access to medicines and public health in general, but rather that the *restrictive* interpretation and implementation of certain TRIPs provisions significantly reduced governments' options for ensuring such access in affordable terms, particularly in developing countries. Hence, although concerns were often raised about the negative implications of TRIPs itself on the worldwide accessibility of affordable new drugs, the aim of the Campaign and of developing countries was not so much to overhaul TRIPs, but rather to protect and use the flexibilities contained in it. It is in this sense that the Declaration was a victory, in that it succeeded precisely in claiming back such flexibilities. Not surprisingly, it did not pose a challenge to TRIPs; quite the contrary, by reiterating members' commitment to TRIPs it helped to further legitimise it.

Immediately after the Declaration there was a flurry of statements from all the actors involved, each appearing to welcome the Declaration as a satisfactory development. For their part, most developing countries and Campaign NGOs saw the Declaration as a powerful legal and political statement which opened valuable policy space for governments to deal with public health concerns (I1 and I3, 2006; MSF 2001b). On the other hand, pharmaceutical business actors also welcomed the Declaration, at least publicly, although on the grounds that it recognised that TRIPs and patents were legitimate tools for developing new medicines and were part of the solution for ensuring better public health (I16 and

117, 2006; PhRMA 2001; EFPIA 2001b; Noehrenberg 2003). Similarly, the US and EU also welcomed the Declaration, highlighting the importance of TRIPs and IP protection to the issues of access to medicines and public health, whilst taking the opportunity to hail TRIPs as an important indication of the ability of the WTO to respond to the concerns of its developing members (EC 2001; USTR 2001b; Vandoren 2002). These reactions were possible because of the language contained in the Declaration which simultaneously upheld TRIPs, confirmed that it provided sufficient flexibility to accommodate measures taken to deal with public health concerns, and spelled out such flexibilities through clarifying provisions related to pharmaceutical IPRs. The pharmaceutical business actors deliberately downgraded the importance of the flexibilities reiterated in the Declaration, although they clearly entailed a *temporary* erosion of their IPRs in that governments could undertake TRIPs-compliant measures, such as compulsory licensing, when they deemed them necessary to protect public health. While these measures added nothing new in terms of TRIPs provisions, they did unequivocally counter the more restrictive interpretation of such provisions that these business actors and certain regime members had been busy promulgating until then.

Overall, however, the Declaration did not fundamentally threaten the standard of their IPRs. Broadly speaking, by reiterating commitment to the TRIPs agreement, the Declaration challenged neither IPRs standards mandated by TRIPs nor the IP–trade linkage established by it, although it did highlight the newly-established IP–public health dimension. In other words, the Declaration sought to adjust public health concerns to the rules of the trade and IP regimes, rather than the other way around. Hence, the Doha Declaration managed at a stroke to vindicate the positions of pharmaceutical business actors and NGOs, formulated as 'IPRs = research = cures' and 'copying = cheap medicines = life' respectively. The extent to which these IP frames will be balanced in practice depends largely on the political will and efforts of business and state actors to tilt the balance either way. A different approach could perhaps have been that of linking pharmaceutical IPRs not only to innovation and the development of new medicines, like TRIPs and the Declaration, but also to *access* to such medicines. In other words, members could have agreed to revoke IP protection for certain medicines in a particular market if and when the right-holders failed to provide sufficient quantities of good quality and, importantly, *affordable* medicines for which they held IPRs in that market. This would not, in fact, have been a far-fetched approach, given that the whole point of the IP protection system is, or should be, to encourage both innovation *and* public access to such innovations.

Negotiations over the language of the Declaration, and its final form, illustrate the tensions that existed between the various actors involved, with some business actors and key developed members keen to ensure that their competitive advantage established by TRIPs was not eroded, and certain developing members and NGOs framing the issue within a discourse of public goods. While some sort of acceptable language was found for the Declaration, the more practical issue raised with regard to finding a solution for countries with insufficient capacity in the pharmaceutical sector to make use of compulsory licensing was postponed for later (paragraph 6 of the Declaration). As we shall see shortly, the paragraph 6 mandate became the new platform for contestations between state and non-state actors within the trade regime until TRIPs was amended in the Hong Kong Ministerial in December 2005. Obviously, the WTO TRIPs amendment process was not the only front on which IP contests were unfolding but, due to its complexity, this chapter focuses on the amendment process. It is organised chronologically, with the first part focusing on contests within the trade regime up to the August 2003 WTO Decision on the Implementation of paragraph 6 of the Doha Declaration on the TRIPs Agreement and Public Health ('the Decision'), and the second on developments unfolding after the Decision until the final amendment of TRIPs just before the WTO Hong Kong Ministerial in December 2005.[1]

5.1   The August 2003 decision: reneging on the Doha Declaration

Put simply, the issue of compulsory licensing for countries with insufficient or no pharmaceutical manufacturing capacities related to their inability to address public health concerns through issuing compulsory licensing, as their counterparts could. This inability stemmed not only from the fact that they did not have the capacity to work these licences domestically, but also because other countries who could were restricted by stipulations found in TRIPs Article 31(f) which, essentially, did not allow compulsory licences for export purposes.[2] This stipulation was not an oversight of the negotiations; rather, it was in line with pharmaceutical business actors' demands for limiting the use and scope of compulsory licences. The issue of compulsory licences for import/export was expected to become more significant with the full phasing-in of TRIPs obligations for pharmaceutical IPRs in 2005 in countries like India: this would substantially curtail the worldwide flow of generic versions of newly-developed medicines. This was not a problem that affected only a few developing WTO members, for nearly 60 developing countries have no manufacturing capacities at all in the pharmaceutical sectors, while some have only the capacity to produce medicines out of ready-made active pharmaceutical ingredients. Only a few developing countries, namely, Argentina, Brazil, Mexico, India, China and South Korea, are capable of manufacturing a patented pharmaceutical through reverse engineering (Ballance et al. 1992; Kaplan and Laing 2005). In addition, the existence of general manufacturing capacities for pharmaceuticals does not necessarily mean that a country has such capacities for a particular medicine; indeed, it is not impossible to conceive of a country with manufacturing capacities reviewing these capacities for a specific medicine, or group thereof, and concluding that it has insufficient capacities to fulfil a particular need. It is for this reason that defining the list of countries to which a potential paragraph 6 solution would apply became, as we shall see, a contentious area of debate within the TRIPs Council meetings during 2002 and 2003.

Despite differences in economic circumstances and immediate public health needs, most developing countries shared a strong interest in securing a broad and flexible solution to the issue of compulsory licensing for import/export. Indeed, their draft proposal for the Doha Declaration of October 2001 already contained two provisions according to which regime members could give effect to compulsory licences intended to address the public health needs of an importing member.[3] This broad solution was seen by developing countries as in accordance with the language of TRIP Article 30, which sets out exceptions to the rights of the patent-holders,[4] but it met with considerable resistance from some developed countries, particularly the US, in the pre-Doha meetings and was eventually eliminated from the text. As we shall see, disagreements over the legal form of a potential paragraph 6 solution became a second area of disagreement at the TRIPs Council meetings during 2002. In addition, a third controversial area emerged with regard to the scope of the diseases and health crises to which the paragraph 6 solution would apply, with certain state and pharmaceutical actors being concerned that too flexible a solution, encompassing many countries and an unlimited scope of diseases, would amount to a serious derogation from TRIPs-mandated IP protection for pharmaceuticals (I16 and I17, 2006).[5] It was mainly over these three issues that the battle was fought for over 18 months, engaging, once again, state and non-state actors, all of whom were attempting to shape the outcome of these contests in a manner conducive to their interests.

As we noted in the previous chapter, the coalition of business actors that came together before the Uruguay Round with the aim of securing globally enforceable IP protection were successful in maintaining the momentum in the early post-TRIPs period, assuming simultaneously the new roles of TRIPs guardians and 'TRIPs plus' advocates. Nevertheless, having secured TRIPs, some business actors within the coalition did not consider global IPRs as an issue that still required sustained coordination efforts of the Uruguay type. Furthermore, some business actors were also concerned that putting too much pressure on developing countries for a 'timely' and 'proper' implementation of their TRIPs obligations could be counterproductive (Matthews 2002b: 24). Signs of fissures in the business coalition were also observable in the many TRIPs-related dispute cases brought to the WTO post-TRIPs, the majority of which involved developed countries acting on behest of specific IP-reliant industries' interests. This is not to say that the coalition unravelled completely post-TRIPs; rather, specific industries and individual companies began to focus more on gaining and locking in their own competitive advantage in the market (Matthews 2002b). As the IP–public health debate overshadowed others from 2001 onwards, some business actors expressed concern that the Doha Declaration and the subsequent work at the TRIPs Council would set a dangerous precedent in the global IP regime, in that other issues could be brought up for revision and amendment by developing countries and civil society actors, with the overall effect of weakening the hard-won IPRs standards as mandated by TRIPs (I18 2006). On the other hand, some powerful (US) companies, including General Motors, a founder member of the IPC, responded to the Campaign message and sought increased availability of generic medicines, albeit primarily to reduce their own medical insurance costs (Sell 2003; Abbott 2006). The IP–trade linkage during the TRIPs negotiations provided a uniting frame for disparate IP interests, but it turned out to provide less comfort or support to specific IP interests, such as pharmaceuticals, as and when they found themselves in the spotlight. Sure enough, given these developments and the sector-specific nature of the IP–access to medicines contests as they unfolded after the Doha Declaration, pharmaceutical business actors found that they had to go it alone (I16 2006).

Civil society actors had been absent during TRIPs negotiations, but they emerged as the key actors in the IP–public health debate; indeed, they were the actors that established the linkage in the first place. Not only were civil society actors successful in establishing and bringing this linkage within the trade regime, but they were also crucial in providing technical expertise to developing countries' delegations in Geneva; indeed, almost all delegates interviewed during the course of this study highlighted the positive contribution that they felt the NGOs had made towards achieving the Doha Declaration. To the extent that the Declaration was a victory for the weaker actors within the regime, its success is attributable in good part to the ties and relationships built and maintained between developing countries' negotiators, academic experts and the network of health NGOs, who collectively constituted 'the capital' where negotiating positions were formulated and coordinated. Nevertheless, after the Declaration, and as deliberations at the TRIPs Council became increasingly technical, the momentum was lost somewhat, with some NGOs diverting attention to other trade issues (Matthews 2006), and others focusing more specifically on HIV/AIDS (I6 2006; I19 2007). But key civil society actors such as CPTech, MSF, HAI and Third World Network continued to lend support and expertise to developing countries' negotiators engaged with the paragraph 6 work, although, as we shall see, the ties between them weakened during the ensuing negotiations.

5.1.1   Charting the key actors' negotiating positions during 2002

To start with, the position of the NGOs and developing countries' coalition with regard to the paragraph 6 mandate converged, in that both parties envisaged a solution that would cover a broad range of diseases and public health needs, minimal procedural requirements and wide eligibility of importing and exporting countries.[6] The preferred route for achieving this flexible and broad solution was through an interpretation of Article 30 of TRIPs which had been advocated by the Campaign NGOs since the Amsterdam Statement before Seattle in 1999 and was included in developing countries' draft of the Doha Declaration in 2001. Some developed members, particularly the US, had opposed this approach during the Doha negotiations and the US explicitly sidelined the Article 30 route in its submission to the first TRIPs Council meeting in March 2002.[7] The position of developing countries in this meeting favoured either an authoritative interpretation of Article 30 that would allow the production and export of pharmaceuticals to address public health needs in other countries, or the deletion of the problematic paragraph (f) of Article 31.[8] For its part, the EC submission at this stage proposed both an interpretation of Article 30 and an amendment of Article

31(f) as possible routes to a workable solution.[9] The US saw merit in the Article 31 approach but, concerned about the consequences of opening and amending specific TRIPs provisions, preferred to address the issue through a moratorium on breaches of Article 31 (f) obligation for purposes of exporting to members experiencing a public health crisis.[10] A moratorium would have left TRIPs untouched but, from the perspective of some developing countries, it was seen as a temporary, unpredictable and legally unstable solution (I2, 2006).

The pharmaceutical business actors, for their part, were concerned about a possible Article 30 approach and preferred a solution based on Article 31 instead (I16, 2006); recall that the latter, specifying the procedures to be followed in case of compulsory licensing, had been one of the most debated articles during TRIPs negotiations and its final version still proved unsatisfactory to the pharmaceutical actors. Nonetheless, the choice of an Article 31 approach was crucial to the industry, given that the Article 30 route would have resulted in a broad and automatic exception that allowed the exporting country to manufacture and export *without* a compulsory licence at all.[11] Generally speaking, for developing countries and NGOs, an Article 30 approach meant speed, flexibility and fewer conditions and procedural requirements, these being precisely the reasons why the pharmaceutical actors preferred the Article 31 route instead. This article does not limit the grounds upon which a licence may be granted, but it does specify procedural and administrative requirements for compulsory licences issued on a case-by-case basis which, in practice, translate into legal and bureaucratic impediments, costs and delays. Indeed, as the Canadian experience with compulsory licensing for pharmaceuticals in the North American Free Trade Agreement (NAFTA) had made clear, patent-holders routinely relied on administrative requirements, judicial reviews and appeals to delay or render compulsory licences unattractive; 'delay was the name of the game' (Vaver and Basheer 2006: 11). Clearly, within the context of the paragraph 6 mandate, procedures, costs and delays that were burdensome from the perspective of developing countries and NGOs were framed by the pharmaceutical business actors as necessary safeguards and measures to protect their legitimate IPRs.

Deliberations about the legal form of the solution continued well into the second half of 2002; a summary compiled by the Secretariat after the June 2002 meeting based on the submissions of the US, EC, African Group, Brazil (on behalf of the developing countries coalition) and the United Arab Emirates (UAE), indicated that consensus was still lacking.[12] Options included an authoritative interpretation of Article 30; an amendment to Article 31; a moratorium on disputes; and a waiver with regard to Article 31 (f). The UAE and developing countries' proposal continued to favour an Article 30 approach at this stage, as did the proposal by the African Group, although, crucially, the latter also indicated that the deletion, an exception or authoritative interpretation of Article 31(f) had some potential. This change of heart on the part of the African Group can be partly explained by pressure exerted by the US and the EU throughout the negotiations (I12 2006), and partly by the adoption of a more expansionary agenda by the African Group at that time. This agenda included both resolving the compulsory licensing issue in the short term and the ambition of establishing pharmaceutical manufacturing capacities in certain African members that had no such capacities in the long term. This was envisaged through, amongst other things, technology transfer and a redefinition of the 'domestic market' limitation of Article 31(f) in terms of pharmaceuticals to mean the 'regional market' when dealing with public health challenges. The aim was to facilitate the establishment of generic pharmaceutical companies within Africa, which, under this mechanism, would have the entire regional market in which to achieve economies of scale (I1 2006).[13] For its part, the US continued to insist on a moratorium on dispute cases or, at most, a waiver of Article 31(f) obligations. At this stage, the EC, too, highlighted the benefits of an Article 31 approach to providing a legally secure mechanism for all parties involved.[14]

With the coalition of developing countries and the African Group failing to devise a common position on a preferred approach, a key development occurred with the change of position of the EC in the June 2002 meeting, at which it downplayed the merits of the other options including, importantly, the Article 30 approach. This change of heart was partly explained by the realisation that the US would not accept a mechanism based on Article 30 (Vandoren and Eeckhaute 2003), and partly due to divisions between the members of the EC and between the different Directorates General within the Commission itself. Members with a substantial proprietary pharmaceutical industry, such as Germany and the UK, were highly supportive of pharmaceutical actors' concerns and hence of the more restrictive Article 31 approach, while others, such as the Netherlands, lent support to the Article 30 approach. After many deliberations, it was the former group of countries that had their way (I20 2006). With the US categorically opposed to the Article 30 approach, the EC abandoning it in June and the African Group indicating that it could agree to an Article 31 route, the chances of a mechanism based on Article 30 were effectively doomed. This remained the case despite continuous support for this approach by a group of developing countries, led by Brazil and India, in the subsequent TRIPs Council meetings. The network of NGOs continued to support this approach too,[15] as did the European Parliament[16] and the WHO, which endorsed this approach explicitly in a TRIPs meeting in September 2002.[17] Despite such support, continuous pressure from the US and EC on the African Group members, with a view to separating them from the developing countries' coalition, bore some fruit. Most notably, neither the South African non-paper nor the Communication from Kenya on behalf of the African Group in the TRIPs Council meeting in November 2002 mentioned explicitly the Article 30 route (I12 2006).[18] In the end, with the unity of developing and least developed countries weakening on the legal mechanism issue, the Article 30 approach had been successfully eliminated by the end of 2002, and with it the chances of a potentially broader and more flexible solution.

While the legal mechanism of the paragraph 6 solution was being narrowed down to an Article 31 approach by the autumn of 2002, other issues, such as those related to safeguards against abuse, the eligibility of importing and exporting countries and the scope of diseases and health crises, were being intensely debated. The issue of safeguards to prevent potential abuse of the paragraph 6 solution was raised early on from both the US and the EU,[19] the latter being particularly insistent, and instrumental in ensuring that these safeguards became part of the final mechanism. The safeguards related primarily to the pharmaceutical industry's concerns with regard to trade diversion and the re-exportation of medicines produced under compulsory licensing to other markets, especially those in developed and high-income developing countries from which it derives the overwhelming part of its sales and profits (I17 2006). The role of the EU in securing these safeguards is partly attributable to its operating a regional exhaustion doctrine which forbids the import of cheaper medicines from outside the EU (Matthews 2004). Its submissions to the TRIPs Council proposed the insertion of similar safeguards to those found in the EU on the basis that the existing TRIPs provisions on enforcement measures were insufficient in the case of a paragraph 6 solution because they did not deal with trade diversion as such.[20] However, the introduction of such safeguards amounted to *limiting* the flexibilities contained in TRIPs for countries that would use the paragraph 6 solution (as opposed to those that would not), given that no safeguards against trade diversion and re-importation of goods produced under compulsory licences were stipulated in Article 31, which sets out the procedural requirements for such licences.

Despite initial resistance by some developing countries (less so by the African Group) to the idea of accepting conditions inserted in the solution that would limit the flexibilities offered by TRIPs,[21] such safeguards and procedural requirements gradually found their way into the first draft of a paragraph 6 presented by the TRIPs Council Chair Peréz Motta on 19 November 2002, just days after a mini-ministerial held in Sydney. These safeguards included the following requirements: (i) the TRIPs Council must be informed of an intention to use the mechanism and given a detailed justification for such a decision; (ii) the patent-holder must be approached for a voluntary licence beforehand; (iii) two licences must be granted (for import and export); (iv) production under licence must be limited to the quantity required by the importing country; and, (v) measures must be taken to prevent trade diversion, and compensation paid to the patent-holder.[22] Importantly, the incorporation of these 'TRIPs plus' procedural requirements came just as efforts towards a broader Article 30 approach were defeated, and despite calls from the NGOs and generic pharmaceutical industry actors that such safeguards would have the effect of turning the paragraph 6 solution into too burdensome a mechanism (I21, 2006).[23]

In addition, these safeguards were part of wider efforts by the proprietary pharmaceutical actors and some advanced developed countries to limit both the range of diseases and the countries eligible to use the paragraph 6 solution. Of all the issues debated at the TRIPs Council during this period, the issue of limiting the range of diseases became by far the most controversial. Since its first submission in March 2002, the US referred to paragraph 1 of the Doha Declaration, which mentioned public health problems 'resulting especially from HIV/AIDS, tuberculosis, malaria and other epidemics' in order to fashion a paragraph 6 solution confined to these diseases.[24] The issue was debated extensively amongst state negotiators, business actors, NGOs representatives and academic experts at an informal meeting organised by Quakers United Nations Office (QUNO) and the government of Norway in July 2002, but it became the major issue in negotiations mainly from the September TRIPs Council meeting onwards (I22 2007). During the July meeting in Norway, both the US and the EU floated the idea that paragraph 1 of the Declaration *intended* to limit the scope of diseases to which the solution would apply, although later this became largely a US cause as the EU eventually withdrew its explicit support for limiting the scope of diseases (I15 and I20, 2006). This was mainly in response to united resistance from developing and African countries which, since the early Council meetings, had argued that the solution would not be limited to a list of diseases and referred to the 'access to medicines for all' language in paragraph 4 of the Declaration to support their argument (I1 2006).[25]

Despite this resistance and the lack of consensus in the TRIPs Council, Chair Peréz Motta issued a note on 17 October 2002 on his own responsibility which, reflecting the US preferred approach to disease coverage, referred to the scope of diseases in paragraph 1 of the Doha Declaration. A week after the note appeared, the Assistant USTR for Africa, Rosa Whitaker, wrote to all African government leaders to support the approach contained in the note, insisting, amongst other things, that its aim was to deal with the serious epidemics faced by Africans (HIV/ AIDS, malaria and tuberculosis) and arguing that 'broadening the solution…would divert attention and resources away from these epidemics at Africa's expense'.[26] Many developing countries' negotiators and NGOs saw the letter as another attempt by the US to break up their unified resistance to limiting the scope of diseases and the number of eligible countries for the paragraph 6 solution (I4 2006). To counter such efforts, developing countries' negotiators responded with a non-paper presented by South Africa on 5 November to the TRIPs Council, which explicitly stated that there should be no restrictions on the eligible countries and scope of diseases to be addressed by a potential paragraph 6 solution.[27] This unified position on the scope of disease issue was strengthened by the Kenyan submission on behalf of the African Group in the following week, which provided detailed legal grounds for rejecting limitations on disease coverage, including the sovereign right of members to determine public health needs, and the overall objective of the solution to promote access to medicines for all.[28]

The US approach, outlined in Council meetings and in Whitaker's letter, was aimed at simultaneously limiting the scope of diseases, mainly to those that are infectious, as well as the number of countries to which the solution would apply. This position reflected concerns raised by pharmaceutical business actors who, keen on limiting the number of products eligible for compulsory licensing, envisaged a solution limited to certain diseases and only to least developed countries. From these actors' perspective, this would be followed by irresponsible compulsory licensing for any disease and drug of choice by countries that would benefit from the solution if these limitations were not introduced, thereby seriously weakening the patent protection terms achieved through TRIPs. These concerns were raised throughout the negotiations; they also appeared in a letter to the USTR in November 2002 in which around twenty research-based pharmaceutical companies strongly urged the USTR to ensure that the disease scope was limited only to medicines for serious epidemics, and not for 'lifestyle' diseases like cancer, heart disease or diabetes.[29] And the USTR continued to insist on limiting the disease scope of the solution, using arguments that such limitation was inherent in paragraph 1 of the Declaration and that broadening the scope would risk the inclusion of non-infectious (lifestyle) diseases and undermine future R&D, in addition to undermining the interest of African members, for whom the solution was principally intended. However, these arguments failed to convince most other members, most importantly the EC, as they were not legally founded in the Declaration. Furthermore, limiting the disease scope would have been TRIP-inconsistent as it would have limited the grounds for issuing compulsory licensing to certain diseases for countries with no manufacturing capacities, but not for those that were fortunate enough to have such capacities.

Some of these arguments were also raised by the NGOs network during November and December 2002, when the issue of limiting disease scope was fiercely debated at the TRIPs Council. The network played an important role in keeping the pressure on the USTR to renounce its stance on the issue, and on negotiators in general by communicating and networking with trade negotiators and through raising public awareness about the implications of accepting such limitations (I23 2006; I19 2007).[30] After the Sydney mini-ministerial and a follow-up informal meeting of the TRIPs Council on 18 November 2002, the first draft of a potential solution circulated by Chair Motta on 19 November continued to refer to language on paragraph 1 of the Declaration, just as the Chair's note of 17 October had done before it.[31] Faced with substantial criticism from developing countries at the TRIPs Council, the Chair released two other drafts on 20 and 24 of November, which explicitly stated that public health problems were not limited to epidemics of the three specific diseases mentioned in paragraph 1 of the Declaration. The US objected strongly to the distribution of these later texts on account of their 'broad' disease scope, although by that stage, as we have noted, the more limited Article 31 approach and the many safeguards aimed at preventing abuse and trade diversion had already reduced the chances of a flexible solution. During the formal and informal meetings at the TRIPs Council that took place at the end of November and during December 2002, the US continued to insist on limiting the application of the solution to certain diseases. In addition, it intensified its campaign to divide the developing countries' group by arguing that countries such as India and Brazil were acting in bad faith and diverting attention from the 'true' purpose of the solution (I4 2006).

5.1.2   From the December 2002 text to the 2003 Decision

With the December 2002 deadline approaching, a compromise draft implementation of paragraph 6 of the Declaration was tabled by Chair Motta on 16 December.[32] The text recognised the public health problems expressed in paragraph 1 of the Declaration, but it did not limit the scope of the solution to any particular diseases. Amongst other things, it proposed a waiver of the obligations of Article 31 (f) with respect to pharmaceuticals in cases of compulsory licences for import until TRIPs was amended to that end, and spelled out the safeguards and measures to be taken by importing and exporting members, as discussed above. Given these measures, many developing countries had considerable reservations about the Motta text but, feeling that other concessions would not be forthcoming, signalled their willingness to accept it, provided no limitation of disease scope were attempted later (I1 and I3, 2006).[33] The NGOs network, viewing the Motta text as limiting the importance of the Declaration and creating uncertainty and unnecessary impediments, was dismayed by this decision and wrote immediately to the negotiators urging them to reject the Motta text.[34] Nevertheless, it was not the developing countries, which had most to lose from the Motta text, but the US who rejected it during the Council meeting on 20 December, purely because it had a very broad scope which went beyond the focus on HIV/AIDS, tuberculosis and malaria.[35] Anticipating adverse reactions, the USTR announced on the same day a unilateral moratorium on dispute settlement actions for countries using compulsory licences for imports based on its preferred outcome of the negotiations. Essentially, the moratorium applied to a narrow list of diseases and excluded developed and high-income developing countries.[36] The EU followed suit with its own moratorium in January 2003 but, unlike the US, it derived its language on the Motta December text.[37]

By many accounts, the US was unable to join the 20 December consensus as it was unacceptable to the US pharmaceutical industry (I7, I17 and I24, 2006). As was discussed above, research-based pharmaceutical actors were concerned that negotiations at the TRIPs Council could, if developing countries had their way, result in a mechanism which would be used to legitimise the granting of compulsory licences on all sorts of drugs and pharmaceutical products to deal with public health issues by a large number of countries that would claim they lacked manufacturing capacities for the pharmaceutical product in question (I16 and I17,

2006).[38] Were these negotiations to be carried out in the spirit of the Declaration, the ensuing solution could, in their view, amount to nothing less than a WTO-legitimised tool for using compulsory licensing for commercial purposes and the protection or encouragement of nascent (pharmaceutical) industry in other members, with adverse and irreparable implications for pharmaceutical IP protection achieved through TRIPs. However, despite these shared concerns, it appears that the Motta December text, while not seen as the best solution, was more acceptable to the European-based pharmaceutical business actors (I17 and I18, 2006). It is difficult to ascertain whether this acceptance stemmed from a realisation of their limited power to influence the EC positions and multilateral negotiations on this scale, from a genuine realisation that it could live with the proposed solution or from a calculated shift of its efforts, with its US counterpart, to the more accessible US front.

For its part, the US continued to represent the interest of its pharmaceutical actors, insisting on limiting the scope of diseases, putting enormous pressure on other governments to change their position and attempting to divide African members from other (exporting) developing countries such as India, China and Brazil (I4, 2006; Noehrenberg 2003).[39] Despite having briefly flirted with the idea of expanding the list of diseases from HIV/AIDS, malaria and tuberculosis to 23 diseases and epidemics in the last hours of the 20 December TRIPs Council meeting, the US showed no enthusiasm for an EC proposal that emerged on 7 January 2003 introducing a presumptive list of 23 diseases to be addressed by the solution that could be further expanded on advice by the WHO.[40] Although the EC negotiators insisted that the proposal was just an attempt to break the deadlock rather than limit the scope of diseases as such, many developing countries and Campaign NGOs criticised the EC for having joined the US on the issue of restricting the scope of diseases and involving the WHO to sweeten the pill (I1, I3, I15, I20 and I25, 2006).[41] For its part, the WHO declined the role of taking public health decisions, as this was generally viewed as the responsibility of sovereign governments.[42] Criticism was also strong because the 'approved' list included mainly diseases for which there existed no drug treatment or for which existing treatments were off-patent, thus diseases for which the 'risk' of compulsory licensing was rather small (MSF 2003). Nonetheless, the proposal was also met with criticism by US pharmaceutical business actors who saw it and the involvement of the WHO as opening a 'Pandora's box'.[43]

With negotiations remaining deadlocked for the first part of 2003 over the disease coverage issue, it became increasingly clear that developing countries, supported by the Campaign NGOs,[44] were not going to accept a limitation on the scope of diseases under any circumstances and that their resistance to such a limitation had a strong legal standing in the Doha Declaration and the TRIPs agreement itself. Given such resistance, during a mini-ministerial held in Tokyo in February 2003 the US floated the idea that it might be willing to concede on the scope of diseases if the solution were limited to African members.[45] This idea was further crystallised in the next few months and at another mini-ministerial held in June 2003 in Sharm el-Sheikh in Egypt, when the US again indicated that it could consider abandoning the idea of a restricted scope of diseases to be covered by the solution, in exchange for limiting the list of countries eligible for a paragraph 6 solution.

This change of heart on the part of the USTR was strongly linked to developments within the US and European pharmaceutical business circles. Until May 2003 both PhRMA and IFPMA still insisted that the proposed solution would be unacceptable without significantly narrowing the scope of diseases and beneficiary importing countries. Indeed, Harvey Bale of the IFPMA was still arguing at that point that the Motta December draft solution was 'a license to steal'.[46] By June 2003, however, the pharmaceutical business actors were moving towards a consensus on how to proceed and were giving signals that they could soften their stance on the issue of restricting the scope of diseases in exchange for limiting the solution to the poorest members. At that point, they started to press the US government to focus on limiting the number of eligible countries based on certain criteria related to a country's GNP, or whether a certain percentage of a country's population was affected by a certain disease.[47] The US PhRMA spokesman, Mark Greyson, confirmed publicly in July 2003 that the US pharmaceutical industry was 'recasting its position on a global trade agreement that would give poor countries access to generic drugs while protecting company investments in name-brand pharmaceuticals'.[48]

The issue of limiting the eligibility of importing countries did not, in fact, emerge during negotiations in the first half of 2003. In line with the general interest in limiting the use of a potential paragraph 6 solution, the US and the EC had already made proposals during the earlier stages of negotiations about possible ways of restricting the number of eligible importing countries.[49] Despite substantial differences in pharmaceutical production capacities, developing countries were able to formulate and generally maintain a common position on the wide eligibility of importing and exporting countries. Nevertheless, efforts to pit African members, who had a strong interest in increasing manufacturing capacities in Africa, against other countries with developed manufacturing capacities such as India, China and Brazil, did give rise to some tensions between the developing countries as a group on this issue. But, given that virtually no country, developing or otherwise, could claim to be self-sufficient in producing the full range of medicines in use, it became increasingly clear during the negotiations that no developing country was going to accept its exclusion as an importer from a potential solution. In addition, the Doha Declaration had addressed public health challenges as experienced by developing countries overall, and these countries were not keen to see themselves grouped in categories of countries devised for paragraph 6 purposes but not officially recognised by the WTO. Indeed, the Motta text of 16 December 2002 had already removed all such categories and established as eligible importing countries all least developed members (automatically) and developing members that would notify the TRIPs Council of their intention to act as an importer.[50] At the same time, the Motta text had also indicated that some members, namely the EC Member States, Australia, Canada, the US and New Zealand, would not use the mechanism as importers at all, although no records exist about how this decision was taken and then made known to the TRIPs Council.

Given the change in the pharmaceutical actors' stance on disease limitation in exchange for limiting importing countries' eligibility by mid 2003 and their general discontent with the safeguards contained in the Motta text, the key issue became one of how to limit eligibility and enhance safeguards without reopening the Motta text that trade negotiators had shown willingness to accept. This change occurred mainly during June and July 2003 as a response to the firm and united opposition to restrictions of disease coverage by developing members and Campaign NGOs. It was also due to fault lines, both between and within large research-based pharmaceutical business companies on the merits of a hard-line and uncompromising stance on an issue that had acquired important public and political dimensions.[51] The solution to the impasse was eventually offered by pharmaceutical business actors and came in the form of the Chairperson Statement ('the Statement') that supplemented the Motta December text as part of what later became the August 2003 Decision. Interestingly, in a hopeless attempt to break the impasse, Chair Motta had already floated the idea of an accompanying statement in an informal February 2003 meeting, but it was soon discounted.[52] The idea of an accompanying statement became attractive only after the pharmaceutical business actors decided to recast their demands for additional limitations and safeguards using more positive language. Instead of insisting on limiting the scope of diseases and/or eligibility of countries, the chosen strategy was that of excluding countries and markets of concern to the pharmaceutical business actors from the solution. The Statement achieved this through listing 47 members (developed and high-income developing countries) that had 'agreed' to opt-out of using the system as importers, partly or completely,[53] and by listing additional safeguards and measures to be taken by members with the aim of preventing the diversion of both finished and active ingredients produced under the system.[54] It is worth recalling that the US market alone accounts for around 60 per cent of total worldwide pharmaceutical industry profits, while around 80 per cent of global pharmaceutical sales are accounted for by the US, Canadian and European market alone (PhRMA 2005; EFPIA 2009). In other words, the aim of the Statement was to prevent these and other high-income countries from resorting to compulsory licensing for import, as well as, through additional safeguards, ensuring that drugs produced under the system by other countries would not be diverted into these markets under any circumstances. The opt-out was presented as uncontroversial, indeed as an act of goodwill on the part of the developed members, as the solution was always meant to address the concerns of developing and least developing countries.[55]

In addition to fencing off markets and adding safeguards to address pharmaceutical business actors' concerns, the Statement also aimed to spell out certain key understandings 'shared' amongst members, especially the understanding that the mechanism was to be used in good faith to protect public health and not as an instrument to pursue industrial or commercial policy objectives. This language was familiar to developing countries' negotiators, who had been told by the USTR in the mini-ministerial held in Montreal in the end of July 2003 that the US would accept the December text if large developing countries, such as Brazil and India, made public announcements that they would not use the solution for commercial purposes (I14 2006). Similar language made its way into the Statement in the form of 'shared understandings' clearly aimed at assuaging pharmaceutical actors' concerns about compulsory licences being used 'inappropriately' or with the aim of supporting member's domestic generic industries, rather than for humanitarian purposes. Such language in the Statement attracted criticism from certain developing members, given that compulsory licensing is generally used to counter restrictive business practices and monopolistic pricing, both of which are legitimate commercial and industrial policies (I1, I3 and I13, 2006). In addition, generic producers would not generally work a compulsory licence other than for profit and commercial purposes. The Statement also charged the TRIPs Council with the new role of overseeing the report-and-review process which, under the banner of transparency, went beyond the requirements contained in the Motta text. It demanded, amongst other things, that importing members include information on how they had established that they lacked manufacturing capacities, as well as offering to other members the possibility of raising concerns regarding the implementation of the Decision with a view to taking 'appropriate action'.

The idea and content, if not the language, of the Statement emerged first within pharmaceutical business circles in the US and was then hammered out in a small group of negotiators including the US, India, Brazil, Kenya, South Africa and Chairperson Vanu Gopala Menon in a series of informal meetings in July and August 2003 (I3, I12, I15 and I16, 2006).[56] The 'five' struck a deal on 21 August and a slightly revised text of the Statement became official on 26 August;[57] thereafter, allowing insufficient time for consideration of the Statement by other governments and amidst accompanying high-level pressure on the capitals to accept it, the TRIPs Council approved the solution on the paragraph 6 issue during its 28 August meeting (I3, I4 and I12, 2006).[58] Whether members were pressurised or convinced about the necessity of accepting the Statement as the price for bringing the US on board, following approval in the TRIPs Council, the final draft of the Motta text and the Statement were presented and adopted at a pre-Cancún meeting of the WTO General Council on 30 August 2003.[59] The 30 August 2003 Decision ('the Decision') was essentially a permanent waiver of members' obligations under Article 31(f) for countries with insufficient pharmaceutical manufacturing capacities facing public health challenges, until such time as that article is amended. Officially, developed and some developing countries welcomed the Decision as a major breakthrough in the negotiations and, as with the 2001 Declaration, as a clear indication of the ability of the WTO to respond effectively to the concerns of developing members.[60] Pharmaceutical business actors also welcomed the Decision while, for their part, most Campaign NGOs were disappointed that developing countries had accepted the Motta text and the Statement that, from their perspective, was a 'monstrosity' and a 'gift bound in red tape'.[61] *Médecins sans Frontières* (MSF) was the first to attempt to use the mechanism set up by the 2003 Decision in May 2004 for the generic production of a triple-fixed dose ARV drug for patients in its HIV/AIDS projects by a Canadian manufacturer, but did not see a single pill produced even after two years had elapsed. MSF subsequently argued that the mechanism was burdensome, inflexible and ultimately unworkable.[62]

5.2 The December 2005 Amendment

Just as the Doha Declaration gave a mandate which locked state and non-state actors in contestations for nearly two years, the Decision also mandated an amendment of Article 31 of TRIPs which continued to engage these actors in contests for an additional two years. Paragraph 11 of the Decision envisaged that such an amendment should be adopted within six months, but the deadline was missed several times as state and non-state actors struggled over the content and form the amendment was to take.[63] As with the Doha Declaration, the African Group emerged again as the main *demandeur* of the amendment process. Indeed, since the IP–public health linkage became officially part of the WTO work programme, there existed a tacit understanding among developing countries that the African Group had 'the moral high ground' in the negotiations at the WTO, given the acuteness of HIV/AIDS endemic there, although none of the victories won in the process would have been possible without the support of other developing countries as a group and Campaign NGOs. Nonetheless, partly as a result of pressure from key regime members, partly due to diverse interests and partly as a result of negotiation fatigue, the unity within the African Group, and between the Group and the developing countries and NGOs to which the Doha success was attributed broke down during the paragraph 6 negotiations. As we noted, Campaign NGOs were disappointed that developing countries had given in to pressure and backtracked on the Doha Declaration; on the other hand, although all developing members had officially adopted the Decision, countries such as the Philippines, Cuba, Argentina, India and Indonesia felt that its requirements were burdensome, and publicly made some of their reservations known during the General Council meeting of August 2003.[64] Within the African Group, Kenya was particularly critical of the Decision and the accompanying Statement and came under considerable pressure to renounce its 'counterproductive' stance during TRIPs Council meetings (I1 and I12, 2006).

When work started on the TRIPs amendment, the aim of the African Group was to take advantage of the existing political will to deal with the issue of public health with a view to ensuring a permanent amendment of TRIPs (I1 and I7, 2006). For their part, key developed members saw the Decision as a fine and hard-struck balance between industry and developing countries' interests and saw no reason to rush towards a TRIPs amendment, while certain developing countries saw the amendment process as an opportunity to deal with and address their concerns about the Decision. Indeed, many of them that had raised concerns over the substance of the solution throughout the paragraph 6 negotiations, most outspokenly Kenya and the Philippines, had accepted the Decision largely on the grounds of expediency and on the understanding that their concerns would be dealt with during the amendment process (I1 and I12, 2006). Hence, negotiations got off to a bad start from the very first TRIPs Council meeting to deal with the issue in mid-November 2003, where they were faced with the position of some key developed members who argued that the amendment was to be but a 'technical' effort that did not require renegotiating the substance of the Decision.[65] Thereafter, with members agreeing to hold informal consultations until the following March 2004 meeting, negotiations went effectively underground.

Indeed, little exists in terms of public records on the negotiations among members thereafter. Because most developed members were of the opinion that the amendment should be no more than a technical exercise, no concrete proposals were made to the TRIPs Council, the only exception being a proposal submitted by the African Group in December 2004. The March 2004 Council meeting came and went, with little progress made in finding common ground and negotiations remaining underground. Disagreement continued over the form the amendment was to take, with the EC favouring an amendment of Article 31 in the actual text of the agreement, while the US preferred a footnote to Article 31, which would have made reference to both the Decision and the Statement. From that point onwards, the issue of written reference to the Statement, as advocated by the US, Switzerland and Japan, became the most contentious issue of the negotiations (I11 and I27, 2006).[66] For their part, the majority of developing countries were opposed to the idea of a written footnote to the Statement because of their concern that such a reference would be tantamount to an unnecessary upgrading of its legal status, while some other developing countries insisted on improving the substance of the Decision (I1, I3 and I12, 2006). With disagreements continuing over these issues, the first deadline of the June 2004 meeting was missed and the TRIPs Council agreed on finalising the amendment by March 2005.

One key development in this period was the proposal submitted by the African Group in the December 2004 TRIPs Council meeting which, unlike the debate over technical and legal issues that had dominated the informal negotiations until then, sought to deal with the substance of the amendment by providing a text which dropped many of the safeguards and procedural requirements of the August Decision.[67] Importantly, the proposal excluded the Statement altogether on the basis that it was unnecessary since it had already served its purpose in producing the required consensus.[68] Essentially, the aim of the proposal was to reduce the level of complexity and potential cost of the mechanism set up by the Decision. From the perspective of the African Group, the proposal was in line with its interpretation of the Decision, which stated that the amendment would be based on that Decision 'when appropriate' (paragraph 11). The proposal enjoyed the support of many developing countries, particularly countries such as India, Brazil, the Philippines, Sri Lanka, Argentina, Kenya and Peru, which had understood the Decision as an interim measure to be refined during the amendment process and had made their reservations about the latter known during the adoption process in 2003.[69] For certain developed members such as the US, EU, Switzerland, Canada and Australia, the proposal amounted to the unacceptable step of reopening the difficult and fragile balance stuck in 2003, with the US in particular raising severe criticism on account of the proposal having excluded some crucial provisions of the Decision and the Statement altogether.[70] These positions were reiterated during the March 2005 TRIPs Council meeting, with little concrete result in terms of reaching consensus.[71]

With the March 2005 deadline missed again, a second key development in the negotiations was the informal draft proposal circulated by the EC in July 2005.[72] In fact, because the US had made it clear that it would not accept renegotiating any element of the Decision or the weakening of the Statement's legal status during the amendment process, only the African Group and the EC were involved in the informal negotiations that started in March 2005. The principle underlying the EC proposal was that the Decision should be incorporated in an Annex and reference made to the latter through adding a new paragraph to Article 31 of TRIPs. The US found the proposal unacceptable because all references to the Statement which had enabled it to join the consensus in 2003 were omitted both from the Article 31 amendment and the proposed Annex.[73] For its part, the African Group found the proposal unacceptable on the grounds that it transformed the Decision word for word in an amendment. During the informal negotiations, the African Group requested that certain elements it deemed important in the Decision, namely those of waiving importing countries' obligation to pay compensation to patent-holders and those related to the 'regional market' option, be incorporated in the body of the amendment (I1 2006). The EC, having experienced great difficulties in harnessing consensus amongst its member states, found this 'pick-and-choose' strategy unacceptable, and the informal negotiations eventually stalled by the end of September 2005 (I15, I20 and I25, 2006).

With both the African proposal and the EC idea failing to move the negotiations forward and the December Hong Kong Ministerial approaching, the US embarked upon a series of informal trilateral consultations with the African Group and the EC (I1 and I12, 2006). The amendment process was not part of the Programme of the Doha Round or Ministerial as such, but amidst worries that progress on agriculture and NAMA negotiations would be insignificant in Hong Kong, there was a considerable incentive for achieving some success on the highly-publicised public health issue. Despite this incentive, the informal trilateral negotiations did not bear much fruit; old positions were reiterated over and over again in the TRIPs Council meetings in October and November 2005, the only novelty being the serious objections raised by members such as India and Brazil at having been left out of the consultations.[74] As late as the end of November 2005, the US was still insisting on a written reference to the Statement, having objected to the idea of 'rereading' the Statement for fear that other statements made before or after it would undermine its strength.[75] Such a position reflected similar concerns raised by pharmaceutical business actors, whose position throughout the negotiations had been that the deal struck in August 2003 be incorporated wholesale in the amendment and the Statement's status maintained, if not elevated (I16, 2006). The negotiations reached their climax in the first week of December 2005, by which point the African Group abandoned its original December 2004 proposal and the US moved away from its request for a written reference to the Statement. Nevertheless, to ensure that the legal status of the latter was protected, a new, elaborate procedure in the form of a 'choreography' of nine steps to be followed at the TRIPs and General Council was devised, whereby the Statement would be read after the amendment and no other statements reflecting other understandings or reservations would made.[76]

By some accounts, the US stepped down from its original position only after the pharmaceutical business actors were convinced that the 'choreography' granted the Statement a substantial interpretative and legal status and thus gave the green light to it (I16 2006). This is so because other (competing) statements that would have had a similar interpretative weight were not permitted. Important statements made in the course of adopting the Decision in 2003, most notably by the

Philippines and Kenya, were deliberately not reaffirmed. Some commentators have argued that, due to the 'choreography', these previous statements may have minimal interpretative value, whereas the Statement could come to be seen as providing the main, if not the sole, supplementary means for interpreting it, even though it is not in the actual text of the agreement.[77] Essentially, the amendment added an Article 31 *bis* where three elements from the Decision were incorporated, namely, limited exceptions to Article 31(f), similar exceptions for countries belonging to regional trading agreements (the majority of whose members are among the least developed members) and a provision to avoid double compensation to the patent-holder, with the rest of the Decision incorporated in an Annex.

A group of 54 NGOs, headed by CPTech, Oxfam and MSF, asked WTO members in a joint statement not to rush towards incorporating a solution whose feasibility in practice was seriously questionable, presumably only to deflect attention from lack of movement or anti-development proposals in other areas of the negotiations.[78] However, once the African Group indicated that it would accept the amendment and the 'choreography' just before the December TRIPs and the subsequent General Council meetings, other developing countries also agreed to go along, reportedly amidst pressure from the US to do so (I26 2006).[79] As set forth in the 'choreography', the amendment was adopted at the TRIPs and the General Council meeting on 6 December 2005. As expected, the deal was greeted as an achievement by developed members and pharmaceutical business actors, while the NGOs and some developing countries' negotiators were critical of the amendment and considered it as a step back from the Doha Declaration and, indeed, the August 2003 Decision (I3 and I12,2006).[80] For this reason, some negotiators in Geneva at the time, on their own initiative, were attempting to dissuade developing countries from formally accepting the 2005 Amendment, a step which would eventually leave in force the 2003 Decision (waiver) (I28 2006). As it happens, the Decision is still in force because the Amendment will be part of the TRIPs agreement once two-thirds of the WTO membership formally accepts it: at the time of writing only 29 countries have done so. The list includes some of the key developing countries that were dissatisfied with it, such as India, the Philippines and Brazil, but not the key members of the African Group. Interestingly, despite the urgency of dealing with the matter, no country notified the TRIPs Council of its intention to use compulsory licences for import or export for a while. The only exception was that of Rwanda, which notified the TRIPs Council in July 2007 that it intended to import TriAvir, a fixed-dose (patented) ARV drug produced under licence by Apotex, Canada's largest generic pharmaceutical company. The first shipment was ready over 15 months later, but Apotex claimed that it was not willing to go through the process again, unless the rules were changed.[81]

As with TRIPs and the Declaration, the Amendment implementation process would provide another chapter in the IP–access to medicines story, as it is in the implementation phase that actors seek to convert rather remote rules into practices that favour certain understandings and interests over others. Moreover, as we have seen in this chapter, both the 2003 Decision and the 2005 Amendment were not arrangements that, from the perspective of some state and non-state actors, offered a satisfactory resolution to the issue of compulsory licensing for patented drugs. It was unlikely, then, that the Amendment would signal the end of the IP–access to medicines contests. In any case, the issue of compulsory licensing was but one of the issues of that debate, although an important one. As we shall see in the following chapter, while this one issue continued to demand considerable efforts at the WTO, contests over IPRs had expanded and intensified in many more regimes and fora.

6
Shifting IP Issues between Regimes and Fora: Contestations Continued

The previous chapters have demonstrated why and how IPRs came to be seen as a trade matter and, later, why IPRs–access to medicines contests became highly politicised in the late 1990s, how state and non-state actors with different normative and material interests participated in these contests over the years and why the latter were 'resolved' the way they were in the Hong Kong TRIPs Amendment in 2005. As we have seen, during the negotiations over the Declaration, the Decision and the Amendment, pharmaceutical business actors and key developed countries continued to consider IP protection for pharmaceuticals as a trade and competitiveness issue, while most developing countries and Campaign NGOs viewed it as a public health and public good issue, although commercial concerns were not irrelevant to developing members and even a few NGOs (such as MSF). As was argued earlier, the Doha Declaration, a victory for the developing members and civil society actors, posed serious challenges neither to the TRIPs-mandated IP standards nor to the IP–trade linkage established by it. The 2003 Decision and the subsequent 2005 Amendment, laden with procedures and requirements to protect the IP interests of pharmaceutical business, were even less successful in doing so.

But regimes are dynamic and contested processes, and contestations over a particular issue are likely to continue as actors who do not share a consensus over how it is 'resolved' may continue to challenge, redefine and reframe it time and again. And, as the last chapter showed, the 2005 Amendment represented an unsatisfactory resolution of the IPRs–access to medicines contests for many of the actors involved, largely due to its highly skewed and burdensome nature. Moreover, as was the case with the TRIPs Agreement and the Doha Declaration earlier on, it was to be expected that contests over pharmaceutical IPRs would continue during the implementation phase of the Amendment, a process during which rules of a more general nature become common practice and instantiate certain interpretations and understandings over others. In any case, even if both the Amendment and its implementation were balanced, the issue of compulsory licences was but one element of the more complex IP–public health debate which, as we shall see in this chapter, far from fading away, has been expanding and overflowing into other regimes and fora.

The conclusion of the TRIPs amendment process in 2005 did not, then, signal the end of the IP–public health contests – or other contests over IPRs for that matter. Indeed, having dealt exclusively with developments at the WTO in the last chapter, two arguments need further attention. Firstly, the IP–public health contests in 2001–2005 were not limited to the WTO forum. As we have seen, bilateral and regional free trade agreements (FTAs), the WHO and various human rights bodies were drawn into the IP–public health debate early on. Of these additional fora, it is the FTAs that have come to constitute a new and important front where IPRs–access to medicines contests have unfolded. Perhaps it would be more accurate to say that they have been important for IP-reliant actors who have been successful in pushing IPRs standards further beyond the already high TRIPs standards without much resistance from their developing country counterparts. So in addition to the WTO negotiations in 2001–2005, FTAs have provided the next most important fora where contests over IP–public health have been fought, unfortunately – from the perspective of developing countries and civil society actors – even less successfully than at the WTO.

Secondly, and as indicated in previous chapters, the IP–public health contests are but one part of wider challenges levelled against the IP–trade linkage established by TRIPs. They have no doubt become the most well-known and politicised challenge, but they are by no means the only one. In retrospect, it can be argued that the IP–public health linkage brought to the fore a deeper and more persistent tension between two opposing discourses over IP protection: one that was formulated (and continues to be championed) by IP-reliant business actors, linking strong and global IP protection to trade competitiveness, and another, supported by some key developing countries and certain civil society actors, that linked IP protection to a set of public goods, of which public health emerged as the most pressing in the late 1990s. In many ways, contests over IPRs and public health helped open up the way for other linkages between IPRs and other issue-areas to come to the fore more forcefully, such as those between IPRs and human rights, development, traditional knowledge and biodiversity. As a result, contests over IPRs have spilt over into other regimes more recently and more regimes have been drawn into and linked to the IPRs regime which, in turn, has become more complex and contested.

These contests, and those over public health for that matter, are still unfolding at the time of writing and, because regime contests are continuous and dynamic, it is hard to predict what their outcome will be. While a full analysis of these other contestations is important in its own right, it falls outside the scope of this study and regrettably cannot be offered here. That said, we cannot fully understand the politics of IPRs and access to medicines, nor their (intermediate) resolution, in isolation from these other contests and without a more comprehensive understanding of the complex global regime that currently governs IPRs. For these reasons, this chapter seeks to achieve two things: in the first part, it tracks the unfolding of contests over IPRs and access to medicines on bilateral and unilateral fronts in the post-Declaration period and beyond. By doing so, it paints a fuller picture of the politics of IPRs and access to medicines by adding to the analysis of contests at the WTO, covered in the preceding chapter, some developments and trends whose beginnings we observed in our analysis of the 1990s. The second part of the chapter extends the analysis beyond the IP–public health debate, by opening up a window into the complex new linkages and contests over other issue-areas that, alongside those over public health, have come to characterise the current global IP regime.

6.1 'IP–trade' versus 'IP–public health': the battle at the bilateral level

Precisely when the strength of the IP–public health linkage at the multilateral level was at its peak during negotiations over the Doha Declaration, both the US and the EU gave a boost to their IP–trade linkage at home and abroad. After deliberations during 2001, in 2002 the US Congress enacted the Trade Promotion Authority Act ('TPA') which called for accelerated compliance with the provisions of the TRIPs agreement, and for any multilateral or bilateral trade agreements to reflect standards of IP protection similar to those found in US laws (US Trade Act 2002 S.2102). Similarly, the Lisbon Agenda for Europe, agreed in 2000, recognised innovation and IP protection as the key to the EU becoming the most competitive and dynamic knowledge-based economy by 2010 (European Council 2000). These developments indicate that the two key actors within the trade regime continued to frame IP protection as a trade and competitiveness issue, despite the many concerns raised over the impact of IPRs on other issue-areas, especially that of public health, during the same period. This continued support for the IP–trade link has had important repercussions, not only on the shape and outcome of the contestations over public health and IP at the WTO discussed in the previous chapters, but also outside it. Most importantly, because of frustration with the lack of concrete results in recent multilateral trade negotiations, both the US and the EU have been eager to liberalise further and faster, via the regional and bilateral trade agreements route. One implication of this strategy, given the established IP–trade linkage as a competitiveness issue in these two major trading countries, has been that many regional and bilateral FTAs contain IP provisions that often go beyond TRIPs, designed with a view to protecting and enhancing the competitive advantage of these two countries and their IP-reliant industries.

The FTA process is complex and multifaceted. It relates closely to developments at the multilateral level (or lack of them) while simultaneously feeding into it. Once in motion, trade bilateralism and regionalism is further perpetuated by state and business actors who feel impelled to join in for fear of missing out: an understandable concern given the discriminatory nature of preferential trade agreements toward non-parties. As we have seen, the US (re)turned to trade bilateralism (and unilateralism) before and during the Uruguay Round, partly as a means of countering resistance to its agenda during the Round. Lack of agreement at the multilateral level during the Seattle and Cancún Ministerial in 1999 and 2003 further exacerbated the bilateral/regional trend within the trade regime. Indeed, after the Cancún Round, the then US Trade Representative, Robert Zoellick, immediately retaliated with the 'competitive liberalisation' programme, whereby the US would move forward in deep trade liberalisation with 'willing' partners, leaving the 'won't do' countries behind (Zoellick 2002). The EU which, incidentally, has always followed the regional route, revamped its regional trade approach to mirror that of the US and moved towards a more bilateral stance with the launch of the Global Europe platform in 2006 (129 2009).

Given the framing of IPRs as a competitiveness and commercial issue by these two key trading partners, and their commitment to bilateralism and regionalism, it should not be surprising that all the FTAs they have concluded contain specific IP chapters, most of which mandate IP standards beyond those mandated by TRIPs. Clearly, these 'TRIPs plus' provisions are not limited to IP protection for pharmaceuticals; however, given the importance the IP–public health debate has assumed since the late 1990s, it is in this area that they have attracted most criticism. Despite the EU having achieved a great degree of internal IP harmonisation, it has not, until recently, demanded similar legislative sophistication on the part of its trading partners, unless they are EU accession countries. The IP chapters in typical EU FTAs, such as EU–Israel (2000), EU–Chile (2000), EU–Mexico (2002) and EU–Jordan (2002), are not issue-specific and generally do not contain provisions dealing with enforcement, remedies or administration; they have mainly requested adherence to multilateral IP treaties, but it is worth noting that some of these are in effect 'TRIPs plus' treaties (Santa-Cruz 2007; Pugatch 2007; El Said 2007). More recently, the EU has moved towards requesting the inclusion of more elaborate and comprehensive IP provisions in its FTAs. For instance, the EU–Korea FTA concluded in September 2009 specifies protection for pharmaceutical test data for five years[1] as do most US FTAs, as well as some concluded by the European Free Trade Association (EFTA), such as those with Chile, Tunisia and Lebanon. However, it is the US FTAs, which often incorporate provisions mirroring those of its own IP law, that 'TRIPs plus' provisions are more obvious. Without exception, all the US FTAs signed since 2000 have included 'TRIPs plus' provisions for data exclusivity and patent extensions (GAO 2007).[2] In addition, a few FTAs effectively prohibit parallel importation of medicines and set restrictions on compulsory licensing, the very issues on which contestations over the Declaration and Decision were based.

For actors who see IP protection as a competitiveness issue and have an interest in and stronger IP protection rules, the inclusion of these and other 'TRIPs plus' provisions in FTAs is better understood as another strategy for achieving their goals in more favourable fora. We saw, for instance, how during the post-TRIPs period these very same actors sought to speed up TRIPs implementation and expand IP protection in areas where TRIPs had 'failed' them, by shifting their efforts in various fora simultaneously: multilaterally, at WIPO, the WTO Review Mechanism and the WTO Dispute Settlement Body, and bilaterally or unilaterally through IP technical assistance programmes and through direct pressure of the Special 301 kind. Not surprisingly, from the late 1990s onwards at the WTO, when contestations and resistance over IPRs were becoming more forceful, these actors sought to secure and entrench higher IP protection standards through the bilateral route, where power dynamics systematically favour the larger trading partner.

From an increasingly complex set of IP chapters in various FTAs concluded by the US and EU, it is possible to identify five main 'TRIPs plus' provisions that either limit TRIPs flexibilities or go beyond TRIPs with respect to IP protection for pharmaceuticals. These are data exclusivity, parallel importing, compulsory licensing (the key issue during the TRIPs amendment process), patent term extensions and patentability criteria. It is worth recalling that TRIPs itself leaves it up to each Member to (i) provide protection for pharmaceutical test data submitted to regulatory authorities for marketing approval (data exclusivity) (Art 39:3), (ii) determine their own system of IP exhaustion (which relates to parallel importing) (Art 6), (iii) determine the grounds for the issue of compulsory licences (Art 31) and (iv) define strict criteria for patentability (Art 27). In addition, TRIPs does not oblige members to compensate patent holders for 'unreasonable' delays during the marketing approval process by offering patent term extensions, nor does it make provisions that link the marketing approval of competitors' drugs to the patent status, as is the case with FTA provisions on patent linkages.

The issue of *data protection* has probably been the most important and politicised of them all, especially because access to original data is crucial for speeding up the entry of generic medicines into the market after the expiration of the patent, or for successfully working a compulsory licence during the patent term. These are the very reasons why proprietary pharmaceutical companies have been only too keen to push for restrictive data protection rules in FTA partner countries. While the TRIPs agreement recognises the importance of data protection, it only requests that data is protected against unfair commercial use. There are a number of options in practice, but the US and the EU have adopted an 'exclusive rights model', which protects data against use for five years and 8+2 years respectively. The more flexible system of unfair competition rules, for instance, has been sidelined as a model for data protection. In practice, most parties to US FTAs are introducing pharmaceutical data protection that mirror the US exclusive rights model whereby access to data is forbidden for five years from the date of marketing approval (in that party). This is the case with all US FTAs signed from 2000 onwards, with the exception of that with Jordan (2000). The EU FTA with South Korea in 2009 also requires a five year exclusivity period. Overall, the problem with data protection of the US/EU type is that it poses a huge obstacle to generic competition and, probably, to access to data for compulsory licensing purposes.

While data exclusivity has been the most politicised 'TRIPs plus' provision so far, those relating to *compulsory licensing* are the more interesting, due to the prolonged contestations over this very issue at the WTO from 2001 until TRIPs was amended in 2005. In addition to placing a limitation on an FTA's party ability to work a compulsory licence if it offers exclusive data protection as discussed above, compulsory licence options are further narrowed down in other ways. For instance, the US FTAs with Jordan (2000), Singapore (2003), Australia (2004), Vietnam and those initiated in 2003 with the South African Customs Union and the Free Trade Area of the Americas (FTAA) (both stalled) limit the grounds upon which a licence can be granted to cases of anti-trust remedies, national emergencies or non-commercial use, although neither TRIPs nor the 2001 Declaration specify any such grounds (Morin 2006).[3] Furthermore, the US FTA with Morocco limits the use of TRIPs flexibilities to particular diseases such as HIV/AIDS, malaria, tuberculosis and other epidemics (Sell 2007), a limitation which, it is worth remembering, was fiercely and successfully opposed during the WTO negotiations. The issue of limiting the use of compulsory licences in the manner discussed here has become particularly worrisome in the post-2005 period when all countries (apart from less developed countries) have to respect all TRIPs obligations. Post-2005 the production of generic versions of patented medicines is completely dependent on either voluntary or compulsory licences.

There are two other ways in which FTAs narrow down TRIPs flexibilities with respect to pharmaceutical patents; these are *patent term extensions* and looser *patentability criteria*. With regard to the former, all US FTAs and that between EFTA and Chile request that parties provide extension to the patent term (the length varies between FTAs) when the marketing approval process delays the marketing of a product or process. Further, in all US FTAs cases apart from the US–Jordan FTA, an additional extension of the patent term is also requested for 'unreasonable' delays in the patent granting process (Roffe and Spennemann 2006). TRIPs itself does not request the granting of such extensions, but patent term extensions are routinely granted in the US and EU on the basis that the patent and marketing approval process (lasting 8–12 years) significantly reduces the effective patent term (nominally 20 years). The problem for developing countries from a public health perspective is two-fold: on the one hand, longer patent terms further delay the entry of cheaper generic medicines and on the other, due to the strain placed on resources, 'reasonable' delays may appear 'unreasonable' to the more developed FTA party, triggering further extensions and delays in generics market entry. Similarly, some FTAs require parties to make available patents for new uses of known products. This is the case with the US FTAs with Australia, Bahrain and Morocco, with the result that patent-holders are allowed to 'evergreen' existing patents by adding another patent term to already known/patent products, and pushing the entry of generic versions further into the future (Roffe and Spennemann 2006).

Amidst all these 'TRIPs plus' provisions, it must be noted that the USTR has adopted a relatively cautious approach when negotiating the pharmaceutical IPRs that were at the heart of negotiations of the Declaration and Decision at the WTO, especially compulsory licensing. This is because the TPA of 2002 that charged the USTR with achieving US-like IP standards abroad also included a provision requesting that the USTR respect the Declaration and the flexibilities contained therein.[4] As a result, the USTR has ultimately backed off from provisions restricting compulsory licensing, but only when explicit concerns were raised by the developing counterparts during FTA negotiations. Equally, no concessions have been made on these two areas for countries the USTR does not consider as 'developing' (GAO 2007).[5] The USTR has reconciled respect for the Doha flexibilities with its mandate of securing high IP protection (for pharmaceuticals) by adopting a view of the Declaration and the Decision as *exceptions*. As USTR Mickey Kantor said, these exceptions 'cannot swallow the rule: strong intellectual property protections remain essential to foster innovation and creativity' (Kantor 2005: 9). Reminiscent of the restrictive interpretation given to TRIPs provisions in the post-TRIPs period, both the USTR and pharmaceutical business actors have adopted a restrictive interpretation of the Declaration which, in their view, affirms the importance of IP protection and TRIPs and does not assign public health a greater priority than IPRs. Hence, despite the TPA provision to respect the Doha Declaration, US FTAs have in effect restricted the policy space of the developing countries involved to ensure access to affordable medicines.[6]

Because 'TRIPs plus' provisions for pharmaceuticals contained within these FTAs ultimately strengthen the position of the patent-holders and limit or delay access to affordable pharmaceuticals, FTAs threaten to undermine gains that developing countries have achieved in multilateral negotiations, such as the Declaration and, less so, the Decision. One of the functions of FTAs from the perspective of actors with interest in and stronger IP protection is to get rid of the 'dead weight' inherent in multilateral negotiations which, incidentally, are recognised as TRIPs flexibilities from the perspective of other actors. Hence, it is not surprising that FTAs negotiated between a party that sees strong pharmaceutical IP protection to be in its interests (such as the US and the EU) and a weaker partner introduce 'TRIPs plus' provisions for pharmaceuticals. This is largely due to the US and the EU being the two largest trading powerhouses in the world. Naturally, at the bilateral level, negotiations favour the larger and stronger trading partner, as the weaker one is effectively on its own, unable to enrol the support of other actors and often only too willing to accept stronger IP rules in exchange for the seemingly more immediate interest of access to the lucrative market of the larger partner. While not surprising, such a trend is worrying from a public health perspective, insofar as the policy space of governments to deliver on this front is further restricted by such provisions. FTAs, then, represent the fora where the IP–public health linkage is losing ground and the IP–trade linkage is further being entrenched.

As if this was not enough, unilateral pressure on pharmaceutical IP protection did not fade away during or after the WTO negotiations. The US Special 301 procedure continued to pressure other countries to 'improve' their pharmaceutical IPRs. Indeed, from 2000 onwards, nearly half of the countries listed in the Special 301 reports were found to have 'inadequate' IP protection for pharmaceuticals, with data exclusivity – a key issue for pharmaceutical companies – emerging as the top concern (GAO 2007). The EC, having contemplated the issues at least since 2003, also decided to set up its own version of the US 'watch list'.[7] The EC strategy is couched mainly in terms of problems with IPRs enforcement in third countries rather than standards *per se*. The EC takes pains to explain that it does not intend to impose unilateral solutions to the problem. But, as is the case with the US Special 301, these strategies are all the more successful for effecting desired changes by their mere existence rather than the actual use of sanctions. And, like the Special 301 reports, the EC 2009 report was also based on EU business complaints about infringements of their IPRs in foreign countries.[8] The targeted countries are similar to those targeted by US Special 301: China headed the EC list in 2009 with the usual suspects, Indonesia, the Philippines, Thailand, Turkey, Argentina, Brazil, India and Russia, following behind.

It is worth noting in passing that this focus on IPRs enforcement, especially on the part of the EC, is not limited to these developments. A new Counterfeiting Trade Agreement (ACTA) has been under negotiation since the end of 2007 between IP-reliant actors with the aim of strengthening the global enforcement of IPRs. There has been severe criticism from civil society groups about the secrecy of the negotiations and concerns that these enforcement standards will go beyond TRIPs standards (as some FTAs already do), arguments that the EC has been particularly keen to reject.[9] Regarding IPRs–access to medicines, one key area where this accelerated IP enforcement agenda has found expression has been in cases of drug seizure in transit through European ports in the last few years. These have generally been in transit from India or China to other developing countries and have involved drugs for which no patents were in force in the exporting or importing country. There were 19 such seizures in 2008 alone and a few more in 2009, raising concerns among health groups about their impact on access to medicines. India raised this issue several times at the TRIPs Council during 2009 and has also threatened to challenge EU legislation at the WTO.[10]

What is clear is that watch lists and IP enforcement agenda is largely directed towards middle or high-income developing countries, that is, countries with profitable markets and/or those with generic pharmaceutical capacities. Indeed, no challenge, bilateral or otherwise, has generally been levelled against the least developed countries, particularly in Africa, for using flexibilities in TRIPs and the Doha Declaration. As was noted in an earlier chapter, the markets these latter countries represent are inconsequential as far as the proprietary pharmaceutical sector is concerned. However, contests have been fierce when middle or high-income developing countries have used, or tried to use, such flexibilities, even when the procedures followed have been legally correct. For instance, considerable pressure was placed on Brazil and Thailand by pharmaceutical companies, the USTR and the EU Trade Commissioner for issuing compulsory licences for antiretroviral and cardiovascular drugs in 2006 and 2007 for the domestic market, although all the correct procedures were in place.[11] Likewise, when a large pharmaceutical company, Novartis, had its application for a patent in India rejected in 2006 due to the new Indian patent law having incorporated some TRIPs flexibilities which restricted the grounds on which patents could be granted, it opened (and lost) a lawsuit reminiscent of the infamous 2001 South African court case.[12] India has often come under fire from various proprietary pharmaceutical companies because it has a large pharmaceutical domestic market, a thriving globally-orientated generics sector and domestic IP laws which have incorporated many of the flexibilities offered by TRIPs. How long it will continue to hold the line on the IP–access to medicines front remains to be seen, especially as an FTA with the EU is expected to be concluded by the end of 2010.

6.2 Beyond IP–public health: other challenges to the IP–trade link

The unilateral and bilateral developments mentioned above can be best seen as 'forum shifting' strategies by IP-reliant business actors and their respective countries, aimed at overcoming TRIPs 'limitations' and further expanding IPRs, often at the expense of other public interests and issue-areas (Helfer 2004; Drahos 2007). However, just as business actors and their home governments have used 'forum-shifting' to achieve their preferred ends, developing countries and certain NGOs have also been active in the post-TRIPs period in shifting IP protection issues of interest to them into other regimes and fora. This has been done by making new linkages between IPRs and other issue-areas that are marginalised by the narrow IP–trade linkage established through TRIPs, access to medicines being one of them. As a result of these linkages, IPRs contests have now spread into other regimes and the latter have been linked and brought into the IPRs regime. New IP rules are now negotiated, existing ones reinterpreted, and declaration, reports, recommendations and statements about IPRs are issued in many fora: the WIPO, regional or bilateral FTAs, the WTO, the World Health Organisation (WHO), the UN Industrial Development Organisation (UNIDO), the UN Food and Agriculture Organisation (FAO), the World Bank, the Convention on Biodiversity (CBD), UNESCO, various human rights commissions (ECOSOC, CHR), the UN Development Programme (UNDP), the G8 and the World Customs Organisation. Of all the new linkages between IPR and other issue-areas, those between IPRs and human rights, development, biodiversity and the protection of traditional knowledge have been the most important ones to date.

The IP–access to medicines linkage that we have considered at length here opened up the possibility of linking the IP regime to other regimes beyond trade: initially, to the public health regime. As was noted in an earlier chapter, at the height of the IP–access to medicines contests in the late 1990s, the WHO, initially prompted by Access Campaign NGOs, passed a series of resolutions which encouraged member states to review options under international agreements to ensure and safeguard access to essential medicines.[13] The WHO continued to be involved in IP–public health contests: for instance, just as negotiations over paragraph 6 solution stalled at the TRIPs Council in May 2003, it produced a report which endorsed the approach of the developing countries and NGOs in those negotiations and, amongst other things, highlighted the negative impact of patent protection on drug pricing and criticised FTAs'

'TRIPs plus' provisions as being detrimental to health care.[14] Further, in the May 2003 World Health Assembly meeting on access to medicines, a group of developing countries, led by Brazil, proposed the creation of an independent commission to examine the relationship between IPRs, innovation, public goods and public health. As a result, the commission set up in 2004 in response to these demands produced, among other things, several proposals for creating a sustainable R&D mechanism for diseases disproportionately affecting developing countries, but for which the existing IP arrangements have largely failed to deliver.[15] The 2008 Global Strategy of the current WHO Intergovernmental Working Group on Public Heath, Innovation and IP has also included proposals for new ways to fund pharmaceutical R&D, such as prizes, patent pools and government funds.[16] Hence, the role of this regime has moved beyond passing resolutions in support of public health commitments to housing new initiatives that seek to fundamentally overhaul the way the pharmaceutical R&D process is funded and the IP system to which it lends itself. While it remains to be seen whether these proposals will fundamentally change the conventional pharmaceutical IP model, it is clear that IPRs are now an important part of this regime's remit, which, in turn, contributes to the growing complexity of the global IPRs regime.

Yet another front was opened with the linkage established between IP protection and human rights in the late 1990s. Again, it was a consortium of different human rights NGOs which prompted the IP–human rights linkage in the late 1900s, challenging the compatibility of TRIPs with human rights obligations (Sell 2006). In response, the UN Human Rights Sub-Commission adopted a resolution on IPRs and human rights which explicitly pointed out the real and potential conflicts between TRIPs obligations and the realisation of economic, social and cultural rights.[17] This was only the first of a large number of resolutions and reports the many bodies of the human rights regime have been only too keen to pass and adopt, all of which have been highly critical of the current IPRs arrangement.[18] Importantly, the conflicts they highlight intersect with many other issue-areas and regimes including health, farmers' rights, education, biodiversity, and the protection of indigenous culture and knowledge. In many ways, the IP–human rights linkage has served as a broad umbrella under which actors engaged in contests over other IP links (such as health or biodiversity) can come together and tap into the strengths of a wider network (Schultz and Walker 2005). More generally, although concrete ways of governing IPRs are not being seriously contemplated in this regime, the tensions between IPRs as a competitive issue, and human rights principles and norms, are used to legitimise and support other linkages established elsewhere.

One such important linkage is that between IPRs and the protection of biodiversity and the environment, also contested in various regimes: those relating to trade and human rights, and the complex regime governing genetic resources. The last of these includes the 1992 Convention on Biodiversity (CBD), the 1961 International Union for the Protection of New Varieties of Plants (UPOV), and the 2001 International Treaty on Plant Genetic Resources for Food and Agriculture. As we have seen, concerns about the conflict between certain IP rules mandated by TRIPs and those set out by the CBD was the first to be raised at the WTO TRIPs Council by some developing countries and sympathetic NGOs, a few years after TRIPs came into force (Watal 2000; Pugatch 2004a). Contests over TRIPs and CBD have intensified since then, especially after the CBD's Conference of the Parties meeting in 2002 and the formation of the Group of Like-Minded Megadiverse Countries of around 70 developing members of the WTO in the same year (Helfer 2004). The fundamental concerns here relate to the adverse impact of stronger 'life-patenting' IP rules mandated by TRIPs on biodiversity and biopiracy. In addition, a closely related linkage has been established between IPRs and the protection of traditional/indigenous knowledge. This complex linkage has different dimensions relating to justice, human rights, culture and biodiversity, which is why it is contested in different fora, including various human rights committees, the WTO TRIPs Council, UNESCO and the CBD. One of the key concerns for countries with substantial indigenous communities and civil society groups representing their interests is that indigenous knowledge, until then considered part of the public domain, has been appropriated unfairly for commercial ends and that new IPRs should be devised to protect it. In the meantime, current IPRs should contain disclosure of the origins of genetic resources or traditional knowledge involved, and facilitate the benefit-sharing with such communities of their commercial value (Pugatch 2004a).

As can be seen, some of these linkages have been established simultaneously and it is common for one linkage to be pursued in many fora simultaneously. Hence, some of the linkages mentioned above have been brought back to WIPO, further extending the overlap and complexity of the IPRs regime. For instance, concerns about IPRs, biodiversity and traditional knowledge were bundled together at WIPO by some developing countries seeking to incorporate this linkage into the negotiations over the WIPO Patent Law Treaty (PLT) in the late 1990s, requesting that the treaty include clauses for the disclosure of origin and benefit-sharing clauses within it (Sell 2006). This attempt was not successful, but actors with interest in biodiversity and indigenous peoples have sought again to incorporate this linkage into the current negotiations for a new Substantive Patent Law Treaty (SPLT) at WIPO. It is worth noting that the latter is yet another initiative of the IP-reliant actors to harmonise the global scope of patent protection upwards, alongside other ongoing efforts to further strengthen IPRs standards.

The WIPO SPLT negotiations have become the platform for the launch of another important linkage, that between IP and development. It is worth recalling that this is not a new linkage: it was attempted, unsuccessfully, by developing countries as part of their efforts towards the New International Economic Order (NIEO) in the 1970s. A group of developing countries (the Group of Friends for Development) led by Brazil and Argentina and supported by civil society groups proposed a Development Agenda for WIPO in 2004. Much to the consternation of IP-reliant actors, the goal of the Agenda is to overhaul WIPO's mandate and reframe IP as a tool for development rather than as an end in itself. If successful, this norm would obviously run counter to the spirit of TRIPs. In 2005, progress on the WIPO SPLT negotiations was made explicitly dependent on progress on the Development Agenda (ICTSD 2005). Like the IPRs–human rights linkage, this link is also broad but is different in that it contains some specific ideas and proposals. Having managed to water down more radical proposals, developed countries resistant to the Development Agenda finally acquiesced to it in October 2007. A new WIPO Committee on Development and Intellectual Property (CDIP) was also created to manage this Agenda, which at the time of writing included some 45 concrete proposals that could be grouped into six clusters, including WIPO's technical assistance, norm-setting and the public domain, technology transfer, access to knowledge and a few more. Obviously, it is too early to say much about the outcome of the Development Agenda, but its very existence is surely a success for actors pushing for it, although the risk of it becoming just rhetoric or, worse, reconfirming the role of strong IPRs in development is real and should not be discounted. Nevertheless, of all the linkages mentioned here this seems to be the more promising, as it can subsume other linkages such as human rights, biodiversity, public health and indeed trade, whilst also addressing directly the issue of protecting the intellectual commons and public domain, the very cornerstone of any IPRs regime.

Judging from these recent developments, contests over IP and public health do not appear to have withered away with the amendment of TRIPs. Work at the WHO, WIPO and developments taking place elsewhere are still unfolding and the prospects of success for developing countries and civil society actors in these forums remain to be seen. What they clearly demonstrate, however, is that the principles, norms and rules guiding global IPRs are far from settled. What we see happening in the current global IPRs regime is the making and remaking of IP linkages between and within regimes, a regime-shifting strategy which all actors seem to have adopted. One result of this development has been the drawing of various regimes previously not concerned with IPRs into the governance of IPRs. Hence, we can best conceptualise the current IP regime arrangement as a *regime complex*, a collective of horizontal, partially overlapping and even inconsistent regimes, marked by the existence of several arrangements that are created and maintained in distinct fora (Raustiala and Victor 2004; Raustiala 2007). As we have seen, the story of the IP regime complex is not one of natural progression. Instead, it is the result of various contests and linkages being strategically made between and within regimes and fora by state and non-state actors with interests and stakes in the shape and direction of the global IP regime.

Of course, some linkages and some actors have been more successful than others. The most important linkage, that between IP and trade institutionalised in TRIPs (and later in FTAs), was a clear success on the part of IP-rich state and business actors, but one which has come back to haunt them, as many actors who are not convinced of governing IPRs as a trade or competitiveness issue are establishing their own IP linkages elsewhere. There is no guarantee, of course, that the IP–trade linkage will be undermined, or that, should this happen, it will be superseded by a more balanced or legitimate one. The outcomes of regime contestations are difficult to predict, particularly when the number of actors involved is large, their interests varied, and consensus absent, as is the case with IPRs. What is clear for now is that, given the importance of knowledge and information in the current global economy, neither the contestations over IPRs nor the regime complex they have helped create, are going to settle any time soon. The outcome of contests over IPRs and access to medicines is intrinsically bound up with how these deeper conflicts are resolved.

7
Conclusions

We started this study arguing that the institution of intellectual property is complex and highly political. Intellectual property protection is essentially about wealth, and its form and substance have been contested since its very beginning. This study has focused on developments that have unfolded within the trade and IP regimes from the 1980s onwards, particularly on the contests over the interplay between intellectual property, global trade rules and public health that emerged in the late 1990s. The aim was that of understanding and explaining what conflicts lay at the source of contests over IPRs and access to medicines, whose interests are served by the arrangement that is being contested, and how the latter unfold and get resolved, or not. In order to make sense of these developments, I put forward a conceptualisation of regimes which understands them as the loci of greater or lesser but inevitable tension between state and non-state actors, that is, as dynamic and contested processes. This concept places the focus primarily *inside* the regime in an effort to better understand what goes on inside it, what shapes the behaviour and interest of regime actors, what the contests are about, how these unfold and get resolved and how they interplay with developments in other regimes and beyond. State and non-state actors involved in regime contests have different material interests and normative understandings as to how a particular issue should be resolved, with each actor, or coalition thereof, attempting to convince others of the legitimacy of their preferred view. In seeking to shape regime contests, the actors engaged in them are motivated, act and coordinate efforts in the material and discursive realms simultaneously, but they do not have equal chances of success. Some actors are better positioned and have better resources at their disposal that give them more leverage over regime contests. But the mere existence of such power does not necessarily guarantee success. Weaker actors can also score victories, especially if they are able to frame issues in ways that resonate with broader ideological changes, enrol the support of other actors by building alliances and networks, exploit opportunities opened up by conflicting interests and lack of unity between other actors, capitalise on institutional advantages present in other fora and make strategic use of political crises as and when they occur. As we saw, this is how the coalition of developing countries and Campaign NGOs managed to secure the Doha Declaration in 2001, although since then their success record has not been as impressive. What follows revisits some of the reasons for such outcomes.

As was argued at the start of this study, the WTO TRIPs agreement is without doubt the most significant development in the politics of international intellectual property of the twentieth century, at least insofar as it set in motion the global harmonisation and enforcement of private intellectual property rights. However, TRIPs has not only failed to settle many of the long-standing unresolved tensions and controversial aspects of intellectual property rights, but by decontextualising and launching them onto a global level, it has helped reveal and magnify them even further. Thus, it is not surprising that recently the tensions and contradictions associated with IPRs have become more acute and the politics of intellectual property has become more intense. Indeed, as we have seen, since it came into force in 1995 TRIPs has increasingly been contested between different actors in several fora and regimes, including those dealing with food security, genetic resources, public health and human rights, and continues to be contested today.

Perhaps the most controversial and politically charged of such contests to date have been those over the interplay between intellectual property, international trade rules and public health. For the purpose of this study, we focused on key junctures, such as the 2001 Declaration, the 2003 Decision and the 2005 TRIPs amendment, understanding that the latter did not signal the end of contests over IPRs and public health, either within the trade regime or elsewhere. This is consistent with our broader conceptualisation of regimes as more or less dynamic and evolving processes, representing the outcomes of a series of contests over diverse issues and many actors over time. In addition, each of these outcomes eventually becomes one of the constituent layers of the regime structure, in turn fuelling, informing and shaping new contests between new and old actors over related issues as and when they arise. We saw how the TRIPs agreement itself was the outcome of the active agency of certain state and non-state actors. Once it came into force, it became part of the structure itself and in turn informed contests over several issues, including those over access to medicines. That set of contests culminated in the WTO Doha Declaration on the TRIPs Agreement and Public Health in 2001 which, for its part, also fuelled and shaped developments that unfolded within the WTO with regard to the single issue of compulsory licensing for pharmaceuticals and beyond.

One key observation that emerges from the analysis of these developments over time is that negotiations over a given issue are continuing: issues are framed, defined, challenged and redefined by various actors over and again. As was noted in Chapter 3, a handful of IP-reliant business actors were extremely successful in framing the need for the global protection of *their* intellectual property in a manner which resonated well with broader material and ideological changes occurring during the early 1980s. Their formulation was politically appealing to certain key developed countries' governments preoccupied with their present and future economic performance and competitive positioning in the global economy. It was these business actors that framed IP protection as an international trade issue and were subsequently successful in persuading the governments of certain key states within the trade regime that it was in the *overall* interest to negotiate global IP protection as a trade issue. The ensuing WTO TRIPs agreement testifies to the victory of these actors, in that it transformed the IP–trade link – by no means the only or the most desirable link – into 'hard' law observable in the majority of countries and enforceable at the global level.

Other state and non-state actors have since then attempted to reframe intellectual property as an issue closely related to human and economic development. The WIPO Development Agenda initiated by a group of developing countries and widely supported by civil society actors exemplifies such attempts, as do proposals for an 'Access to Knowledge' treaty that would link IP to the promotion of certain basic rights such as food, health and education. Of these and other potential links, that made between IP protection and access to medicines has been the most politicised and perhaps the most successful so far, at least insofar as it achieved concrete results with the Doha Declaration and the TRIPs amendment. As had been the case with the origins of TRIPs, the link between IP and access to medicines was not framed and defined by state actors, but by a group of international health and non-health NGOs when the HIV/AIDS crisis reached astonishing heights during the late 1990s. As business actors had done before them, these non-state actors were successful in framing their concerns into a succinct formula which linked IP protection to the high prices of patented medicines and the consequent loss of human health and, indeed, life. This link was appealing to most developing countries, which, already struggling to deal satisfactorily with public health responsibilities and challenges, were finding their policy space increasingly constrained by their commitment to introduce IP protection for medicines and other related IP protection rules as mandated by TRIPs. The ensuing Doha Declaration testifies to the victory of the network between these non-state actors and developing countries, at least insofar as it unambiguously clarified certain TRIPs flexibilities and claimed back some policy space for public health purposes.

These observations point to the significance of non-state actors' political agency and to the importance of successfully defining and framing issues. Indeed, making issues visible in a particular way confers significant advantages to certain actors, as it allows them to set out the terms of the 'game' and exclude other frames and formulations. But these observations are not necessarily new in the disciplines of international relations or international political economy, nor are they specific to intellectual property or trade politics. Non-state actors have always been present, at least as long as the state, and many existing state-centric accounts can be (re)written from a non-state actor perspective (Halliday 2001). And, indeed, increased attention is being paid to understanding the role of these actors in their recent shaping of the edifice of global polity. Similarly, the role of ideas and discourse in shaping actors' interests, strategies and outcomes has been discussed from several theoretical perspectives, and in some cases the ability to define and frame issues or knowledge astutely, rather than the use of coercion, has proven more successful in bringing about macro changes (Braithwaite and Drahos 2000).

With regard to intellectual property, we noted that non-state actors have always played a prominent role in shaping the nature of IP norms and rules through repeatedly framing and reframing IP protection issues. It was free trade supporters and other IP-abolitionists who framed IP protection as a hindrance to free trade in the late 1800s. In the meantime, industrialists and artists worked hard towards defining the norms and rules governing international IP protection and achieved considerable victories through the Paris and Berne Conventions signed in the 1880s, which endorsed some of these principles, although not without qualifications (Machlup 1958; Penrose 1951). Later on, when the 'knowledge cartels' of the early 1900s were discredited after World War II and a new form of non IP-reliant corporate governance emerged, IP protection was framed as an antithesis to competition and was subsequently weakened (Porter 1999). During the 1970s, when IP was framed as a development issue as part of calls for a New International Economic Order, business actors responded by reframing IP as a trade issue. The ensuing WTO TRIPs agreement clearly embodied this latter definition. The long history of IPRs gives weight to arguments about the importance of successful framing and of the role played by non-state actors in shaping governance structures.

What is new today, however, is the faster rate at which these developments unfold, the growing number of actors involved and the increasing range of venues in which IP is being contested. As we have seen, this has clearly been the case with the contests over intellectual property since TRIPs came into force in 1995 that have been engaging state and non-state actors in several fora simultaneously. They have been fuelled largely by the unbalanced manner in which TRIPs dealt with contentious IP issues. At the same time, they have been facilitated by an increased interdependence in human affairs in the recent decades, one consequence of which has been that regime borders have become more permeable and vague. Issues now travel more easily within and between regimes, and new and old actors are more inclined to engage in regime-shifting. Again, forum- and regime-shifting is not necessarily an IP phenomenon alone, but the complex nature of intellectual property and its impact on a number of other important issue-areas such as scientific research, technology, environment, health, education, trade and agriculture, make it easier for state and non-state actors to engage in alliance-building and regime- or forum-shifting.

As we saw, TRIPs itself was the result of skilful regime-shifting on the part of some IP-reliant business and state actors, which moved IP protection away from WIPO to the GATT/WTO in the early 1980s. There is little doubt that the TRIPs agreement was the victory of a handful of IP-reliant business actors. This was not simply because of their structural power, but also because of their ability to organise transnationally, to successfully enrol the support of key state actors, and frame their concerns and interests in a manner that resonated with broader ideological and material changes taking place at the same time. Lack of IP protection in other countries was framed as 'theft' and 'piracy' and hence as an unfair non-tariff barrier that hampered the flow of free trade. This framing came at a time when the move towards knowledge-based economies in certain key developed countries, and the ascendance of ideas that promoted markets and free enterprise, created the favourable conditions that placed the concerns of these business actors at the forefront of their governments' agendas. At a stroke, the discourse of these business actors: (i) justified the negotiation of global IP protection within the trade regime; (ii) appealed to key developed state actors concerned with their competitiveness in the global market; and, (iii) sought to strike a similar chord with other state actors preoccupied with their economic development through framing strong IP protection as a prerequisite for FDI, innovation and technology transfer. In addition to deploying such discourse, the Intellectual Property Committee (IPC), one of the key business actors in global IP issues since the 1980s, spearheaded an impressive alliance-building campaign that brought together key IP-reliant business actors across the world. Within the trade regime, developing countries were on the defensive against this formidable coalition of state and non-state business actors, unorganised and without a truly competing discourse, while other non-state actors were completely absent.

If we add here the use of coercive unilateral trade measures and negotiating dynamics at the WTO, it is not surprising that TRIPs came to embody a narrow, commercial view of global IP protection that paid insufficient attention to the complex interplay between intellectual property and the provision of other complementary goods. Indeed, TRIPs does not represent a broadly shared consensus amongst knowledge producers, owners, users and policy-makers, nationally or globally, about how knowledge goods should be best produced, protected, controlled, owned and diffused (Maskus and Reichman 2004). What it mainly does is lock in the (temporary) competitive advantage in IP goods of certain business actors who, as we have seen in the case of pharmaceutical companies at least, are not especially innovative themselves. As we have discussed, TRIPs and other subsequent IP instruments that have increased IP protection even further upwards have not struck the right balance between protecting private rights and advancing the global public interest in innovation, diffusion, competition and the provision of other public goods. Essentially, these concerns fuelled the resistance and counter-response of certain developing countries and non-state actors post-TRIPs, both within the trade regime and in other regimes and fora over several issues, including that of access to medicines.

Contests over IP and access to medicines make for a more complex picture than that of the negotiation of TRIPs itself. Despite the fact that they relate to only one area affected by TRIPs rules, these contests engaged many more actors and unfolded faster than before in various interrelated levels and fora simultaneously. The emergence of the IP-public health debate is attributable both to concerns over the impact of TRIPs protection standards on dealing with public health and those over the rapidly shrinking flexibilities that TRIPs itself afforded for health and other public purposes. The latter was the direct result of the post-TRIPs strategies of the coalition of IP-reliant business actors and certain state actors that had brought about TRIPs. They perceived themselves to have suffered losses of the type usually associated with the 'dead weight' of multilateralism, and were only too keen to speed up TRIPs implementation. This being their position, they actively pursued their goals through means such as IP technical assistance, WTO review mechanism, WTO dispute settlement and bilateral and unilateral trade pressure to further stretch IP protection standards upwards and sideways. Incidentally, one consequence has been the further encroachment of private IPRs into the public domain. This was true of several business actors, but pharmaceutical business actors were particularly active, and their post-TRIPs strategies had the unintended consequence of further fuelling the resistance and counter-response of other actors within the trade regime and beyond.

Against the backdrop of growing concern over global public health challenges, and particularly over the escalation of HIV/AIDS crisis, the (transnational) network of Access Campaign NGOs was successful in framing complex IP issues into a formula that was simple and appealing to both state actors and the lay public. Essentially, by linking strong IP protection for pharmaceuticals to the high cost of HIV/AIDS drugs (to include later all patented drugs) in developing countries, and to the alarming advance of disease and increasing death rates, strong private IPRs were framed as an obstacle to the enjoyment of human health and life. Importantly, the Campaign NGOs had a realistic and narrow aim: they did not advocate the complete overhaul of TRIPs, but rather that the flexibilities aimed at safeguarding the public domain should be respected and observed. Their framing, in essence, advocated the use of TRIPs flexibilities to enhance access to affordable medicines in the developing world. Through using language such as 'medical apartheid' and 'patent versus patients' and making astute use of the media they appealed to the public at large which, in turn, lent support to the Campaign and increased pressure on politicians and decision-makers domestically and internationally. As we noted, the IP–access to medicine link initially made by Campaign NGOs had great appeal to, and was readily embraced by, most developing countries that had grown more critical of TRIPs and were finding their public health policy space increasingly circumscribed in the post-TRIPs period. Over only three or four years, Campaign NGOs and certain developing countries managed to create a strong network that, deploying expert technical IP language and garnering and maintaining the support of the public at large, was able to offer a compelling counter-frame to that offered by certain state and business actors, and one that was both legitimate and legally sound.

Concerns raised by the Campaign NGOs also resonated with the redefinition of the concept of national security on the part of the developed countries, which had come to consider epidemics and ill health beyond their borders as a challenge to the well-being of their citizens, as well as to the stability of world affairs more generally. Although there existed a consensus on the part of the developed countries that global public health issues were serious enough to warrant immediate attention, their preferred list of solutions did not include the watering down of TRIPs obligations or IP protection for pharmaceuticals. Developed countries with a substantial proprietary pharmaceutical industry largely continued to frame IP protection as a trade and competitiveness issue. This framework was sustained and facilitated by the broader mainstream discourse which justifies IPRs as necessary for continued innovation. Indeed, for their part, proprietary pharmaceutical business actors responded to the emergence of the IP–access to medicines debate precisely through appealing to the utilitarian argument that, without IP protection, there would be no cures and new drugs at all. We have seen how the Doha Declaration did not challenge the IP–trade link embodied in TRIPs; on the contrary, it reaffirmed governments' commitment to TRIPs and reaffirmed the role IP protection plays in research and innovation. The victory of the network of 'weaker' actors resides only in the fact that the Declaration unambiguously clarified and claimed back the flexibilities TRIPs afforded to governments facing public health challenges (including compulsory licensing), flexibilities that hitherto had been actively restricted and misconstrued. As we have noted, weaker (in terms of material power) actors can outmanoeuvre their stronger 'rivals' and score some victories, as the WTO Doha Declaration on TRIPs and Public Health in 2001 demonstrates.

What is striking when observing the ways in which state and non-state actors interacted during TRIPs and IP–public health contests is the remarkably similar strategies adopted by business and civil society actors. As we have noted, all actors engage in contests by making strategic use of the power available to them and adopt strategies in both the material and discursive realms. With regard to contests over IP and public health, both business actors and NGOs engaged in network and alliance-building; the networks thus created made strategic use of political opportunities and contingencies and used ideas astutely to frame their concerns in ways which allowed them to alter their relative power position, thereby enabling them to graft their preferred discourse onto policy debates and eventually influence policy outcomes (Sell 2003). It is not surprising that these non-state actors adopted similar strategies, especially if we accept that the distinction commonly made in international relations between business and civil society actors based on instrumental versus normative orientations is defunct (Sell and Prakash 2004). In other words, there are no fundamental differences between the motives of business and NGO networks: normative frameworks and instrumental objectives inform the strategies of both.

An additional observation relates not only to the similarity but also to the complexity of these strategies. We have noted that the actors we have studied were engaged in contests that unfolded simultaneously in various regimes and fora, a strategy referred to as regime-shifting. Issues now travel more easily within and between regimes and many regimes overlap; this has resulted in certain issues-areas, like IPRs, being governed by regime complexes. This is a new trend in global governance which deserves attention in its own right. For our purposes, regime complexes make governance complicated, but they also offer new opportunities for actors to shift issues or policy concerns in different regimes or fora that enhance their chances of success. Again, forum- or regime-shifting in IP issues is not new; key state and business actors have more than once skilfully shifted IP issues across various fora within a regime and to other regimes altogether in order to reach their preferred goals. What is remarkable in recent IP developments is that weaker actors have also resorted to forum- and regime-shifting. Links and conflicts between TRIPs obligations and issues related to biodiversity, traditional knowledge and genetic resources have been brought in and contested within the trade regime and within the IP regime, as well as other regimes that deal with these issue-areas specifically. On the IP–public health front, we noted the strategic use made of the WHO and several human rights bodies by the network of developing countries and Campaign NGOs through exploiting the comparative institutional advantages they offered, just as proprietary pharmaceutical business actors and their home countries were doing the same through the WTO, WIPO and the use of trade bilateral and unilateral measures.

Shifting issues into different regimes and fora shows both that state and non-state actors are keen to capitalise on the advantages that the differences between the norms, rules and power dynamics of various regimes may offer them, and that these actors are aware that regime contests are fluid (Helfer 2004). However, regime-shifting can be a double-edged sword insofar as it expands weaker actors' opportunities to 'win' contests while simultaneously making these victories more vulnerable to new challenges and contests unfolding elsewhere. This is so because, as has been argued repeatedly, regime negotiations and contestations are continuous and play out in unequal terms. Eventually, the network of actors with the most resources for engaging in and sustaining multi-regime contests, and that are the most capable of using power strategically, is more likely to shape the future edifice of global intellectual property. In the short term, the temporary nature of negotiating wins requires actors, particularly the weaker ones, to adopt strategies that both safeguard and realise such wins, especially if the victory is scored at the level of principle, as was the case with the Doha Declaration. As we noted, the Declaration did not introduce changes in the regulatory sphere. It mainly provided an ordering of principles, with the duty to protect intellectual property subordinated to the right of states to protect public health, but the open-ended nature of such principles required that they be institutionalised and secured through practices and concrete rules, or risk becoming redundant (Drahos 2007).

Not only did the network of developing countries and NGOs not have a post-Doha strategy aimed at safeguarding the Doha victory, but they soon found that proprietary business actors and key state actors, the US in particular, were challenging the ordering of principles the Doha Declaration provided by seeking to shift the contest to the bilateral level. We saw how the US FTAs have acknowledged the Doha Declaration in principle, but also how the pharmaceutical IP rules and standards agreed in the Declaration have the effect of actually restricting access to affordable medicines for the respective developing counterpart(s). At the bilateral (trade) level, negotiations between actors are much more likely to favour those who are (economically) stronger, as weaker actors have next to no opportunities to network, enrol the support of other actors or (re)frame issues. Negotiations are generally over concrete rules in various areas and stronger IP rules are often accepted in exchange for the seemingly more immediate interest of access to the lucrative market of the stronger actor. In addition to such developments on the bilateral front, the contests set in motion by the Declaration over the rules of compulsory licensing for pharmaceuticals on the multilateral front were also gradually taking the form of a complex set of rules which essentially derogated from the spirit of the Declaration. The WTO Decision of 2003 and the TRIPs amendment that followed in December 2005 were primarily concerned with safeguarding the IP interest of proprietary pharmaceutical companies rather than enhancing access to affordable medicines in developing countries and, more broadly, creating more competitive pharmaceutical markets worldwide.

As with other contests, both agency and structure affected the outcome of the post-Doha contests over the issue of compulsory licensing that were unfolding within the trade regime. As was argued in an earlier chapter, regardless of references to development, the actual rules of the trade regime have generally favoured the strongest and largest members. Hence, given that the major regime members continued to link IP protection to their trade competitiveness embodied in TRIPs after the Declaration, it is not surprising that negotiations over TRIPs compulsory licensing rules have largely come to be seen as contests over safeguarding and improving such competitive positioning. Judging from the outcome of these contests, we noted that the network of developing countries and NGOs did not manage to transform a victory in the realm of principles into a rule-based solution that actually institutionalised them.

This was so not only because the trade regime is primarily about capturing economic opportunities and improving the competitive positioning of its major members which, incidentally, happen to have a comparative advantage in intellectual property goods such as pharmaceuticals. It is also because weaker actors were not successful in improving their overall relative bargaining position. As we discussed in detail, the network deteriorated somewhat after the signing of the Declaration, both in strength and membership. Some NGOs either left the network when the negotiations became highly technical, or diverted their attention to other trade issues and more specific issues related to the HIV/AIDS epidemic. On the other hand, the unity between developing countries also weakened over time, not only because of their varied interests and negotiation fatigue, but also due to the continuous pressure and tactics deployed by stronger members with the aim of dividing them. This is not to say that they lost on all levels; several victories were secured, but these were achieved either when the network formulated a united, strong and legally grounded position, as was the case with disease coverage and eligible countries, or when they were successful in using opportunities opened up by the lack of common positions between key actors, as was the case with the written reference to the Chairman's Statement. Obviously the 2005 Amendment is better than it might have been in the absence of these modest wins. Nevertheless, it represents a complex rule-based solution that essentially does no more than bend and adjust certain governments' policies related to public health (pharmaceutical compulsory licences for export/import) to fit in with the rules of international trade and intellectual property, rather than working the other way around. This complex set of rules certainly falls short of the initial goal of the network, which was to secure an expeditious, flexible and broad solution that in time could have brought about the development of responsive state practices and customs in the domain of public health and IP issues (Drahos 2007).

Instead, the impact of the 2003 Decision and 2005 Amendment remains to be seen, and it may well prove difficult to implement in practice. As we noted earlier, apart from the small quantity of drugs shipped to Rwanda in 2008, little has changed in practice with regard to compulsory licences for import/export that can be attributed to the 2005 TRIPs amendment. Some HIV/AIDS drugs experienced a fall in prices as contests over IPRs and public heath unfolded, but that effect has not stretched to other essential medicines or to new generation HIV/AIDS drugs. In other words, the problem has not yet been resolved, although one ought to make the point that access to medicines also depends on other factors in addition to their price. In any case, this is not the final chapter of the IP and public health contests, even if it is the final chapter of this book. Such contests are still unfolding at the time of writing, and many more continue over several IP issues in other regimes and fora. More broadly, certain developing countries and international NGOs are continuing to use regime-shifting as a strategy to deal with many of the IP issues either dealt with unsatisfactorily in TRIPs or omitted altogether, in their determination to rebalance, supplement and revise the agreement. Issues such as genetic resources, plant varieties, biodiversity, patentability of life forms and traditional knowledge are currently being contested in various regimes. While it may be that shifting some of these issues to other regimes is mere window-dressing, more often than not regime-shifting is being used by actors in order to truly shape principles, norms and rules in ways that were not possible in the original regime (Helfer 2004). Counter-regime norms, soft and hard law can thus be generated in 'safer' regimes or fora which, in turn, can be integrated into the new rounds of IP lawmaking at the WIPO and WTO.

Increased opportunities, however, come at a cost. Many of these norms and rules promulgated elsewhere are inconsistent with each other. Sometimes, this is precisely the aim of the actors behind them, that is, to create inconsistencies that subvert the mainstream discourse (Helfer 2004). More broadly, potential or real conflict between norms and rules is a key characteristic of a regime complex, as is the lack of a clear hierarchy between them. This raises the important question of how such conflict may be resolved in practice and what rules and norms come to take precedence over others. The 2001 Doha Declaration represents a case of regime actors trying to order the principles and norms that govern IPRs. However, as we have seen, the Declaration did not finally and conclusively resolve the conflict between IP protection and access to medicines, and contests continued thereafter. From a narrow, functionalist point of view, increased complexity and inconsistency may render a regime ineffective, at least in the short term. In the case of IPRs, neither a regime that solely links higher IP protection to trade, nor the current regime complex, appear capable of regulating IPRs in ways that successfully resolve the tension between the public and private domain which lies at the heart of IPRs.

That said, regime-shifting and regime complexes could also be seen as a positive development, insofar as they result from contestations between actors holding competing normative frames and understandings, and to the extent to which they enable actors holding marginalised understandings to participate in and shape, to some degree, the nature of a regime. As we have seen, both strong and weak actors can and do make use of regime-shifting, legal inconsistencies and fragmented governance structures. However, these actions require a great deal of expensive expertise and resources, which undoubtedly disadvantages weaker actors. Hence, the degree to which these strategies will be successful in bringing about a more balanced global IP regime remains to be seen, but the chances do not appear to be great at this moment in time. This may be the case for as long as stronger actors that have so far pushed for higher global IP protection continue to frame strong, global IPRs as key to their competitiveness and economic advancement. As we have seen, the current IP arrangement ensures wealth for some, rather than health for all. Contests over IPRs will continue, but the resolution of complex, prolonged and unequal contests unfolding in multiple regimes and fora does not bode well for a balanced solution. Instead, their resolution requires that all actors pause and engage in a broader rethink of what the *social purpose* of enforcing IPRs is, or ought to be.

Intellectual property is about wealth, it is about how knowledge and information – the new capital – is owned, controlled and distributed. Given the importance that this form of capital has assumed in the current shift towards the knowledge economy, contests over the principles, norms and rules of the emerging global intellectual property regime are not only here to stay, but will also become more pertinent and intense in the near future. But knowledge is also a public good and impinges on the provision of other public goods, hence it cannot and should not be treated simply as a competitiveness or trade issue. The tension between providing incentives for innovation, creativity and technological advancement, on the one hand, and enhancing public utility, diffusion and access to knowledge goods, on the other, is old, but nonetheless it has never been fully resolved. Periods of strong and weak IP protection have alternated, with the result that no consensus exists on how best to balance these opposing forces. Now that these tensions have been projected on to the global level, it is even less clear what a balanced global IP regime should be like, a challenge not known or dealt with by previous generations. What is clear in the current situation, however, is that global IPRs have been narrowly linked to the commercial interests of a few state and business actors. For this reason, many of the contests brought by certain state and non-state actors, currently unfolding in various regimes, are important, at least insofar as their main goal is to claim back and safeguard the public domain from being encroached upon even further. In the final analysis, the public domain is the very cornerstone of the institution of intellectual property. This means that constructing a global IP arrangement that fully takes into account the many public interests implicated in IP protection, including public health, is a pressing task for the present era. It needs to be addressed quickly, before the current arrangement becomes a deeply entrenched layer of the structure that is consequently much harder to change.

Notes

2 Intellectual Property Rights and Pharmaceuticals

1. It must be noted that no IP law has ever aimed or achieved total exclusion. As we shall see later, not only are IP laws designed to grant entitlements for a limited period of time, but they are also limited by several clauses to allow partial diffusion of knowledge protected by the law. Furthermore, certain intellectual goods cannot be the object of private ownership, such as everyday ideas or knowledge, or discoveries of facts or laws found in nature. Nonetheless, both categories are susceptible to interpretation and hence, at different times, the contours of public and private intellectual subject matter have been drawn differently.
2. These figures refer to new molecular entities (NMEs) and new chemical entities (NCEs); the terms are used to express the difference between these genuinely new and radical discoveries and other 'new' medicines presented in the market but which offer only minor changes or improvements compared to medicines already marketed.
3. That is to say that US$400 million of the US$802 million estimate is the estimated revenue that might have been generated had the money spent on R&D been invested elsewhere.
4. An EC DG Competition report on the EC pharmaceutical sector in 2009 found that over the eight-year investigation period, €430 million was spent litigating disputes relating to 68 medicines, each case lasting on average 2.8 years (EC 2009). These figures are bound to be rather higher in the US.
5. For these reasons, there are those in the US government and pharmaceutical sector who claim that they (and the US population) are funding major medical research while the rest of the world free-rides. According to a study in the US, the extrapolated diminished returns due to price controls in the OECD countries were in the range of US$18–27 billion annually, which was converted into an R&D reduction of about US$5–8 billion or a loss of three or four new medicines annually (US ITA 2004: 12).
6. A compulsory license is an authorisation granted by a government to a third party to exploit an invention without the permission of the patent holder.

3 Linking IPRs to Trade: The Making of TRIPs

1. Pfizer's CEO, Ed Pratt, became a key individual in bringing about the IPRs–trade link. Indeed, he himself has referred to his involvement in events leading up to the TRIPs Agreement as being his greatest achievement (Matthews 2002a).
2. The only provision for dispute settlement was added to the Paris Convention in 1967 (Article 28), which stipulated that member states could bring cases of violations of obligations under the Convention to the International Court

of Justice (ICJ). Despite such provision, not all countries accepted the compulsory jurisdiction of the ICJ in IP matters and furthermore, those that did considered patent disputes as too trivial to bring before the ICJ. No IP-related case has ever been considered there (Emmert 1990).

3. Indeed, as Yeutter (USTR from 1985 to 1988) himself accepted 'it was the United States and Europe, more than any other GATT members, which understood that strong and effective protection of international property rights was vital to continued trade expansion...' Yeutter, in Gorlin 1999, foreword.

4. However, trademark industries, led by Levi Strauss Corporation, that had organised into the Anti-Counterfeiting Coalition at the end of Tokyo Round (1979), had also made the link between trade and IPRs (Dutfield 2003a).

5. Gorlin's recommendations in his 'A Trade-Based Approach for the International Copyright Protection for Computer Software' were incorporated almost wholesale into the ACTN Task Force on Intellectual Property report to the ACTN in October 1985 (Sell 1999).

6. In an interview given to Drahos and Braithwaite (2002: 117), USTR Clayton Yeutter commented on explaining to Pratt and Opel the need to get the other Quad countries (the EU, Japan and Canada) to support the IPRs–trade link at the GATT: 'I am convinced on intellectual property but when I go the Quad meetings, they are under no pressure from their industry. Can you get it?'

7. The copyright-reliant industries were initially reluctant to adopt the GATT option because they were generally satisfied with copyright standards worldwide; their problem was with the enforcement of those rights. The International Intellectual Property Association (IIPA), representing all US IP copyright interests, was created in 1984 precisely to advocate an agenda for the USTR's section 301 mandate, as it preferred bilateral measures and sanctions under Section 301 as the most flexible and effective means of improving enforcement of IP abroad (Ryan 1998a; Matthews 2002a).

8. Council Regulation 2641/84, September 1984. However, according to a European Court opinion (15 November 1994) the Community did not have competence to enter into agreements with non-member countries with a view to protecting intellectual property (although it had competence over harmonising internal IP standards, subject to voting). The Court maintained that this was so regardless of the fact the EC *had resorted* to autonomous measures falling within the ambit of commercial policy, namely the opening of procedures under commercial policy instruments and the suspension of generalised tariff preferences (European Court Opinion 61994V0001, 1994, emphasis added).

9. The IPC included a number of the largest pharmaceutical companies. Its initial 13 members were: Bristol-Meyers, DuPont, FMC Corporation, General Electric, General Motors, Hewlett-Packard, IBM, Johnson & Johnson, Merck, Monsanto, Pfizer, Rockwell International and Warner Communications.

10. Its members were the US, the EEC, Japan, Canada, Switzerland, Sweden and Australia (see Drahos and Braithwaite 2002).

11. In all three cases, pharmaceutical patent protection was the main issue on which the USTR initiative was based. Although Korea had amended its patent law for pharmaceutical and chemical products, US pharmaceutical

companies remained dissatisfied and resubmitted a section 301 complaint against Korea again in 1988, charging that Korean companies were pirating patented products; European companies voiced the same concerns to their governments. In the Argentine case, the 1988 investigation by the USTR was withdrawn a year later on a promise by the Argentine government to constructively address the issue of patents for pharmaceuticals (see Ryan 1998a; Watal 2001).

12. Under the 1988 Trade Act, the USTR is required to provide an annual report listing, under Special 301 provision, countries who are the most onerous offenders, with whom negotiations carry the threat of retaliatory sanctions. Once a country is identified as a priority country, the USTR must initiate an investigation within 30 days, determine the actionability of foreign activity and devise a policy response within six months from the start of the investigations. These strict time limits reflect the expressed desire of the private sector to toughen US resolve on IP issues. In addition to the priority list, the USTR also compiles annually a 'priority watch' list, where countries with serious IP protection shortfalls but that are not a target of deadlined negotiations are ranked. The Special 301 list of countries is announced in February each year and is the result of close cooperation between the USTR and business associations, which duly submit their report of losses and violations of their IPRs abroad. We recall that the IIPA set this trend in 1985, when it submitted to the USTR a report on losses to its companies in a group of countries; since 1988, several IP-reliant sector associations submit their dossier to the USTR, including PhRMA (Ryan 1998a; Sell 2003).

13. Brazil had weakened its opposition since the Montreal Ministerial in December 1988; India did so soon afterwards amidst fierce criticism, especially from within the country (although opposition to the IPRs agenda was divided between those representing multinational interests who demanded amendments to India's IP laws and those that objected to India even joining the Paris Convention). By many accounts, India stepped back due to direct pressure from the US, both high level pressure and through Section 301 action (see Ramanna 2002).

14. Despite the common structure of the EEC-US proposal, some significant differences existed, especially on exceptions to the patentable subject matter. The US proposal (alongside that of Switzerland and Japan) offered no exceptions, but the EEC proposal included exceptions for inventions contrary to public policy and health, plant or animal varieties or the biological processes used in their production (incorporated later in TRIPs Article 27(3)). These exceptions, also being advocated by developing countries, were used to construct the image of the EEC as bridging differences between the latter and the US; in actual fact, there was no agreement between European countries over the patentability of life, and the proposed exceptions follow closely the relevant provisions of the European Patent Convention of 1973 (Sell 2003: 112).

15. These were Argentina, Brazil, Chile, China, Colombia, Cuba, Egypt, India, Nigeria, Peru, Tanzania, Uruguay, Pakistan and Zimbabwe.

16. According to Gorlin (1999), apart from the Quad, the composition of the group varied according to the issue being discussed. Australia, the Nordic countries, Switzerland, Hong Kong, Argentina, Brazil, India, Malaysia and

Thailand were regular participants and New Zealand, Singapore, Chile, Indonesia, Tanzania and Uruguay were also present.

17. Pipeline protection refers to full protection for pharmaceutical products which are patented (but still awaiting marketing approval) in other countries *before* the entry into force of the TRIPs agreement. This means that if a pharmaceutical product is patented in 1993 in the US (but is still awaiting marketing approval from the US FDA), then it will not benefit from patent protection as stipulated in TRIPs in countries not yet required to comply with TRIPs, such as India, where patents did not have to be provided for pharmaceutical products until 2005. The aim of the pharmaceutical companies was to extend global patent protection to as many of their products (in the pipeline) as possible.

18. Unlike the 'pipeline' protection sought by the US pharmaceutical companies, the mailbox provision is intended to freeze the novelty requirement for the granting of pharmaceutical patents for products which were filed after the TRIPs agreement came into force (1995), but which would not benefit from patent protection in countries where this protection would not be available until a later date if the mailbox mechanism were not provided. For example, if a pharmaceutical company files a patent application for a product in the EU in 1995, it can also file a patent application through the mailbox in, say, India, although the latter is not obliged to provide patents until 2005. When India starts processing applications for pharmaceutical patents in that year, it will have to consider mailbox applications made between 1995 and 2005, not through examining 'prior art' as of 2005, but by reference to the prior art as it existed at the time the application was made (1995). When a patent is granted, this will last for 20 years from the date of the mailbox filing (1995). In addition to providing for mailbox application, the TRIPs agreement also obliges states that do not need to comply with TRIPs until a later date to provide market exclusivity (for five years) for products for which a mailbox application has been made and which has obtained marketing approval in another country (the EU in our example). The effect of these two provisions, as the GATT secretariat explained to the pharmaceutical companies, who were distressed over the long transition periods granted to developing countries, is that 'for all practical purposes the economic effect on the grant of product patents for pharmaceuticals will be as if the obligation to grant product patents were effective in *all* countries on the day of entry into force' of the TRIPs agreement (Gorlin 1999: 103 emphasis added).

4   Contestations Post-TRIPs and the Emergence of the IP–Access to Medicines Debate

1. The first of these studies, undertaken by Rapp and Rozek, was actually funded by the US Pharmaceutical Manufacturers' Association with a view to presenting arguments on the necessity of strong intellectual property protection in fostering economic development (see Weissman 1996).

2. 'TRIPs plus' refers to obligations of a higher standard than those specified in TRIPs as well as to obligations which are missing or ambiguous in the TRIPs

text. Some of these involve extending patents and copyright to new kinds of subject-matter; eliminating or narrowing permitted exceptions, including those still provided for in US and European IPR laws; extending protection terms; introducing new TRIPs-mandated IPR rules earlier than the transition periods allowed by TRIPs; and ratifying new WIPO treaties containing TRIPs plus measures (see Drahos 2002).

3. See for instance, IPC (1994), IFPMA (1995), TABD (1998), EFPIA (1999), UNICE (1999) and PhRMA (1999).

4. The WTO and WIPO signed a Cooperation Agreement in 1995, in which WIPO assumed obligations to provide legal and technical assistance to developing WTO members on TRIPs matters, regardless of their WIPO membership status. From 1996 to 2000, the WIPO international bureau drafted around 214 IP laws for 119 developing countries, in addition to commenting or amending provisions for 235 draft laws for 134 developing countries (see WIPO 2001).

5. According to Shaffer (2004: 476), in the wake of TRIPs the US 'regularly sent lawyers for the U.S. pharmaceutical and copyright industries to Geneva as "faculty" of the WIPO...to teach developing country representatives about intellectual property matters and to draft "model" laws for their consideration. Industry successfully lobbied Congress to allocate funds for these "educational" efforts'.

6. See, for instance, reasons to support this strategy given by an IPC lawyer and lobbyist, Charles Levy (2000), as well as by Eric Smith of the IIPA (1996).

7. For instance, the US and the EC and member states participated as a claimant or defendant in around 88 per cent of GATT cases, excluding those cases where they were third parties (see Shaffer 2004). With regard to IP cases, we noted in Chapter 3 that IP norms and rules developed primarily in these two countries.

8. For a public record of complaints by research-based pharmaceutical companies of alleged losses in India due to its failure to provide mailbox and exclusive marketing rights, see a letter by Harvey Bale, Director of PhRMA, to the USTR attached to the September 1997 Panel Report (WT/DS50/R). Similarly, a letter from Alan Hesketh, Manager of Global Intellectual Property in Glaxo-Wellcome (UK), to the EC is also attached to the Panel Report of August 1998 (WT/DS79/R). According to Matthews (2002: 97), the interests of the research-based pharmaceutical companies in the US and EC case against India were represented through the India International Task Force which was chaired by a Glaxo-Welcome expert in the UK.

9. See WT/DS36/4, IP/D/2/Add.1, 7 March 1997.

10. INTERPAT is an association of proprietary pharmaceutical companies focused exclusively on global pharmaceutical IP issues and committed to the improvement of intellectual property laws around the world. Member companies are multinational, research-oriented pharmaceutical companies; it essentially works as a network or working group composed of the heads of patent departments of 29 proprietary pharmaceutical companies, including AstraZeneca, Bristol-Myers Squibb, AVENTIS, Merck, Boehringer Ingelheim, Wyeth, Schering-Plough, Eli Lilly, Novartis, Pfizer, GlaxoSmithKline, Sanofi and Abbott Laboratories. The organisation has regular meetings to discuss initiatives focused on fostering the

improvement of laws by advocating governmental actions to improve, strengthen and harmonise intellectual property regimes throughout the world. Work groups targeting specific areas of the world develop initiatives for their specific regions. A current key issue for INTERPAT is the world-wide implementation of the TRIPs (see Gorlin 1999:1 fn1; INTERPAT 2000). According to Matthews (2002a: 87), the little-known INTERPAT has been operating since the early 1970s.

11. See the Panel Report WT/DS50/R of 5 September 1997 and the Appellate Body Report WT/DS50/AB/R of 19 December 1997.

12. See the Panel Report WT/DS114/R of 17 March 2000.

13. For the distinction made by the Panel on how provisions related to testing did not conflict with the 'normal exploitation' of a patent while the 'stock-piling' provisions did, see WT/DS114/R, paragraphs 7.56 and 7.57.

14. It must be noted that, according to EFPIA (1999), IFPMA (1999) and UNICE (2000), *only* experimental use of pharmaceutical data constituted excep-tions allowed under TRIPs Article 30; this would effectively exclude other Bolar provisions in addition to 'stockpiling' but, as we have noted already, such extremely narrow interpretation was greatly hampered by the exist-ence of provisions in the US Hatch-Waxman 1984 Act.

15. Brazil was the first developing country to commit to providing universal and free access to AIDS drugs in 1996. The US actions came under fierce crit-icism from some international NGOs that were worried about the impact of the case in Brazil's AIDS/HIV programme. See Dispute 224, Brazil files a complaint on US Patent Code, available at http://www.wto.org/english/tratop_e/dispu_e/cases_e/ds224_e.htm, accessed on 10 March 2010.

16. Compiled from information from the USTR listings during 1996, 1997, 1998, 1999 and 2000, available at www.ustr.org.

17. See, for instance, Botswana's statement, which highlighted the importance of technical assistance to help with implementing WTO agreements, par-ticularly in terms of 'developing legislation and safeguards for intellec-tual property rights', WT/MIN(96)/ST/76. See also statements made by the Dominican Republic WT/MIN(98)/ST/117, Kenya WT/MIN(98)ST/43 and Bangladesh WT/MIN(98)ST/60.

18. During TRIPs negotiations, a middle ground was found on the extension of the WTO Dispute Settlement Procedures to TRIPs in terms of 'non-violation' complaints, namely that these complaints would not apply to TRIPs for a period of five years, with a decision to be taken at the end of 1999. Demands to preserve the exclusion came from the African Group (submission by Kenya on behalf of the African Group WT/GC/W/302 August 1999), Colombia (WT/GC/W/316 September 1999), Venezuela (WT/GC/W/282 August 1999) and Canada (WT/GC/W/256 July 1999). For its part, the US was strongly opposed to any extension and deemed it best to allow the moratorium to die a natural death by 2000. See the US submission to the General Council WT/GC/W/115 in 1998.

19. The EC and its Member States remained the main *demandeur* on the GI front; in addition to the EC, countries such as India, Morocco, Egypt, Mexico, Venezuela, Nigeria, Cuba and Turkey were all keen to expand the scope of GI to include cheese, beer, chocolate, embroidery, artisanal handicrafts and so on. See Otten (1998) and Watal (2000).

20. For some developing countries' position on benefit sharing, see submissions by Cuba, Honduras, Paraguay and Venezuela (WT/GC/W/329). India had raised such concerns since 1996 in a submission to the WTO Committee for Trade and Environment (Watal 2000). For proposals related to patentability see, for instance, a communication from Kenya on behalf of the African Group (WT/GC/W/302). Venezuela, on the other hand, joined by some African countries, proposed the exemption of all the medicines in the WHO essential drug list (see Venezuela's submission WT/GC/W/282).
21. See two US submissions to this end: WT/GC/W/115 (1998) and WT/GC/W/323 (1999).
22. See the EC submission WT/GC/W/193 and the submission by Japan WT/GC/W/242.
23. On the amendment of Article 27.3(b), for instance, see communications from Brazil IP/C/W/228 (2000), from India IP/C/W/195 (2000) and from Mauritius on behalf of the African Group IP/C/W/206 (2000).
24. The concept of 'farmers' rights' was developed by Pat Mooney of the Rural Advance Foundation International (RAFI) in 1985 as a counter-norm to the concept of 'breeders' rights' incorporated in the UPOV Convention. Farmers' rights were eventually incorporated in the UN CBD Convention (see Braithwaite and Drahos 2000).
25. The involvement of MSF with the Campaign gave it not only more legitimacy, but also much needed resources; MSF passed all the financial awards associated with its Nobel Peace Price in 1999 to the Access to Medicines Campaign. A brief list of what came to be known as the Access Campaign includes, apart from the above, the Treatment Access Campaign, Health Gap, ACT UP Philadelphia, ACT UP Paris and the Thai Network of People Living with HIV/AIDS.
26. Pharmaceutical companies involved in the lawsuit were: The Pharmaceutical Manufacturers' Association of South Africa, Alcon Laboratories, Bayer, Bristol-Myers Squibb, Byk Madaus, Eli Lilly (SA), Glaxo Wellcome (SA), Hoechst Marion, Ingelheim Pharmaceuticals, Janssen-Cilag Pharmaceuticals, Knoll Pharmaceuticals (SA), Lundbeck (SA), Merck, MSD, Novartis (SA), Novo Nordisk, Pharmacia & Upjohn, Rhone-Poulenc Rorer (SA), Roche, Schering-Plough, SA Scientific Pharmaceuticals, SmithKline Beecham Pharmaceuticals, Universal Pharmaceuticals, Wyeth, Xixia Pharmaceuticals, Zeneca (SA), Bayer AG, Boehringer-Ingelheim International GmbH, Boehringer-Ingelheim KG, Bristol-Myers Squibb Company, Byk Gulden Lomberg Chemische Fabrik GmbH, Dr Karl Thomae GmbH, Eli Lilly and Company, F Hoffman-La Roche AG, Merck KGaA, Merck & Co, Inc, Rhone-Poulenc Rorer S.A., SmithKline Beecham. See MSF Press Statement, 1 March 2001, *MSF Demands Pharmaceutical Industry Stop Obstructing Access to Medicines in South Africa*, available at http://www.doctorswithoutborders.org/press/release.cfm?id=658&cat=press-release, accessed 8 December 2010.
27. See EC note on the WHO's Revised Drug Strategy, Doc No 1/D/3/BW D (98) of October 1998, available at http://www.cptech.org/ip/health/who/eurds98.html, accessed on 10 March 2010.
28. See Resolution WHA 52.19 of 24 May 1999.
29. See Resolution WHA 54.10 and WHA 54.11 of 21 May 2001. These resolutions addressed the need to strengthen national policies so as to increase the

availability of generic drugs and to evaluate the impact of TRIPs on access to drugs, development of new drugs and local manufacturing capacity.

30. See President Clinton Announces New Cooperative Effort to Help Poor Countries Gain Access to Affordable Medicines, Including for HIV/AIDS Treatment, 1 December 1999, available at http://clinton3.nara.gov/WH/ New/WTO-Conf-1999/factsheets/fs-012.html, accessed on 10 March 2010.

31. See The White House, 10 May 2000, Executive Order no 13155, Access to HIV/AIDS Pharmaceuticals and Medical Technologies, available at http://frwebgate.access.gpo.gov/cgi-bin/getdoc.cgi?dbname=2000_ register&docid=fr12my00-170.pdf, accessed on 10 March 2010. In the US, PhRMA's President Alan Holmer stated that the Order set an 'undesirable and inappropriate precedent, by adopting a discriminatory approach to intellectual property laws, and focusing exclusively on pharmaceuticals. We recognise that AIDS is a major problem, but weakening intellectual property rights is not the solution' (as quoted in Sell 2002: 509). The order was upheld by the George Bush Administration.

32. See the UN Security Council Resolution 1308, 17 July 2000, page 2, available at http://daccess-dds-ny.un.org/doc/UNDOC/GEN/N00/536/02/PDF/ N0053602.pdf?OpenElement, accessed on 10 March 2010.

33. UN General Assembly Resolution 55/2, 8 September 2000. The Millennium Development Goals include three public health objectives: to reduce child mortality rate by two thirds; maternal mortality ratio by three quarters; and to halt and begin to reverse the spread of HIV/AIDS, malaria, and other major diseases by 2015.

34. Proposals for the creation of a global fund to deal with HIV/AIDS and other pandemics were discussed at the G8 meeting in 2000 and the Global Fund to Fight AIDS, Tuberculosis and Malaria was created in 2002. The Fund is organised as a partnership between governments, civil society, the private sector and affected communities, and is mainly a financial instrument, rather than an implementing entity. It finances programmes when it is assured that its assistance does not replace or reduce other sources of funding, either those for the fight against AIDS, tuberculosis and malaria or those that support public health more broadly. See The Global Fund website www.theglobalfund.org/en/, accessed on 8 March 2010.

35. See Resolution 2000/7 of the 52nd Session of the Sub-Commission E/CN.4/ Sub.2/Res/2000/7, 17 August 2000, available at www.ohchr.org. (See also 'TRIPs Regime at Odds with Human Rights Law, Says UN Body', Third World Network, SUNS 4728, available at www.twnside.org.sg/title/odds. htm, accessed on 10 March 2010.

36. See, for instance, the resolution sponsored by Brazil just as its patent law was challenged at the WTO Dispute Settlement Body by the US; UN Commission on Human Rights 'Access to Medication in the Context of Pandemics such as HIV/AIDS' Resolution (E/CN.4/RES/2001/33) adopted on 23 April 2001 and others adopted in 2001, 2002 and 2003 (E/CN.4/Sub.2/RES/2001/21, E/CN.4/RES/2002/2000 (Resolution 32) and E/CN.4/RES/2003/L.11/Add.3 (Resolution 29) available at www.ohchr.org).

37. The Accelerated Access Initiative was set up through collaboration between five proprietary pharmaceutical companies (Boehringer-Ingelheim, Bristol-Myers Squibb, GlaxoSmithKline, Merck, and Hoffmann-La Roche, joined

later by Abbott Laboratories and Gilead Sciences), and several UN organisations (WHO, UNAIDS, UNICEF and UNFPA). See the press release from UNAIDS dated 11 May 2000, available at www.essentialdrugs.org/edrug/archive/200005/msg00027.php, accessed on 10 March 2010.

38. See Barton Gellman, 'A Turning Point that Left Millions Behind', The Washington Post, 28 December 2000, available at www.washingtonpost.com/wp-dyn/content/article/2006/06/09/AR2006060901310.html, accessed on 10 March 2010. In addition, NGOs have argued that such price reductions require considerable threats and extraordinary measures and political mobilisation, which make price reduction an unreliable tool for dealing with health crises. See CPTech et al. (2001).

39. In mid 2000, some US Congressmen introduced a bill to promote the availability of affordable HIV/AIDS medicines in Sub-Saharan Africa, and in early 2001 members of the US Congress announced their opposition to the ongoing lawsuit (see www.house.gov/schakowsky/press/pr7_27_2000watersaidsbill.shtml, accessed on 10 October 2007). Government leaders from Denmark, Germany, the Netherlands and Belgium also expressed their public support for withdrawal of the lawsuit and in March 2001, the European Parliament passed the resolution 'Access to medicines for AIDS patients in the Third World' that called on the pharmaceutical companies to withdraw from the case (available at http://eur-lex.europa.eu/LexUriServ/site/en/oj/2001/c_343/c_34320011205en03000302.pdf, accessed on 10 March 2010). See also Cooper *et al.* 2001.

40. Interview with CPTech officer, CPTech Office in Geneva, 10 February 2006. See also Love (2001). 'Intellectual Property Rights and the South African Medicines Act' presented at the Symposium on Intellectual Property, Development, and Human Rights', University of Florida Fredric G Levin College of Law, 24 March 2001.

41. See 'TRIPs Council to Hold Discussion on Essential Medicines', *BRIDGES* Weekly, April 2001, ICTSD, available at www.ictsd.org/html/weekly/10-04-01/story1.htm, accessed on 10 October 2007.

42. See Special discussion on intellectual property and access to medicines, WTO TRIPs Council meeting 18–22 June 2001, WTO document IP/C/M/31, 10 July 2001, available at www.wtocenter.org.tw/SmartKMS/fileviewer?id=13012, accessed on 10 March 2010.

43. See Daniel Pruzin 'WTO Talks on TRIPs, Public Health Declaration Stall over Compromise Text', in *International Trade Daily*, 24 October 2001, available at www.cptech.org/ip/wto/doha/bna10242001.html, accessed on 10 March 2010.

44. One study referred to a PhRMA report of August 2001, 'Facts and Figures on Patenting and Access in Africa', while the other to a paper published by Attaran and Gillespie-While (2001) in the *Journal of Medical Association* in October; both were widely circulated by pharmaceutical business actors in the run-up to the Doha Ministerial.

45. Draft Ministerial Declaration IP/C/W/312, 4 October 2001; Proposal by the African Group, Bangladesh, Barbados, Bolivia, Brazil, Cuba, Dominican epublic, Ecuador, Haiti, Honduras, India, Indonesia, Jamaica, Pakistan, Paraguay, Philippines, Peru, Sri Lanka, Thailand and Venezuela; Draft

Ministerial Declaration, IP/C/W/313, 4 October 2001, Contribution from Australia, Canada, Japan, Switzerland and the United States.

5 TRIPs Revisited

1. WT/L/540 and Corr.1, Decision of the General Council of 30 August 2003, 'Implementation of Paragraph 6 of the Doha Declaration on the TRIPs Agreement and Public Health';also WT/L/641, Decision of the General Council of 6 December 2005, 'Amendment of the TRIPs Agreement'.

2. Article 31(f) of the TRIPs agreement on Other Use without the Consent of the Right Holder stipulates that 'any such use shall be authorized predominantly for the supply of the domestic market of the Member authorizing such use'.

3. See paragraph 5 and 9 of the Draft Ministerial Declaration IP/C/W/312, 4 October 2001, Proposal by the African Group, Bangladesh, Barbados, Bolivia, Brazil, Cuba, Dominican Republic, Ecuador, Haiti, Honduras, India, Indonesia, Jamaica, Pakistan, Paraguay, Philippines, Peru, Sri Lanka, Thailand and Venezuela.

4. TRIPs Article 30 'Exceptions to Rights Conferred' states that 'Members may provide limited exceptions to the exclusive rights conferred by a patent, provided that such exceptions do not unreasonably conflict with a normal exploitation of the patent and do not unreasonably prejudice the legitimate interests of the patent owner, taking account of the legitimate interests of third parties'.

5. Similar concerns were raised by then USTR Robert Zoellick in a letter to trade ministers dated 27 December 2002 (available at www.cptech.org/ip/wto/p6/zoellick12272002.html, accessed on 10 March 2010).

6. See the Statement on the Considerations or Paragraph 6 Modalities delivered by Kenya on behalf of the African Group, Brazil, Cuba, the Dominican Republic, Honduras, India, Indonesia, Jamaica, Malaysia, Sri Lanka and Thailand at the first TRIPs Council Session on 5 March 2002, available in TRIPs Council Meeting Minutes IP/C/M/35, 22 March 2002. NGOs circulated a substantial number of analytical papers throughout the negotiations; an early position was presented in a joint letter sent by MSF, Oxfam, CPTech, Health Gap, Third World Network and Essential Action to the Members of the TRIPs Council on 18 January 2002, 'Joint Letter to the TRIPs Council', available at www.accessmed-msf.org/prod/publications.asp?scntid=12220021732142&contenttype=PARA&, accessed on 10 November 2007.

7. See Communication from the United States 'Paragraph 6 of Doha Declaration on the TRIPs Agreement and Public Health' IP/C/W/340, 14 March 2002.

8. See the Statement on the Considerations for Paragraph 6 Modalities delivered by Kenya at the March 2002 TRIPs Council meeting, supra note 6.

9. See the Communication from the European Communities and their Member States 'Concept Paper Relating to Paragraph 6 of the Doha Declaration on the TRIPs Agreement and Public Health' IP/C/W/339, 4 March 2002.

10. See the US Submission supra note 7 and Vandoren and Eeckhaute (2003) (both of whom work for EC DG Trade and were involved with the paragraph 6 negotiations).
11. This was so because Article 30 provides for limited exceptions to the exclusive rights conferred by a patent, provided that such exceptions do not unreasonably conflict with a normal exploitation of the patent and do not unreasonably prejudice the legitimate interests of the patent owner. In the case of compulsory licences for export/import, arguments were raised that an Article 30 approach would have permitted the exporting country to establish an exception in its patent law, limited to exporting pharmaceuticals, to address public health crises in other Member states. This was not considered to prejudice the rights of the patent-holder, given that the importing country would have either issued a compulsory licence (in which case the patent-holder had no claims) or the pharmaceuticals in questions were not patented there at all (in which case the patent-holder had no protection in the first place). The US took the position that Article 30 exceptions were meant for such things as non-commercial experimental use and for statutory exceptions already permitted in members' laws; it considered that other exceptions, including those suggested above, would seriously prejudice the interests of the patent holders (see the second communication of the US to the TRIPs Council 'Paragraph 6 of the Doha Declaration on the TRIPs Agreement and Public Health' IP/C/W/358, 9 July 2002). It appears that the WTO dispute case between Canada and the EU with regard to Bolar exceptions (analysed briefly in the last chapter), and the relatively strict interpretation of exceptions to patent-holders' rights as provided for in Article 30 by the Panel, had some impact on support for the view that Article 30 could not accommodate an exception as broad as that being proposed with regard to compulsory licensing for public health crises.
12. See the Note by the Secretariat 'Proposals on Paragraph 6 of the Doha Declaration on the TRIPs Agreement and Public Health: Thematic Compilation' IP/C/W/363, 11 July 2002. The submissions of individual countries or groups of countries are also available: Kenya on behalf of the African Group IP/C/W/351; EC and its member States IP/C/W/352; United Arab Emirates IP/C/W/354; Brazil on behalf of the delegations of Bolivia, Brazil, Cuba, China, Dominican Republic, Ecuador, India, Indonesia, Pakistan, Peru, Sri Lanka, Thailand and Venezuela (the Philippines also associated itself with this proposal at the TRIPs Council meeting) IP/C/W/355 and the US, IP/C/W/358.
13. When the Chair draft solution appeared in December 2002 (see below) the paragraph addressing the African Group's request that 'domestic market' in 31(f) should also refer to customs unions or free trade areas had been reformulated. The draft Decision allowed for the 'domestic market' requirement in Article 31(f) to be waived for regional trade agreements (RTA), but it set out clearly which RTAs this rule would apply to, including a requirement that at least half of the membership of the RTA was to be made up of least developed countries. See ICTSD 'WTO Members still battling over TRIPs and Health', *BRIDGES*, Volume 6, No 43, 20 December 2002, available at www.ictsd.org/weekly/02-12-20/story1.htm, accessed on 10 November 2007.

14. See the US and EC submissions in the June 2002 TRIPs Council meeting, supra note 12.
15. See, for instance, MSF 'Why Article 30 Will Work. Why Article 31 Will Not', available at www.msfaccess.org/resources/key-publications/key-publication-detail/?tx_ttnews[tt_news]=1402&cHash=ef850f5e46, 24 June 2002, accessed on 10 March 2010.
16. In October 2002 the European Parliament proposed an amendment to the European Commission's proposed Directive on Medicinal Products for Human Use Directive 2001/83/EC, with the aim of allowing the manufacture for export of generic versions of patented medicines in response to a compulsory licence issued by a third country to meet that country's healthcare needs. The text of Amendment 196 can be found at www.europarl. europa.eu/omk/omnsapir.so/calendar?APP=PDF&TYPE=PV2&FILE=p00210 23EN.pdf&LANGUE=EN, accessed on 10March 2010.
17. See the WHO statement at the TRIPs Council meeting on 17 September 2002, available at TRIPs Council meeting minutes, IP/C/M/37, 11 October 2002, in which it was stated that 'Among the solutions being proposed, the limited exception under Article 30 is the most consistent with this public health principle. This solution will give WTO Members expeditious authorization, as requested by the Doha Declaration, to permit third parties to make, sell and export patented medicines and other health technologies to address public health needs'.
18. See the South African Non-Paper on Substantive and Procedural Elements of a Report to the General Council under Paragraph 6 of the Declaration on the TRIPs Agreement and Public Health JOB(02)/156, 5 November 2002, and Communication from Kenya, the Coordinator of the African Group IP/C/W/389, 14 November 2002.
19. See the submissions from the US and the EU to the June 2002 TRIPs Council Meeting, IP/C/W/358 and IP/C/W/352 respectively.
20. TRIPs enforcement measures are contained in part III of the Agreement, Articles 41–61; see especially article 44. The EU argued that these applied mainly to counterfeiting, while trade diversion was altogether another issue. See an EU Memo 'Sustainable Trade: Access to Medicines – Main elements of the Chair's 16 December 2002 Draft Compromise Decision (Perez Motta text), Brussels, 9 January 2003, available at http://ec.europa. eu/trade/issues/global/medecine/memo090103_en.htm, accessed on 24 November 2007. This argument was strikingly similar to that raised in the EU's case against Canada at the WTO in 2000 discussed in the last chapter; importantly, on that occasion the Panel stated unambiguously that it was the responsibility of the patent-holder, not of government, to stop trade diversion practices by means of resorting to private infringement action (see the Panel Report WT/DS114/R of 17 March 2000, paragraph 7.46).
21. See the submission by Kenya on behalf of the African Group and that by Brazil on behalf of a group of developing countries submitted to the TRIPs Council in its March 2002 meeting (IP/C/W/351 and IP/C/W/355 respectively).
22. The Chair's text can be found at www.cptech.org/ip/wto/p6/wto11192002. html, accessed on 10 March 2010.

23. See, for instance, a statement by CPTech, MSF, Oxfam and the Third World Network: 'Say No to Poisonous Proposals' of 25 November 2002 available at www.cptech.org/ip/wto/p6/ngos11252002.html, and a note by CPTech directed to TRIPs Council Members '7 Reasons to Reject A Bad Deal' of 27 November 2002, available at www.cptech.org/ip/wto/p6/cptech-7reasons. html, both accessed on 10 March 2010. Generic pharmaceutical industry associations in Europe, Canada, India and the US also lobbied their home governments to ensure a flexible paragraph 6 solution.

24. See the submission by the US to the TRIPs Council meeting of 14 March 2002, IP/C/W/340.

25. Paragraph 4 of the Doha Declaration reads: 'We agree that the TRIPs Agreement does not and should not prevent members from taking measures to protect public health. Accordingly, while reiterating our commitment to the TRIPs Agreement, we affirm that the Agreement can and should be interpreted and implemented in a manner supportive of WTO members' right to protect public health and, in particular, to promote access to medicines for all. In this connection, we reaffirm the right of WTO members to use, to the full, the provisions in the TRIPs Agreement, which provide flexibility for this purpose'.

26. See Rosa Whitaker (Assistant USTR) letter to African Governments 'Compulsory Licensing of Pharmaceuticals: Summary of the U.S. Proposal', 25 October 2002, available at http://lists.essential.org/pipermail/ip-health/2002-November/003690.html, accessed on 10 March 2010.

27. See the South African Non-Paper on Substantive and Procedural Elements of a Report to the General Council under Paragraph 6 of the Declaration on the TRIPs Agreement and Public Health JOB(02)/156, 5 November 2002.

28. See Communication from Kenya, the Coordinator of the African Group IP/C/W/389, 14 November 2002.

29. See 'Drug Companies Push for Limitations on Disease Coverage in Drug Patent Deal', *Inside US Trade*, 22 November 2002. See also 'Zoellick Faces Heath from Congress on Scope of TRIPs and Health Deal', *Inside US Trade*, 6 December 2002, available at www.cptech.org/ip/wto/p6/insideustrade12062002.html, accessed on 10 March 2010.

30. Many activities were organised by the network in Geneva, including pantomimes and shows in the street, in addition to meetings with developing and developed countries' negotiators and reports. See also CPTech, MSF, Oxfam, & Third World Network 'NGOs: Say No to Poisonous Proposals on Paragraph 6', 25 November 2002, and Letter from CPTech, Oxfam, MSF and HAI to WTO Delegates Regarding December 16, 2002 Chairman's Text for 'Solution' to Paragraph 6 of the Doha Declaration on TRIPs and Public Health, 19 December 2002, both available at www.cptech.org/ip/wto/p6/, accessed on 10 March 2010.

31. The Chair's text of 19 November 2002 can be found at www.cptech.org/ip/wto/p6/wto11192002.html, accessed on 10 March 2010.

32. A copy of the draft decision of 16 December 2002 text, JOB (02)/217, can be found at www.cptech.org/ip/wto/p6/wto12162002.html, accessed on 10 March 2010. The Motta text of 16 December is identical to the Decision eventually agreed on 30 August 2003.

33. In fact, many members stressed that if the text was changed on disease coverage they would also be insisting on modifications elsewhere, in particular with respect to safeguards on the import side. See the African Group Statement of 20 December 2002, TRIPs Council Meeting Minutes, IP/C/M/38, 5 February 2003, also available at www.ictsd.org/ministerial/cancun/docs/AfricaGroup_TRIPs.pdf accessed on 18 December 2007.

34. See a memo sent to the TRIPs negotiators by CPTech 'Reject 16 December Chairman's text on paragraph 6 – Nine reasons' on 16 December 2002, available at www.cptech.org/ip/wto/p6/cptech12162002.html, accessed on 10 March 2010.

35. In a last minute attempt on 20 December 2002, the US attempted to insert a footnote to the Motta text of 16 of December 2002 which would expand its previously proposed list of diseases from three (HIV/AIDS, malaria and tuberculosis) to 23 and 'other epidemics of comparable gravity and scale', including those that might arise in the future. Developing countries rejected this proposal, arguing that it would restrict the mandate given by the Doha Declaration, which refers more generally to 'measures to protect public health'. See ICTSD *Bridges* update, 2 January 2003 'WTO Fails to Meet TRIPs & Health Deadline Due To US Opposition', available at www.ictsd.org/ministerial/cancun/TRIPs_update.htm, accessed on 16 November 2007. The representative of the United States, Ambassador Linnet Deily, regretted the inability of her delegation to join the consensus on the Chairman's draft text of 16 December, indicating that her delegation was willing to join the consensus on all parts of the draft, *except* that on the scope of diseases. See TRIPs Council, Minutes of Meeting on 25–27, 29 November and 20 December 2002, IP/C/M/38, 5 February 2003, paragraph 34. See also 'US Wrecks Cheap Drugs Deal: Cheney's Intervention Blocks Pact to Help Poor Countries After Pharmaceutical Firms Lobby White House', *The Guardian*, 21 December 2002; 'U.S. Sticks to Hard Line on TRIPs, as Supachai Tries to Broker Deal', *Inside U.S. Trade*, 20 December 2002; Press Release WTO General Council 'Supachai disappointed over governments' failure to agree on health and development issues' 20 December 2002, available at www.wto.org/english/news_e/pres02_e/pr329_e.htm, accessed on 10 March 2010.

36. The scope of diseases was limited to 'HIV/AIDS, malaria, tuberculosis, and other types of infectious epidemics, including those that may arise in the future' while eligible countries excluded the developed countries and other high income developing countries such as Barbados, Brunei, Cyprus, Hong Kong, Israel, Kuwait, Liechtenstein, Macao, Malta, Qatar, Singapore, Slovenia, Taiwan, and the United Arab Emirates, on the grounds that these countries have sufficient production capacity in the pharmaceutical sector or sufficient financial resources to address such public health problems without resorting to compulsory licences. See 'U.S. Announces Interim Plan to Help Poor Countries fight HIV/AIDS and other Health Crises in Absence of WTO Consensus', 20 December 2002, USTR at http://usinfo.state.gov/ei/Archive/2003/Dec/31–901735.html, accessed on 16 November 2007.

37. See ICTSD 'EU Initiative Seeks to Break Deadlock in TRIPs and Health Negotiations' *Bridges* Volume 7, No 1, 15 January 2003, available at www.ictsd.org/weekly/03-01-15/story1.htm, accessed on 26 November 2007.

38. Similar concerns were raised by the USTR at the time, Robert Zoellick in a press conference on 16 January 2003, quoted in 'WTO Reneges on Drug Patents: prescription for pain' by James Love in *Le Monde Diplomatique*, 3 March 2003.

39. Eric Noehrenberg of IFPMA also argued that high and mid-income developing countries such as Brazil, Argentina and Hungary had 'hijacked this process...have turned the debate away from AIDS drugs for poor countries, instead, trying to deform this process into promoting copies of all drugs for all countries, including industrialized countries. This debate has reached truly absurd proportions in the last weeks...' (Noehrenberg 2003: 380). See also remarks by USTR Robert Zoellick in the Media Round Table in Pretoria, South Africa on 13 January 2003: '...even though this was designed for countries...that didn't have the capacity to produce pharmaceuticals on their own, all of a sudden everyone else wants to get it too. OK? So Brazil and India and people who frankly may not have Africa's best interests at heart decide, well, we need to be able to get this'. These and other remarks are available at www.gov.mu/portal/sites/ncb/agoa/speech/roundtbl.doc, accessed on 10 March 2010.

40. See Communication from the European Communities and their Member States 'Paragraph 6 of the Doha Declaration on the TRIPs Agreement and Public Health' JOB(03)/9, 24 January 2003. The proposal mentioned coverage of 'at least HIV/AIDS, malaria, tuberculosis, yellow fever, plague, cholera, meningococcal disease...typhoid fever, typhus, measles, shigellosis, haemorrhagic fevers and arboviruses. When requested by a Member, the World Health Organization shall give its advice as to the occurrence in an importing Member, or the likelihood thereof, of any other public health problem'. The EU was trying to merge two proposals put forward last year, that is, the US proposal on the 23 diseases and another by the EU, that notifications under the solution should also be submitted to the WHO, although both had been rejected by developing countries. See ICTSD 'EU Initiative Seeks to Break Deadlock in TRIPs and Health Negotiations', *Bridges* Volume 7, No 1, 15 January 2003 available at www.ictsd.org/weekly/03-01-15/story1.htm, accessed on 26 November 2007. See ICTSD 'TRIPs Council Back at Square One on Medicines Issue', *Bridges*, Volume 7, No 4, 6 February 2003, available at www.ictsd.org/weekly/03-02-06/story2.htm, accessed on 18 December 2007.

41. For reaction by Campaign NGOs see, for instance, MSF's letter to Pascal Lamy on 14 January 2003, available at www.cptech.org/ip/wto/p6/msf01142003.html, accessed on 10 March 2010 and a joint statement by MSF, HAI and OXFAM 'Access to medicines in poor countries: How the EU is backtracking on its Doha commitments', 10 February 2003, available at www.cptech.org/ip/wto/p6/ngos02102003.html, accessed on 18 December 2007.

42. WHO officials claimed that Pascal Lamy (then EU Trade Commissioner) had not consulted WHO on this issue and that the WHO was strongly opposed to any limitation of diseases. See an interview with Germain Velasquez, WHO official, 'The European Union would like to give itself a good conscience' on 10 January 2003, available at www.cptech.org/ip/wto/p6/velasquez01102003.html, accessed on 18 December 2007; see also 'WTO

Tries to Break Deadlock on Medicines Access' by Frances Williams in *The Financial Times*, 10 March 2010.

43. Harvey Bale of the IFPMA according to ICTSD 'EU Initiative Seeks to Break Deadlock in TRIPs and Health Negotiations', *Bridges*, Volume 7, No 1, 15 January 2003, available at www.ictsd.org/weekly/03-01-15/story1.htm, accessed on 18 December 2007. Some industry sources also claimed that the proposal would 'basically wipe out protection for all drugs', quoted in 'WTO Tries to Break Deadlock on Medicines Access' by Frances Williams in *The Financial Times*, 28 January 2003.

44. See, for instance, a statement by the CPTech: 'US Government efforts to limit the scope of diseases in the implementation of the Doha Declaration on TRIPs and Public Health have outraged the public health community, and have been presented in a highly dishonest way by the White House and USTR, damaging US reputation abroad', 5 March 2003, Sign-On Letter to US Trade Representative Zoellick Circulated by Health GAP and Medecins Sans Frontières, 19 December 2002, MSF Statement 'Sell-out at WTO on Doha declaration?', 12 February 2003, all available at www.cptech.org/ip/wto/p6/#older, accessed on 10 March 2010. The USTR came under pressure from some Congressional Democrats to soften his stance on restricting the scope of diseases and urged respect for commitments undertaken at Doha. See 'Members of Congress urge broad compromise on TRIPs and public health', *WTO Reporter*, 19 February 2003.

45. See 'Tokyo Meeting Fails to Dislodge Impasse on TRIPs and Health', *Inside U.S. Trade*, 21 February 2003.

46. See 'No shift on drugs at trade talks – Industry chief', *Reuters*, 22 May 2003.

47. Some 22 US and European pharmaceutical companies and three trade associations eventually wrote to the USTR on 16 June 2003 about how these criteria were to be applied, in order to restrict the number of countries eligible to use the solution to least developed and some low-income developing countries. The text of the letter is available on http://lists.essential.org/pipermail/ip-health/2003-September/005213.html, accessed on 10 March 2010. See also ICTSD 'US Rumoured to Consider Change in Tactic on TRIPs and Health', *Bridges*, Volume 7, No 24, 3 July 2003, available at www.ictsd.org/weekly/03-07-03/story4.htm, accessed on 18 December 2007.

48. See 'Drug companies seek deal on medicine access', *The Washington Times*, 1 July 2003. See also 'Pharmaceutical Companies Close to New Joint Position on TRIPs', *Inside U.S. Trade*, 11 July 2003.

49. For instance USTR deputy Rosa Whitaker's letter of October 2002, mentioned above, as well as the US unilateral moratorium of December 2002, clearly showed that the US understood the solution to be aimed at poor and low-income countries only. One idea floated during negotiations in order to limit the solution to countries that lacked sufficient manufacturing capacities came from the US: this required devising a specific procedure to clarify which countries qualify. Reportedly, this idea was abandoned as sufficient data on manufacturing capacities across countries were not available (see GAO 2007). Although the EC negotiators interviewed (see also Vandoren and van Eeckhaute 2002) argued that the EC had never intended to limit the number of eligible importing countries, at least at one point during the negotiations, the EC did propose a complex solution to differentiate

between countries that had the capacity to produce active pharmaceutical ingredients from those that only had the capacity to use these ingredients into pharmaceutical formulations. See the EC non-paper 'Paragraph 6 of the Doha Declaration on the TRIPs Agreement and Public Health: Elements for a Compromise Solution', JOB(02)/157, also reprinted in *Inside U.S. Trade*, 1 November 2002.

50. See paragraph 1 of the Draft Decision of 16 December 2002, JOB (02)/217, available at www.cptech.org/ip/wto/p6/wto12162002.html, accessed on 10 March 2010.

51. Indeed, the progress on the Cancún Ministerial as a whole was held hostage to progress made on the TRIPs and compulsory licensing issue, although the issue was not part of the Ministerial Programme as such. Despite common concerns and general agreement about the need to restrict the solution as much as possible, individual pharmaceutical companies differed on how this should be achieved; some pharmaceutical actors were also worried that too uncompromising a stance against so many governments could prove to be counterproductive, especially given the symbiotic relation between pharmaceutical companies and governments (I16, I17 and I24, 2006).

52. The proposed statement reportedly stressed that delegations saw the system established by the paragraph 6 solution 'as being essentially designed to address national emergencies or other circumstances of extreme urgency' and that 'countries have recognised the need to avoid undermining the importance of intellectual property protection for the development of new medicines' (see ICTSD 'Last-Minute Attempt to Save TRIPs and Health Discussions' *Bridges*, Volume 7, No 5, 12 February 2003, available at www. ictsd.org/weekly/03-02-13/story2.htm, accessed on 19 December 2007). NGOs, and MSF in particular, criticised the statement as yet another attempt to renege on Doha and limit the solution to national emergencies rather than public health challenges in general (see MSF Statement 'Sell-out at WTO on Doha declaration?', 12 February 2002, available at www.cptech.org/ip/wto/ p6/msf02122003.html, accessed on 10 March 2010). Confusion also arose as to which parties had expressed willingness to accept the statement, with Chair Motta claiming that India or the African Group had accepted it and others discounting these claims (see Jamie Love 'Bad tempers in Geneva, who is telling the truth?', 12 February 2003, available at www.cptech.org/ ip/wto/p6/cptech02122003.html, accessed on 10 March 2010). The issue of the statement was not mentioned at all at the Tokyo mini-ministerial on 14–16 February 2003.

53. The Statement can be found in WTO General Council meeting minutes, WT/GC/M/82, 13 November 2003, as well as under document number JOB(03)177, available at www.cptech.org/ip/wto/p6/note-from-chairman. pdf, accessed on 10 March 2010. The countries that opted out were: Australia, Austria, Belgium, Canada, Denmark, Finland, France, Germany, Greece, Iceland, Ireland, Italy, Japan, Luxemburg, the Netherlands, New Zealand, Norway, Portugal, Spain, Sweden, Switzerland, the United Kingdom and the United States. Additionally, ten countries expecting to access to the EU agreed to use the system as importers only in cases of national or other extreme cases or urgency, upon which accession they would opt-out completely. These are: the Czech Republic, Cyprus, Estonia, Hungary, Latvia,

Lithuania, Malta, Poland, the Slovak Republic and Slovenia. Finally, fourteen other countries agreed to use the system only in cases of national emergency. These include high income developing countries: Hong Kong, China, Israel, Korea, Kuwait, Macao China, Mexico, Qatar, Singapore, the Separate Customs Territory of Taiwan Penghu Kinmen and Matsu, Turkey and the United Arab Emirates.

54. The Statement stressed again the need to prevent diversion of both generic drugs and active ingredients produced under the mechanism to the developed countries' markets. While Motta's December text had stated that special packaging should only be required 'provided that such distinction is feasible and does not have a significant impact on price', the Statement noted that members shared an understanding that 'in general special packaging and/or special colouring or shaping should not have a significant impact on the price of pharmaceuticals'. The statement also made reference to an attachment which included best practices followed by pharmaceutical companies (Novartis, Pfizer and Merck) in terms of countering the risk of diversion through special labelling, different packaging and colouring.

55. However, the opt-out was not a selfless act: by opting out as importers, developed countries were simply giving preference to their domestic generic producers as and when a compulsory licence would be issued to address a public health concern. This argument is valid mainly for the developed countries that opted out rather than for high-income developing countries and EU-accession countries which opted out under considerable pressure from the US and EC (I16 and I26, 2006). In any case, the decision to opt out was not discussed domestically or internationally and, given that the legal status of the Statement is unclear, many countries, developing and otherwise, have questioned whether they will be allowed to opt back in. This issue became particularly important with concerns over the risk of avian flu increasing from 2005 onwards (see 'Avian Flu Issues Could Arise at TRIPs Council Meeting', IP-Watch, 25 October 2005 and 'Pandemic Fears Raise Questions about WTO Health Waiver Opt-Out', *IP-Watch*, 27 October 2005, both available at www.ip-watch.org, accessed on 19 December 2007.

56. Research-based pharmaceutical companies' views on issues to be addressed by the Statement are clearly delineated in a letter sent to USTR Zoellick on 19 August 2003, available at http://lists.essential.org/pipermail/ip-health/2003-September/005213.html, accessed on 10 March 2010. According to James Love of CPTech, the final form of the Statement was also approved by Pfizer CEO Hank McKinnell and the office of Karl Rove, a close adviser of George W Bush's administration; see 'No gift to the poor: Strategies used by US and EC to protect big pharma in WTO TRIPs negotiations', 1 December 2005, available at http://workingagenda.blogspot.com/2005/12/no-gift-to-poor-strategies-used-by-us.html, accessed on 10 March 2010.

57. See 'The U.S. and Key States Reach WTO Drugs Pact' by Richard Waddington, *Reuters*, 27 August 2003 and 'WTO Members Expected to Agree on TRIPs and Health Pre-Cancun' ICTSD *Bridges*, Volume 7, No 29, 28 August 2003, available at www.ictsd.org/weekly/03-08-28/story2.htm, accessed on 19 December 2007.

58. See Minutes of the TRIPs Council Meeting held on 28 August 2003, IP/C/M/41.

59. Decision of the General Council, 30 August 2003, IP/C/W/405.
60. See Statement of the USTR Robert Zoellick on TRIPs and access to medicines on 30 August 2003, available at www.ustr.gov, accessed on 19 December 2007; the EU press release on 'Access to essential medicines: EU strongly welcomes WTO deal on generic medicines', Brussels, 30 August 2003, available at http://ec.europa.eu/trade/issues/global/medecine/medic010903_en.htm, accessed on 10 March 2010. For developing members' statements see Minutes of the WTO General Council Meeting held on 30 August 2003, WT/GC/M/82.
61. For industry's reaction, see EFPIA Statement on Compulsory Licensing for Export 'Paragraph 6' of the Doha Declaration on TRIPs and Public Health, 30 August 2003 and Statement from Herzfeld, PhRMA's Senior Vice President, International Affairs in relation to successful conclusion of the negotiations on TRIPs and Public Health, 30 August 2003. For reaction by Campaign NGOs, see Joint NGO Statement 'TRIPs and Public Health WTO Deal on Medicines: a "Gift" bound in red tape', 10 September 2003, MSF Statement 'Access to Medicines at the WTO: Countries Must Save Lives Before Celebrating Success', 11 September 2003, and MSF's 'Comments on the Draft Chairman's Statement of 21 August 2003', 26 August 2003, all available at www.cptech.org/ip/wto/p6/#older, accessed on 10 March 2010.
62. MSF (2006) 'Neither Expeditious nor a Solution: the WTO August 30 Decision is unworkable (An illustration through Canada's Jean Chrétien Pledge to Africa)'. The XVI International AIDS Conference, August 2006, Toronto, Canada, available at www.accessmed-msf.org/documents/WTOaugustreport.pdf, accessed on 12 February 2009.
63. Paragraph 11 of the Decision stated '... The TRIPs Council shall initiate by the end of 2003 work on the preparation of such an amendment with a view to its adoption within six months, on the understanding that the amendment will be based, where appropriate, on this Decision and on the further understanding that it will not be part of the negotiations referred to in paragraph 45 of the Doha Ministerial Declaration'.
64. See Minutes of the General Council Meeting on 30 August 2003 WT/GC/M/82, 13 November 2003. One of these countries, the Philippines, made a strong statement at the TRIPs Council Meeting on 28 August on its understanding of the Decision and accompanying Statement, which countered many of the requirements and language contained in these two documents with very flexible language and interpretation. Other countries like Brazil, India and Kenya also supported that position (although not on the record) and the negotiator came under a lot of pressure from the USTR, and eventually the Philippine Presidential Office, not to make any similar statement to the General Council meeting (I12, 2006).
65. See ICTSD 'TRIPs Council Shows Little Progress on Health and Biodiversity' *Bridges*, Volume 7, No 40, 26 November 2003, available at www.iprsonline.org/ictsd/news.htm, accessed on 10 March 2010.
66. See also the position of these members expressed in various TRIPs Council meetings, available at Minutes of the March 2005 meeting IP/C/M/47, June 2005 Meeting IP/C/M/48 and October and November 2005 meeting, IP/C/M/49.

67. See 'Implementation of Paragraph 11 of the 30 August 2003 Decision', Communication from Nigeria on behalf of the African Group, 29 November 2004, IP/C/W/437, 10 December 2004.

68. See 'Africa Group Proposes Amendment to TRIPs Agreement in Relation to Access to Medicines' *South North Development Bulletin*, 3 December 2004, available at www.twnside.org.sg/title2/twninfo177.htm, accessed on 10 March 2010. See also ICTSD 'TRIPs Council Considers Public Health, Biodiversity' *Bridges* Volume 8, No 42, 8 December 2004, available at www. ictsd.org/weekly/04-12-08/story1.htm, accessed on 21 December 2007.

69. As noted before, Kenya and the Philippines were particularly insistent that promises should be made by developed countries and the WTO Secretariat that their concerns would be dealt with fully during the amendment process, given the urgency of coming up with a expeditious solution (the waiver). The representative of Kenya publicly recalled these promises and the pressure before and during the Decision in the TRIPs Meeting of 31 March 2005, whereupon the US replied that it was unaware of such promises. See the TRIPs Council Meeting of 8–9 and 31 March 2005, IP/C/M/47, 3 June 2005.

70. For a public record of this position, see Comments on Implementation of the 30 August 2003 Agreement (Solution) on the TRIPs Agreement and Public Health, Communication from the United States, 9 March 2005, IP/C/ W/444, 18 March 2005.

71. See the Minutes of the TRIPs Council Meeting of 8–9 and 31 March 2005, IP/C/M/47, 3 June 2005. See also *IP-Watch* 'TRIPs Public Health Amendment Deadline Missed', 31 March 2005, available at www.ip-watch.org/weblog/index.php?p=37&res=800_ff&print=0, accessed on 10 March 2010.

72. See Draft Communication from the European Communities, Proposal for an Amendment of the TRIPs Agreement to Incorporate the Decision Implementing Paragraph 6 of the Doha Declaration on the TRIPs Agreement and Public Health, available at www.cptech.org/ip/wto/p6/ec-TRIPsamendmentproposal.html, accessed on 10 March 2010.

73. See 'African Countries Reject EU TRIPs Amendment' *Inside U.S. Trade*, 7 October 2005, available at http://lists.essential.org/pipermail/ip-health/2005-October/008373.html, accessed on 10 March 2010.

74. See Minutes of the TRIPs Council meetings during October and November 2005, IP/C/M/49.

75. The idea of rereading the Statement was floated by the TRIPs Council Chair in May 2005 and then again by the EC in June 2005, but the US and pharmaceutical companies insisted that such a procedure would amount to downgrading the legal status and weight of the Statement. See 'U.S. Cool to Compromise Aimed at Resolving TRIPs and Health Fight', *Inside U.S. Trade*, 27 May 2005 and 'WTO Members Make No Headway on TRIPs as EU Proposal Still Held Up' *Inside U.S. Trade*, 17 June 2005, both available at http://lists.essential.org/pipermail/ip-health/, accessed on 10 March 2010.

76. The full text of the 'choreography' can be found in 'Rushing through a "permanent solution" for TRIPs and Health, Third World Network, 9 December 2005, available from the CPTech website http://lists.essential.org/pipermail/ip-health/2005-December/008774.html, accessed on 10 March 2010.

77. See ICTSD 'Members Strike Deal on TRIPs and Public Health; Civil Society Unimpressed' *Bridges*, Volume 9, No 42, 7 December 2005, available at www. ictsd.org/weekly/05-12-07/story1.htm, accessed on 21 December 2007.
78. Joint Statement by 54 NGOs 'WTO Members Should Reject Bad Deal on Medicines', 3 December 2005, available at www.cptech.org/ip/wto/p6/ ngos12032005.html, accessed on 10 March 2010.
79. The Decision of the General Council, 6 December 2005, WT/L/64. The decision enters into force once two thirds of the WTO membership has formally accepted it.
80. See, for instance, the WTO press release 'Intellectual Property: Members OK Amendment to Make Health Flexibility Permanent', 6 December 2005, available at www.wto.org/english/news_e/pres05_e/pr426_e.htm,; EC press release 'EU welcomes permanent WTO solution on generic medicines', Brussels, 6 December 2005, available at http://europa.eu; USTR press release 'United States Welcomes Negotiations Leading to Positive Outcome on Enhancing Access to Medicines', 6 December 2005, available at www. ustr.org, IFPMA press release 'TRIPs Amendment Permanently Resolves Export Compulsory License Issue', 6 December 2005, available at www. ifpma.org/News/NewsReleaseDetail.aspx?nID=3951; Statement of CPTech on TRIPs amendment, 6 December 2005, available at www.cptech.org/ ip/wto/p6/cptech12062005.html; MSF press release 'Amendment to WTO TRIPs Agreement Makes Access to Affordable Medicines Even More Bleak', 6 December 2005, available at www.msf.org, all accessed on 10 March 2010.
81. Roberts, 'CAMR success?... Not exactly' Canada: Center for Intellectual Property Policy, July 2008, available at www.cipp.mcgill.ca/blog/category/ wto/, accessed on 13 February 2009.

6   Shifting IP Issues between Regimes and Fora: Contestations Continued

1. See the EU–Korea FTA text http://trade.ec.europa.eu/doclib/docs/2009/october/tradoc_145180.pdf, accessed on 24 March 2010.
2. Some US-led completed FTAs include: US–Jordan (2000), US–Morocco (2004), US–Bahrain (2004), US–Oman (2006), US–Peru (2006), US–Chile (2003), US–CAFTA (2004), US–Colombia (2006), US–Korea (2007), US–Panama (2006), US–Singapore (2003) and US–Australia (2004). More can be added if bilateral investment treaties (BITs) and bilateral (but not free trade) agreements are counted, such as those negotiated by the US with Vietnam, Cambodia and Laos (see Fink and Reichenmiller 2005).
3. One observation that can be made is that Singapore and Australia are not developing countries and, furthermore, have both opted out of the paragraph 6 Decision; nevertheless, limiting the grounds upon which these and other developed countries can issue compulsory licenses, including compulsory licenses for export to other countries experiencing public health problems, can have negative consequences for the ability of the developing countries that want to use the paragraph 6 mechanism in the future, as sources of generic pharmaceuticals produced under a compulsory licence are effectively being reduced.

4. This provision was added as an amendment at the request of Senator Kennedy, Senator Feinstein and Senator Feingold (CIEL 2007). US Congress guidance on negotiating objectives for trade agreements includes a provision 'to respect the Doha Declaration on the TRIPs Agreement and Public Health, adopted by the World Trade Organization (WTO)' 19 U.S.C. S.3802.

5. In addition, the USTR has also issued a side letter with most FTAs negotiated after the Declaration, which attempts to provide assurances that public health and access to medicines have been taken into account. Nevertheless, because they are not incorporated into the text of the FTA, the legal status of these letters is not clear. Some experts and civil society actors have argued that they have been issued simply to assuage Congressional concerns and have some clarification value, but they do not have the same legal weight as the 'TRIPs plus' obligations often imposed in the text of the agreement (see Oxfam Briefing Note 'Undermining access to medicines: Comparison of five US FTAs', June 2004, available at www.oxfam.org.uk/resources/policy/health/downloads/undermining_access_ftas.pdf, accessed on 24 March 2010, and Correa 2006b). USTR officials have commented on more than one occasion that side letters merely signal the belief of the parties that IP rules of the FTAs will not interfere with the protection of public health, but also that they do not create any kind of exception that would allow FTAs parties to ignore obligations undertaken in the FTA IP chapters (GAO 2007; Fink and Reichenmiller 2005).

6. These concerns have recently also been raised by certain US Congressional representatives; see, for instance, a report by the Committee on Government Reform – Minority Staff, of the US House of Representatives 'Trade Agreements and Access to Medicines under the Bush Administration' (Special Investigations Division) 1 June 2005, available at http://oversight.house.gov/documents/20050609094902-11945.pdf, accessed on 27 December 2007.

7. See EC (2005) 'A strategy for the enforcement of intellectual property rights in third countries', (2005/C 129/03), 26 May 2005, available at http://eurlex.europa.eu/LexUriServ/site/en/oj/2005/c_129/c_12920050526en00030016.pdf, accessed on 1 March 2010. The strategy was communicated in 2004 and there had been an earlier survey of IPRs infringements in 2003 (see 'Survey on the enforcement of intellectual property rights in third countries, July 2003, available at http://trade.ec.europa.eu/doclib/docs/2010/february/tradoc_145794.pdf, accessed on 1 March 2010).

8. See Enforcement Survey (2006), available at http://trade.ec.europa.eu/doclib/docs/2010/february/tradoc_145795.pdf, and Commission Staff Working Document, 'IPR Enforcement Report' (2009), available at http://trade.ec.europa.eu/doclib/docs/2009/october/tradoc_145204.pdf, both accessed on 1 March 2010.

9. See for instance, IP-Watch (31 January 2010) 'ACTA Negotiators Report No Breakthroughs On Transparency', available at www.ip-watch.org/weblog/2010/01/31/acta-negotiators-make-no-breakthroughs-on-transparency/, Electronic Frontier Foundation (undated) 'What is ACTA', available at www.eff.org/issues/acta, both accessed on 1 March 2010. For EC, see its dedicated webpage http://ec.europa.eu/trade/creating-opportunities/trade-topics/intellectual-property/anti-counterfeiting/, accessed on 1 March 2010.

10. South Bulletin, 'Seizures of Drugs in Transit: Why Europe's Law and Actions are Wrong', Issue 41, 22 September 2009, available at www.southcentre.org/index.php?option=com_content&view=arti cle&id=1073%3Asb41-a3&catid=144%3Asouth-bulletin-individual-articles&Itemid=287&lang=en; Third World Network, 'TRIPs 'Council takes up public health, TRIPs/CBD, drug seizure issues', SUNS 6806, 4 November 2009, available at www.twnside.org.sg/title2/health.info/2009/twnhealthinfo20091101.htm; Intellectual Property Watch, 'Drug Seizures In Frankfurt Spark Fears Of EU-Wide Pattern', 5 June 2009, available at www.ip-watch.org/weblog/2009/06/05/drug-seizures-in-frankfurt-spark-fears-of-eu-wide-pattern/; ICTSD Intellectual Property Programme, 'Brazil Slams EU for Seizure of Generic Drugs', Volume 13, No4, 4 February 2009, available at http://ictsd.org/i/news/bridgesweekly/39772/, all accessed on 1 March 2010.

11. See Compulsory Licensing Controversy in Thailand, a webpage maintained by Washington College of Law Program on Information Justice and Intellectual Property, containing all documents and statements regarding the Thai compulsory licensing experience, available at www.wcl.american.edu/pijip/thai_comp_licenses.cfm;, accessed on 1 March 2010. See also Flynn (2008).

12. For more information on the Novartis case, see the Novartis Lawsuit Against India's Patent Law dedicated webpage maintained by CPTech, available at www.cptech.org/ip/health/c/india/, accessed on 1 March 2010.

13. WHA (1999) Resolution WHA 52.19, 24 May 1999; WHA (2001) Resolutions WHA 54.10 and WHA 54.11, 21 May 2001.

14. See A56/17 'Intellectual property rights, innovation and public health', Report by the Secretariat, 12 May 2003, available at www.who.int/gb/ebwha/pdf_files/WHA56/ea5617.pdf, accessed on 27 December 2007.

15. See the WHA Resolution WHA56.27 of 28 May 2003 'Intellectual property rights, innovation and public health', available at www.who.int/gb/ebwha/pdf_files/WHA56/ea56r27.pdf, accessed on 27 December 2007.

16. WHA (2008) Report of the Intergovernmental Working Group on Public Health, Innovation and Intellectual Property, A61/9, 19 May 2008 available at www.who.int/gb/ebwha/pdf_files/A61/A61_9-en.pdf, accessed on 10 March 2010.

17. ECOSOC (UN Economic and Social Council) (2000) Sub Committee on the Promotion and Protection of Human Rights, Resolution 2000/7, UN Doc E/CN.4/Sub.2/RES/2000/9 (17 August 2000)

18. See, for instance, ECOSOC Sub-Committee on the Promotion and Protection of Human Rights (2001), Resolution 2001/21, E/CN.4/Sub.2/RES/2001/21 (16 August 2001) and CHR (Commission on Human Rights) (2003) Resolution 2003/29, E/CN.4/RES/2003/29, (22 April 2003).

Bibliography

Abbott, F. (1998) 'The enduring enigma of TRIPS: a challenge for the world economic system' *Journal of International Economic Law* 1(4): 497–521.

Abbott, F. (2006) 'The Cycle of Action and Reaction: Developments and Trends' in P. Roffe, G. Tansey and D. Vivas-Eugui (eds) *Intellectual Property and Health Negotiating Health: Intellectual Property and Access to Medicines* (London: Earthscan).

Abbott, F., T. Cottier and F. Gurry, (eds) (1999) *The International Intellectual Property System: Commentary and Materials*, Part I and II (London: Kluwer Law International).

Achilladelis, B. (1999) 'Innovation in the Pharmaceutical Industry' in R. Landau, B. Achilladelis and A. Scriabine (eds) *Pharmaceutical Innovation – Revolutionizing Human Health* (Philadelphia: Chemical Heritage Press).

Adede, A. O. (2003) 'Origins and History of the TRIPs Negotiations' in C. Bellmann, G. Dutfield and R. Melendez-Ortiz (eds) *Trading in Knowledge: Development Perspectives on TRIPs, Trade and Sustainability* (London and New York: Earthscan).

Anawalt, H. C. (2003) 'Intellectual Property Scope: International Intellectual Property, Progress, and the Rule of Law' in O. Granstrand (ed.) *Economics, Law and Intellectual Property: Seeking Strategies for Research and Teaching in a Developing Field* (London: Kluwer Academic Publishers).

Angell, M. (2004) *The Truth about the Drug Companies: How They Deceive Us and What to Do about It* (New York: Random House).

Aoki, K. (1994) 'Authors, inventors and trademark owners: private intellectual property and the public domain' *Columbia VLA Journal of the Law and Arts* 18: Part I 1–73; Part II 191–267.

Arrow, K. (1962) 'Economic Welfare and the Allocation of Resources for Invention' in R. Nelson (ed.) *The Rate and Direction of Inventive Activity: Economic and Social Factors* (Princeton, NJ: Princeton University Press).

Arrow, K. (1996) 'The economics of information: an exposition' *Empirica* 23(2): 119–128.

Attaran, A. (2004) 'How do patents and economic policies affect access to essential medicines in developing countries?' *Health Affairs* 23(2): 155–166.

Attaran, A. and J. Sachs (2001) 'Defining and refining international donor support for combating the AIDS pandemic' *The Lancet* 357(9249): 57–61.

Attaran, A. and L. Gillespie-White (2001) 'Do patents for anti-retroviral drugs constrain access to aids treatment in Africa?' *Journal of the American Medical Association* 286: 1886–1892.

Bale, H. E. (1998) 'The conflicts between parallel trade and product access and innovation: the case of pharmaceuticals' *Journal of International Economic Law* 1(4): 637–653.

Ballance, R., J Pogany and H. Forstner (1992) *The Worlds Pharmaceutical Industries: an International Perspective on Innovation, Competition and Policy* (Aldershot: Edward Elgar).

Benkler, Y. (2001) 'A Political Economy of the Public Domain: Markets in Information Goods versus the Marketplace of Ideas' in R. C. Dreyfuss, D. L. Zimmerman and H. First (eds) *Explaining the Boundaries of Intellectual Property: Innovation Policy for the Knowledge Society* (Oxford: Oxford University Press).

Berger, J. M. (2002) 'Tripping over patents: AIDS, access to treatment and the manufacturing of scarcity' *Connecticut Journal of International Law* 17(Spring): 157–233.

Bhagwati, J. (2002) 'Afterword: the question of linkage' *The American Journal of International Law* 96(1): 126–134.

Bieler A. and Morton A. (2001) 'The gordian knot of agency—structure in international relations: a neo-gramscian perspective' *European Journal of International Relations* 7 (1): 5–35.

Blakeney, M. (2006) 'A Critical Analysis of the TRIPs Agreement' in M. P. Pugatch (ed.) *The Intellectual Property Debate: Perspectives from Law, Economics and Political Economy* (Cheltenham: Edward Elgar).

Borrus, M. (2002) *The Global Pharmaceutical Market* (Berkley: University of California Press).

Bourdieu, P. (1987) 'The force of law: towards a sociology of the juridical field' *Hastings Law Journal* 38(July): 805–853.

Boyle, J. (1996) *Shamans, Software, and Spleens: Law and the Construction of the Information Society* (Cambridge, MA: Harvard University Press).

Boyle, J. (2003) 'The second enclosure movement and the construction of the public domain' *Law and Contemporary Problems* 66: 33–74

Braga, C. A. and C. Fink (1997) 'The Economic Justifications for the Grant of Intellectual Property Rights: Patterns of Convergence and Conflict', reprinted in (1999) F. Abbott, T. Cottier and F. Gurry (eds) *The International Intellectual Property System: Commentary and Materials*, Part One (London: Kluwer Law International).

Braithwaite, J. and P. Drahos (2000) *Global Business Regulation* (Cambridge: Cambridge University Press).

Braudel, F. (1981) *The Structures of Everyday Life: The Limits of the Possible* (London: Routledge and Kegan Paul).

Chew, R., G. T. Smith and N. Wells (1985) *Pharmaceuticals in Seven Nations* (London: Office of Health Economics).

CIEL (2007) 'Putting Health on the Fast Track: Compliance with the Doha Declaration on Public Health as a Principal Negotiating Objective for Trade Promotion Authority' The Centre for International Environment Law, Geneva, Switzerland.

Clement, N. C., G. C. Vera, J. Gerber, W. A. Kerr, A. J. MacFadyen, S. Shedd, E. Zepeda and D. Alarcon (1999) *North-American Economic Integration – Theory and Practice* (Cheltenham: Edward Elgar Press).

CMR (Centre for Medicines Research) (2010) *The CMR International Pharmaceutical R&D Factbook* (Chicago: Thomson Reuters)

Cohen, A. D. (1998) 'Exceptions to Experimental Use and Limited Patent Term Extension in Israel' *Patent World* May/June: 24–27.

Cooper, H., R. Zimmerman and L. McGinley (2001) 'Patents Pending: AIDS Epidemic Traps Drug Firms in a Vice: Treatments vs. Profits' *Wall Street Journal* New York, 2 March 2001.

Correa, C. (2002) 'Implications of the Doha Declaration on the TRIPS agreement and public health' World Health Organisation, Geneva, Switzerland.

Correa, C. (2006b) 'Implications of bilateral free trade agreements on access to medicines' *WHO Bulletin*, 84(5).

Cottier, T. (1991) 'The prospects for intellectual property in GATT' *Common Law Market Review* 28: 383–414.

CPTech, Essential Action, Oxfam, Treatment Access Campaign and Health Gap (2001) 'Comment on the Attaran/Gillespie-White and PhRMA Surveys of Patents on Antiretroviral Drugs in Africa', http://wwwcptechorg/ip/health/africa/dopatentsmatterinafricahtml, date accessed 10 October 2007.

Danzon P. and A. Towse (2003) 'Differential Pricing for pharmaceuticals: reconciling access, R&D and Patents' *International Journal of Health Care Finance and Economics*, 3, 183–205.

Danzon, P. (2000) 'The Pharmaceutical Industry' in B. Bouckaert and G. de Geest (eds) *The Encyclopaedia of Law and Economics* (Cheltenham: Edward Elgar).

Danzon, P. and E. Keuffel (2005) 'Regulation of the Pharmaceutical Industry National Bureau on Economic Research' paper presented at Conference on Regulation, 9–10 September, Cambridge, Massachusetts, USA.

Danzon, R., A. Epstein and S. Nicholson (2003) 'Mergers and Acquisitions in the Pharmaceutical and Biotech Industries' paper presented at the Organizational Economics of Health Care Conference, http://ssrncom/abstract=468301, date accessed 8 June 2007.

Destler, I. M. (1992) *American Trade Politics* (New York: Institute for International Economics and the Twentieth Century Fund).

DiMasi, J. A., R. W. Hansen, H. G. Grabowski and L. Lasagna (1991) 'Cost of innovation in the pharmaceutical industry' *Journal of Health Economics* 10: 107–142.

DiMasi, J. A., R. W. Hansen and H. G. Grabowski (2003) 'The Price of Innovation: new estimates of drug development costs' *Journal of Health Economics* 22: 151–185.

Drahos, P. (1995) 'Global property rights in information: the story of TRIPS at the GATT' *Prometheus* 13(1): 6–19.

Drahos, P. (1996) *A Philosophy of Intellectual Property* (Aldershot: Ashgate).

Drahos, P. (1997) 'Thinking strategically about intellectual property rights' *Telecommunications Policy* 21(3): 201–211.

Drahos, P. (2001) 'BITs and BIPs: bilateralism in intellectual property' *Journal of World Intellectual Property* 4(6): 791–808.

Drahos, P. (2002) 'Developing countries and international intellectual property standard-setting' *Journal of World Intellectual Property* 5: 765–789.

Drahos, P. (2003) 'Expanding Intellectual Property's Empire: the role of FTAs' Regulatory Institutions Network, Australian National University, Australia.

Drahos, P. (2004) 'Trading in public hope' *Annals of the American Academy of Political and Social Science* 592: 18–38.

Drahos, P. (2007) 'Four lessons for developing countries from the trade negotiations over access to medicines' *Liverpool Law Review* 28: 11–39.

Drahos, P. and J. Braithwaite (2002) *Informational Feudalism: Who Owns the Knowledge Economy?* (London: Earthscan).

Dreyfuss, R. C. and A. F. Lowenfeld (1997) 'Two achievements of the Uruguay Round: putting TRIPs and dispute settlement together' *Virginia Journal of International Law* 37(2): 268–333.

Dutfield, G. (2003a) *Intellectual Property and the Life Sciences Industries: a Twentieth Century History* (Aldershot, UK: Dartmouth Publishing).

Dutfield, G. (2003b) 'Trading in Knowledge: Introduction' in C. Bellmann, G. Dutfield and R. Melendez-Ortiz (eds) *Trading in Knowledge: Development Perspectives on TRIPs, Trade and Sustainability* (London and New York: Earthscan).

Dutfield, G. and U. Suthersanen (2004) 'Harmonisation or Differentiation in Intellectual Property Protection? The Lessons of History' Quakers United Nations Office, Occasional Paper 15, Geneva, Switzerland.

EC (2001) Fourth Stakeholders Meeting on Trade and Access to Medicine (Brussels, Belgium).

EC (2009) The Pharmaceutical Sector Inquiry Report, DG Competition, available at http://ec.europa.eu/competition/sectors/pharmaceuticals/inquiry/communication_en.pdf, accessed on 10 March 2010

EFPIA (1999) 'Position Statement – Taiwan: Trade Barriers to International Pharmaceuticals', European Federation of Pharmaceutical Industries and Associations, September 1999, Brussels, Belgium, www.efpia.org (home page) date accessed 25 August 2007.

EFPIA (2001a) 'Five Common Misunderstandings about Patents, TRIPs, Compulsory Licensing, Paralell Trade and Local Production Brussels', European Federation of Pharmaceutical Industries and Associations, September 2001 http://wwwefpiaorg/Content/Defaultasp?PageID=179, date accessed 25 August 2007.

EFPIA (2001b) 'Pharmaceutical Industry Statement Regarding Doha Politics Declaration on TRIPs Agreement and Public Health' 14th November, Brussels, Belgium, www.efpia.org (home page) date accessed 25 August 2007.

EFPIA (2004) 'Annual Report Brussels, European Federation of Pharmaceutical Industries and Associations', European Federation of Pharmaceutical Industries and Associations, Brussels, Belgium, www.efpia.org (home page) date accessed 25 August 2007.

EFPIA (2009) 'Pharmaceutical Industry in Figures: 2009 update', European Federation of Pharmaceutical Industries and Associations, Brussels, Belgium, http://www.efpia.eu (home page) date accessed 10 March 2010.

Elliot, L. and C. Denny (2002) 'US Wrecks Cheap Drugs Deal: Cheney's Intervention Blocks Pact to Help Poor Countries After Pharmaceutical Firms Lobby White House' *The Guardian* 21 December 2002, UK.

El Said, M. (2007) 'The European TRIPs-Plus model and the Arab world: from co-operation to association – a new era in the global IPRs regime?' *Liverpool Law Review* 28: 143–174.

Emmert, F. (1990) 'Intellectual property in the Uruguay round – negotiating strategies of the western industrialized countries' *Michigan Journal of International Law* 11(Summer): 1317–1399.

Enyart, J. (1990) 'A GATT Intellectual property code' *Les Nouvelles* (25 June): 53–56.

European Council (2000) Lisbon European Council Meeting: Presidency Conclusions, 23–24 March 2000, Lisbon, Portugal.

Fidler, D. (2004) *SARS, Governance and the Globalization of Disease* (Basingstoke: Palgrave).

Finger, J. M. and P. Schuler (2000) 'Implementation of Uruguay round agreements: the development challenge' *World Economy* 23(4): 511–525.

Fink, C. and P. Reichenmiller (2005) 'Tightening TRIPs: the Intellectual Property Provisions of Recent US Free Trade Agreements', World Bank, International Trade Department, Trade Note, February 2005.

Fisher, R. (1999) 'Technological Progress and American Rights: Trade Policy and Intellectual Property Protection', Testimony of Deputy USTR, Subcommittee on International Economic Policy and Trade House Committee on International Relations, 13 October, Washington DC, USA.

Fisk, C. (2003) 'Authors at work: the origins of the work-for-hire doctrine' *Yale Journal of Law and Humanities* 15: 1–69.

Flynn, M. (2008) 'Brazil's Use of Compulsory Licenses for AIDS Medicines' Paper presented on the American Sociological Association Annual Meeting Sheraton, 31 July 2008, Boston, USA.

Ford, J. (2002) 'A social theory of trade regime change: GATT to WTO' *International Studies Review* 4(3): 115–138.

Fortune (2009) Fortune 500-Pharmaceuticals http://money.cnn.com/magazines/fortune/global500/2009/industries/21/index.html, date accessed 10 March 2010.

Gadbaw, R. and T Richards, (eds) (1988) *Intellectual Property Rights: Global Consensus, Global Conflict?* (Boulder CO: Westview).

Gale, F. (1998) 'Cave 'Cave! Hic Dragone's': a neo-Gramscian Deconstruction and reconstruction of international regime theory' *Review of International Political Economy* 5(2): 252–283.

GAO (2007) 'Intellectual Property: US Trade Policy Guidance on WTO Declaration on Access to Medicines May Need Clarification', United States Government Accountability Office, GAO-07-1198, Washington DC, USA.

GATT (1986) *Punta del Este Ministerial Declaration*, GATT BISD (33d supplement), Geneva, Switzerland.

Goozner, M. (2004) *The $800 million Pill: the Truth about the Cost of New Drugs* (Berkeley, California: University of California Press).

Gorlin, J. (1999) An analysis of the pharmaceutical-related provisions of the WTO TRIPS (Intellectual Property Agreement), Intellectual Property Institute, London, UK, www.ip-institute.org.uk/ (home page) date accessed 10 March 2010.

Gould, D. M. and W. C. Gruben (1996) 'The role of intellectual property rights in economic growth' *Journal of Development Economics* 48(2): 323–350.

Grabowski, H. and J. Vernon (1992) 'Brand loyalty, entry and price competition in pharmaceuticals after the 1984 Drug Act' *Journal of Law and Economics* 35(2): 331–350.

Haas, E. B. (1980) 'Why collaborate? issue-linkage and international regimes' *World Politics* 32(3): 357–405.

Haggard, S. and B. A. Simmons (1987) 'Theories of international regimes' *International Organization* 41(3): 491–517.

Hall, P. (1986) *Political Power of Economics Ideas* (Princeton, NJ: Princeton University Press).

Halliday, F. (2001) 'The Romance of Non-State Actors' in D. Josselin and W. Wallace (eds) *Non-State Actors in World Politics* (Basingstoke: Palgrave).

Hasenclever, A., P. Mayer and V. Rittberger (1997) *Theories of International Regimes* (Cambridge: Cambridge University Press).

Hasenclever, A., P. Mayer and V. Rittberger (2000) 'Integrating theories of international regimes' *Review of International Studies* 26: 3–36.

Hein, W. and L. Kohlmorgen (2007) 'Transnational Norm-Building in Global Health: The Important Role of Non-State Actors in Post-Westphalian Politics' in MacLean S, Brown S and Fourie P (eds) *Health for Some: The Political Economy of Global Health Governance* (Basingstoke: Palgrave MacMillan).

Helfer, L. R. (2004) 'Regime shifting: the TRIPs agreement and new dynamics of international intellectual property lawmaking' *Yale Journal of International Law* 29(Winter): 1–83.

Henderson, E. (1997) 'TRIPs and the Third World: the example of pharmaceutical patents in India' *European Intellectual Property Review* 11(November): 651–663.

Hettinger, E. C. (1997) 'Justifying Intellectual Property' in A. D. Moore (ed.) *Intellectual Property: Moral, Legal and International Dilemmas* (Oxford: Rowman & Littlefield Publishers).

Hindley, B. (2006) 'The TRIPs Agreement: The Damage to the WTO' in M. P. Pugatch (ed.) *The Intellectual Property Debate: Perspectives from Law, Economics and Political Economy* (Cheltenham UK: Edward Elgar).

Hoekman, B. M. (1993) 'New issues in the Uruguay Round and beyond' *The Economic Journal* 103(421): 1528–1539.

Hoekman, B. M. and M. M. Kosteci (1995) *The Political Economy of the World Trading System* (Oxford: Oxford University Press).

Howse, R. (2002) 'From politics to technocracy-and back again: the fate of the multilateral trading regime' *The American Journal of International Law* 96(1): 94–117.

Hudec, R. E. (1991) *Enforcing International Trade Law: the Evolution of the Modern GATT Legal System* (New Hampshire: Butterworth Legal Publishers).

Hughes, J. (1997) 'The Philosophy of Intellectual Property' in A. Moore (ed.) *Intellectual Property: Moral, Legal and International Dilemmas* (Oxford: Rowman & Littlefield Publishers).

I1 (2006) Trade negotiator of the Permanent Mission of Kenya to the United Nations Office and other International Organizations in Geneva, interviewed on 13th July, Geneva, Switzerland.

I2 (2006) Official in the South Centre Trade and Development Programme, interviewed on 17th July, Geneva, Switzerland.

I3 (2006) Trade negotiator of the Permanent Mission of Brazil to the United Nations Office and other International Organizations in Geneva, interviewed on 17th July, Geneva, Switzerland.

I4 (2006) Trade negotiator of the Permanent Mission of India to the United Nations Office and other International Organizations in Geneva, Geneva, interviewed on 12th July, Geneva, Switzerland.

I5 (2006) Two legal officers, UNCTAD, Technology Transfer and Intellectual Property Section, Geneva, interviewed on 14th July, Geneva, Switzerland.

I6 (2006) Representative of Intellectual Property Watch, Geneva, interviewed on 13th July, Geneva, Switzerland.

I7 (2006) Official of the WTO TRIPs Council, WTO, Geneva, interviewed on 14th February, Geneva, Switzerland.

I8 (2006) MSF officer of the 'Access to Medicines' Campaign, MSF Brussels, Interviewed on 20th June, Brussels, Belgium.

I9 (2006) Oxfam officer of the 'Cut the Cost of Medicines' Campaign, phone interview on 8th May.

I10 (2006) WHO official from the Department of Essential Drugs and Medicines Policy, WHO, Geneva, interviewed on 10th February, Geneva, Switzerland.

I11 (2006) Trade negotiator from the US Permanent Mission to the United Nations Office and other International Organizations in Geneva, interviewed on 14th July, Geneva, Switzerland.

I12 (2006) Former Philippine trade negotiator, the Permanent of the Philippines to the United Nations Office and other International Organizations in Geneva, interviewed on 18th July, Geneva, Switzerland.

I13 (2006) Officer of the Quakers United Nation Office (QUNO), QUNO Geneva Office, interviewed on 11th July, Geneva, Switzerland.

I14 (2006) Official in the South Centre Programme on Intellectual Property, Geneva, interviewed on 15th February, Geneva, Switzerland.

I15 (2006) Interview with an official (1) from the EC DG Trade, the EC Commission, Brussels, interviewed on 21st June, Brussels, Belgium.

I16 (2006) Representative of the International Federation of Pharmaceutical Manufacturers Association (IFMPA) in Geneva, interviewed on 6th February, Geneva, Switzerland.

I17 (2006) Official from the European Federation of Pharmaceutical Industries Association (EFPIA), Brussels, interviewed on 22nd June, Brussels, Belgium.

I18 (2006) Representative of the IP Working Group of UNICE, Brussels, telephone interview on 26th June.

I19 (2007) Representative of CPTech NGO (US), interviewed on 19th February, Geneva, Switzerland.

I20 (2006) Official (2) EC DG Trade, Brussels, interviewed on 21st June, Brussels, Belgium.

I21 (2006) Official of the European Generic Medicines Association (EGA), Brussels, phone interview on 13th June.

I22 (2007) Consultant for the Geneva Quakers United Nations Office (QUNO) UK, phone interview on 15th November.

I23 (2006) Representative of MSF, UK, email exchanges throughout 2006.

I24 (2006) Trade negotiator from the Permanent Mission of South Africa to the United Nations Office and other International Organizations in Geneva, interviewed on 18th July, Geneva, Switzerland.

I25 (2006) Official (3) EC DG Trade, Brussels, interviewed on 17th June, Brussels, Belgium.

I26 (2006) Former Indian trade negotiator, interviewed on 13th February Geneva, Switzerland.

I27 (2006) Trade negotiator from the Permanent Mission of Japan to the United Nations Office and other International Organizations in Geneva, interviewed on 7th February, Geneva, Switzerland.

I28 (2006) Trade negotiator from the Permanent Mission of the Philippines to the United Nations Office and other International Organizations in Geneva, interviewed on 17th July, Geneva, Switzerland.

I29 (2009) Official EC DG Trade, Brussels, interviewed on 18th April, Brussels, Belgium.

ICTSD (2005) 'WIPO Development Agenda Status Unclear', *Bridges* (September/October), No. 9: 22.

IFPMA (1995) 'GATT TRIPS and the Pharmaceutical Industry: a Review' International Federation of Pharmaceutical Manufacturers and Associations, Geneva, Switzerland, www.ifpma.org (home page) date accessed 10 August 2007.

IFPMA (1999) 'IFPMA position paper: WTO Millennium Round' International Federation of Pharmaceutical Manufacturers and Associations, Geneva, Switzerland, www.ifpma.org (home page) date accessed 10 August 2007.

IFPMA (2006) 'IFPMA commentary on Oxfam's report "Patents versus Patients: Five Years after the Doha Declaration"' International Federation of Pharmaceutical Manufacturers and Associations, Geneva, Switzerland http://www.ifpma.org/News/NewsReleaseDetailaspx?nID=6097 date accessed 25 August 2007.

IMS (2009) 'Generic Medicines: Essential contributors to the long-term health of society' available at http://www.imshealth.com/imshealth/Global/Content/Document/Market_Measurement_TL/Generic_Medicines_GA.pdf, accessed on 10 February 2009.

IMS (23 June 2004) 'Generics flourish as innovation stalls' IMS Health, www.imshealth.com (home page) date accessed 10 March 2010.

Interpat (2000) 'Submissions on Behalf of INTERPAT Concerning Proposals Affecting the Patent System in the Interim Report of the Intellectual Property and Competition Review Committee Canberra' , Intellectual Property and Competition Review Committee, IP Australia, Government of Australia: 1–7, http://wwwipaustraliagovau/pdfs/ipcr/Sub11pdf date accessed 4 October 2007.

IPC (1994) 'Views of the Intellectual Property Committee on the Uruguay Round Intellectual Property (TRIPs) Agreement' Intellectual Property Committee, April 1994, Washington DC, USA.

Jawara, F. and A. Kwa (2004) *Behind the Scenes at the WTO: the Real World of International Trade Negotiations* (London and Bangkok: Zed Books and Focus on the Global South).

Jungmittag, A. and G. Reger (2000) 'Dynamics of the Markets and Market Structure' in A. Jungmittag, G. Reger and T. Reiss (eds) *Changing Innovation in the Pharmaceutical Industry: Globalization and New Ways of Drug Development* (Berlin: Springer).

Kantor, M. (2005) 'US Free Trade Agreements and Public Health' Submission to the WHO Commission on Intellectual Property Rights, Innovation and Public Health (CIPIH), Geneva, Switzerland, www.who.int (home page) date accessed 21 December 2007.

Kaplan, W. and R. Laing (2005) 'Local Production of Pharmaceuticals: Industrial Policy and Access to Medicines' The World Bank, New York, USA, http://siteresourcesworldbankorg/HEALTHNUTRITIONANDPOPULATION/Resources/281627-1095698140167/KaplanLocalProductionFinalpdf, date accessed 10 November 2007.

Katzenberger, P. and A. Kur (1996) 'TRIPs and Intellectual Property' in F. K. Beier and G. Schricker (eds) *From GATT to TRIPs – The Agreement on Trade-Related Aspects of Intellectual Property Rights* (Munich: The Max Planck Institute for Foreign and International Patent, Copyright and Competition Law).

Keeley, J. F. (1990) 'Toward a Foucauldian analysis of international regimes' *International Organization* 44(1): 83–105.

Kinsella, N. S. (2001) 'Against intellectual property' *Journal of Libertarian Studies* 15(2): 1–53.

Kongolo, T. (2001) 'Public interests versus the pharmaceutical industry's monopoly in South Africa' *Journal of World Intellectual Property* 4(5): 609–627.

Krasner, S. D. (1982) 'Structural causes and regime consequences: regimes as intervening variables' *International Organization* 36: 185–205.

Kratochwil, F. and J. Ruggie (1986) 'International organisation: a state of the art on an art of the state' *International Organization* 40: 753–775.

Kuhlik, B. N. (2004) 'The assault on pharmaceutical intellectual property' *The University of Chicago Law Review* 71(1): 93–109.

Labonté, R., C. Blouin and L. Forman (2009) 'Trade and Health' in A. Kay and O. D. Williams (eds) *Global Health Governance: Crisis, Institutions and Political Economy* (Basingstoke: Palgrave Macmillan).

Lang, A. T. (2006) 'Reconstructing embedded liberalism: John Gerard Ruggie and constructivist approaches to the study of the international trade regime' *Journal of International Economic Law* 9(1): 81–116.

Leebron, D. W. (2002) 'Linkages' *The American Journal of International Law* 96(1): 5–27.

Levy, C. S. (2000) 'Implementing TRIPs – a test of political will' *Law and Policy in International Business* 31(3): 789–795

Levy, D. and D. Egan (2003) 'A neo-Gramscian approach to corporate political strategy: conflict and accommodation in the climate change negotiations' *Journal of Management Studies* 40(4): 803–829.

Levy, D. and P. J. Newell (2005) 'A Neo-Gramscian Approach to Business in International Environmental Politics: an Interdisciplinary, Multilevel Framework' in D. Levy and P. J. Newell (eds) *The Business of Global Environmental Governance* (Cambridge, MA: The MIT Press).

Levy, M. A., O. R. Young and M. Zürn (1995) 'The study of international regimes' *European Journal of International Relations* 1(3): 267–330.

Lipson, C. (1982) 'The transformation of trade: the sources and effects of regime change' *International Organization* 36(2): 417–455.

Love, J. (2001) 'Intellectual Property Rights and the South African Medicines Act' Paper presented at the Symposium on Intellectual Property, Development, and Human Rights. University of Florida Frederic G. Levin College of Law, March 24.

Lu, Z. J. and W. S. Comanor (1998) 'Strategic pricing of new pharmaceuticals' *The Review of Economics and Statistics* 80(1): 108–118.

Macdonald, S. (2002) 'Exploring the Hidden Costs of Patents' in P. Drahos and R. Mayne (eds) *Global Intellectual Property Rights: Knowledge Access and Development* (Basingstoke: Palgrave MacMillan).

Machlup, F. (1958) 'An Economic Review of the Patent System', reprinted in (1999) F. Abbott, T. Cottier and F. Gurry (eds) *The International Intellectual Property System: Commentary and Materials, Part One* (London: Kluwer Law International).

Mansfield, E. (1986) 'Patents and innovation: an empirical study' *Management Science* 32(2): 173–181.

Martin, W. and L. A. Winters (eds) (1996) *The Uruguay Round and the Developing Countries* (Cambridge: Cambridge University Press).

Maskus, K. (2000) 'Intellectual Property Rights in the Global Economy' Institute for International Economics, Washington DC, USA.

Maskus, K. (ed.) (2004) *The WTO, Intellectual Property Rights and the Knowledge Economy* (Cheltenham, UK: Edward Elgar).

Maskus, K. and J. Reichman (2004) 'The globalization of private knowledge goods and the privatization of global public goods' *Journal of International Economic Law* 7(2): 279–320.

Maskus, K. E. (2001) 'Parallel Imports in Pharmaceuticals: Implications for Competition and Prices in Developing Countries' Final Report to World Intellectual Property Organization (Geneva, Switzerland).

Matsushita, M. (1992) 'A Japanese perspective on intellectual property rights and the GATT' *Columbia Business Law Review* 79: 81–95.

Matthews, D. (2002a) *Globalising Intellectual Property Rights: the TRIPs Agreement* (London and New York: Routledge).

Matthews, D. (2002b) 'Trade-Related Aspects of Intellectual Property Rights: will the Uruguay Round consensus hold?' Centre for the Study of Globalisation and Regionalisation CSGR Working Paper (99/02).

Matthews, D. (2004) 'WTO decision on implementation of Paragraph 6 of the Doha Declaration on the TRIPs agreement and public health: a solution to the access to medicines problem?' *Journal of International Economic Law* 7(1): 73–107.

Matthews, D. (2006) 'NGOs, Intellectual Property Rights and Multilateral Institutions' Queen Mary Intellectual Property Research Institute, London, UK.

Matthews, D. and V. Munoz-Tellez (2006) 'Bilateral technical assistance and TRIPs: the United States, Japan and the European communities in comparative perspective' *Journal of World Intellectual Property* 9(6): 629–653.

May, C. (2000) *A Global Political Economy of Intellectual Property Rights: the New Enclosures?* (London and New York: Routledge).

May, C. and S. K. Sell (2006) *Intellectual Property Rights: a Critical History* (London: Lynne Reinner Publishers).

McCalman, P. (2001) 'Reaping what you sow: an empirical analysis of international Patent Harmonization' *International Economics* 55: 161–186.

Morin, J. F. (2006) 'Tripping up TRIPs debates: IP and health in bilateral agreements' *The International Journal of Intellectual Property Management* 1(1/2): 37–53.

Mossinghoff G. J. (1991) 'Pharmaceutical research is expensive but well worth the cost' *Endocrinology* 128(1):3–4.

Mossinghoff, G. and T. Bombelles (1996) 'The importance of intellectual property protection to the American research-intensive pharmaceutical industry' *The Columbia Journal of World Business* (Spring): 39–48.

Mossoff, A. (2001) 'Rethinking the development of patents: an intellectual history 1550–1800' *Hastings Law Journal* 52(August): 1255–1322.

Moynihan, R. and R. Smith (2002) 'Too much medicine? almost certainly' *British Medical Journal* 324: 859–860.

MSF (2001a) 'Statement by MSF on TRIPs and Affordable Medicines' TRIPs Council Session on Access to Medicines, 18th September, Geneva, Switzerland, http://wwwaccessmed-msforg/prod/publicationsasp?scntid=19920011011399&contenttype=PARA&, date accessed 6 November 2007.

MSF (2001b) 'Green Light to Put Public Health First at WTO Ministerial Conference in Doha', Joint Statement by MSF, Oxfam, Third World Network, CPTech and Consumers International, 14th November, http://wwwaccessmed-msforg/prod/publicationsasp?scntid=141120011626104&contenttype=PARA&, date accessed 4 November 2007.

MSF (2003) 'Reneging on Doha' Report, Medicins sans Frontieres, Brussels, Belgium.

MSF (2006) 'Neither Expedious nor a Solution: the WTO August 30th Decision is unworkable' (An illustration through Canada's Jean Chrétien Pledge to Africa)

The XVI International AIDS Conference, August 2006, Toronto, Canada, http://wwwaccessmed-msforg/documents/WTOaugustreportpdf, date accessed 28 August 2007.

MSF, HAI and CPTech (1999a) 'An Open Letter to WTO Member States' November 8th, http://listsessentialorg/pharm-policy/msg00291html, date accessed 26 August 2007.

MSF, HAI and CPTech (1999b) 'Amsterdam Statement to WTO Member States on Access to Medicine' November 25–26, http://wwwcptechorg/ip/health/amsterdamstatementhtml, date accessed 26 August 2007.

Murumba, S. (1998) 'Globalizing intellectual property: linkage and the challenge of a justice-constituency' *University of Pennsylvania Journal of International Economic Law*, (Summer) Symposium: Linkage as a Phenomenon, 435–460.

Musungu, S. and G. Dutfield (2003) 'Multilateral Agreement and a TRIPs-plus World: the World Intellectual Property Organisation (WIPO)', Issue Paper 3 QUNO and QIAP, Geneva and Ottawa.

Noehrenberg, E, (2003) 'TRIPs, the Doha Declaration and public health' *Journal of World Intellectual Property* 6(2): 379–383.

Noehrenberg, E. (2004) 'Intellectual property and public health: will it be peace or war' *Journal of World Intellectual Property* 7(2): 253–256.

Nogués, J. (1990) 'Patents and Pharmaceutical Drug – Understanding the Pressures on Developing Countries' PRP Working Papers, World Bank, Washington DC, USA.

Okediji, R. (2003) 'Public welfare and the role of the WTO: reconsidering the TRIPs agreement' *Emory International Law Review* 17(2): 819–918.

Okediji, R. (2004) 'Back to bilateralism? pendulum swings in international intellectual property protection' *University of Ottawa Law and Technology Journal* 1: 125–147.

Ostergard, R. L. (1999) 'The political economy of the South Africa-United States patent dispute' *Journal of World Intellectual Property* 2(6): 875–888.

Ostry, S. (1990) *Governments and Corporations in a Shrinking World: Trade and Innovation Policies in USA, Europe and Japan*, (USA: Council of Foreign Relations Press).

Ostry, S. (1997) *The Post Cold War Trading System: who's in first?* (Chicago: The University of Chicago Press).

Ostry, S. (2000) 'Looking Back to Look Forward: the Multilateral Trading System after Fifty Years' in WTO Secretariat (ed.) *From GATT to the WTO: the Multilateral Trading System in the New Millennium* (The Hague: Kluwer Law International and the WTO).

Otten, A. (1998) 'Implemenation of the TRIPs agreement and prospects for its further development' *Journal of International Economic Law* 1(4): 523–536.

Oyejide, T. A. (2000) 'Low-Income Developing Countries in the GATT/WTO Framework: the First Fifty Years and Beyond' in WTO Secretariat (ed.) *From GATT to the WTO: the Multilateral Trading System in the New Millennium* (The Hague: Kluwer Law International and the WTO).

Payne, A. J. (2006) *Key Debates in New Political Economy* (London: Routledge).

Penrose, E. T. (1951) *The Economics of the International System* (Baltimore, MD: John Hopkins Press).

PhRMA (1999) 'Industry Profile' Pharmaceutical Research and Manufacturers of America, Washington DC, USA www.phrma.org (home page) date accessed 10 March 2010.

PhRMA (2001) 'WTO Doha Declaration Reaffirms Value of Intellectual Property Protection' 14th November, Pharmaceutical Research and Manufacturers of America, Washington DC, USA www.phrma.org (home page) date accessed 10 March 2010.

PhRMA (2003) 'Pharmaceutical Industry Profile – New Medicines, New Hope Pharmaceutical' Research and Manufacturers of America, Washington DC, USA www.phrma.org (home page) date accessed 10 March 2010.

PhRMA (2005) 'Pharmaceutical Industry Profile 2005 – From Laboratory to Patient: Pathways to Biopharmaceutical Innovation' Pharmaceutical Research and Manufacturers of America, Washington DC, USA www.phrma.org (home page) date accessed 10 March 2010.

Porter, T. (1999) 'Hegemony and the Private Governance of International Industries' in A. C. Culter, V. Haufler and T. Porter (eds) *Private Authority and International Affairs* (Albany: State University of New York Press).

Public Citizen (2001) 'Rx R&D Myths: The Case Against the Drug Industry's R&D "Scare Card"', Washington DC, USA, http://www.citizen.org (home page) date accessed 17th August 2007.

Public Citizen (2002) 'Would Lower Prescription Drug Prices Curb Drug Company Research & Development?' Washington DC, USA, http://www.citizen.org (home page) date accessed 17th August 2007.

Pugatch, M. P. (2004a) *The International Political Economy of Intellectual Property Rights* (Cheltenham: Edward Elgar).

Pugatch, M. P. (2004b) 'Intellectual Property and Pharmaceutical Data Exclusivity in the Context of Innovation and Market Access' ICTSD-UNCTAD Dialogue on Ensuring Policy Options for Affordable Access to Essential Medicines Bellagio, Italy, http://wwwiprsonlineorg/unctadictsd/bellagio/docs/Pugatch_Bell agio3pdf, date accessed 28 August 2007.

Pugatch, M. P. (2007) 'A Transatlantic Divide: the US and EU's Approach to the International Regulation of Intellectual Property Trade-Related Agreements', ECIPE Working Paper No 02/2007, European Centre for International Political Economy, Brussels, Belgium.

Ramanna, A. (2002) 'India's Patent Policy and Negotiations in TRIPs: Future Options for India and other Developing Countries', National Conference on TRIPS – Next Agenda for Developing Countries, Shyamprasad Institute for Social Service, 11–12 October, Hyderabad, India. http://www.iprsonline.org/ictsd/docs/ResourcesTRIPSanita_ramannadoc, date accessed 13 August 2007.

Ramirez, P. and A. Tylecote (1999) 'Technological change in the pharmaceutical industry: A literature review from the point of view of corporate governance', COPI Report, Sheffield University, Report prepared for EC DGXII, Sheffield, UK.

Rapp, R. T. and R. P. Rozek (1990) 'Benefits and costs of intellectual property protection in developing countries' *Journal of World Trade* 24(5): 75–102.

Raustiala, K. (2007) 'Density and conflict in international intellectual property law' *UC Davis Law Review* 40: 1021–1038.

Raustiala, K. and Victor D. G. (2004) 'The regime complex for plant generic resources' *International Organization* 58(2): 277–309.

Reichman, J. H. (1997a) 'From free riders to fair followers: global competition under the TRIPs agreement' *New York University Journal of International Law and Politics* 29: 11–93.

Reichman, J. H. (1997b) 'Enforcing the enforcement procedures of the TRIPs agreement' *Virginia Journal of International Law* 37(2): 276–335.

Reichman, J. H. (1998) 'Securing Compliance with the TRIPs Agreement after US vs. India' *Journal of International Economic Law* 1(4): 585–601.

Reichman, J. H. (2000) 'The TRIPs agreement comes of age: conflict or cooperation with the developing countries?' *Case Western Reserve Journal of International Law* 32(44): 442–470.

Robinson, J. (1969) *The Accumulation of Capital* (London: MacMillan).

Roffe, P. and C. Spennemann (2006) 'The impact of FTAs on public health policies and TRIPs flexibilities' *International Journal of Property Management* 1(1–2): 75–93.

Roffe, P., C. Spennemann and J. von Braun (2006) 'From Paris to Doha: the WTO Doha Declaration on the TRIPs Agreement and Public Health' in P. Roffe, G. Tansey and D. Vivas-Eugui (eds) *Negotiating Health: Intellectual Property and Access to Medicines* (London, Earthscan).

Ruggie, J. G. (1982) 'International regimes, transactions, and change: embedded liberalism in the postwar economic order' *International Organization* 36(2): 379–415.

Ruggie, J. G. (1998) *Constructing the World Polity: Essays on International Institutionalization* (London: Routledge).

Ryan, M. P. (1998a) *Knowledge Diplomacy: Global Competition and the Politics of Intellectual Property* (Washington: Brooking Institution Press).

Ryan, M. P. (1998b) 'The function-specific and linkage-bargain diplomacy of international intellectual property lawmaking' *University of Pennsylvania Journal of International Economic Law* (Symposium: Linkage as Phenomenon – an Interdisciplinary Approach) 19 (Summer 1998): 353–370.

Santa-Cruz, M. (2007) 'Intellectual Property Provisions in European Union Trade Agreements: Implications for Developing Countries' International Centre for Trade and Sustainable Development (ICTSD), Issue Paper 20, Geneva, Switzerland.

Santoro, M. (1992) 'Pfizer: protecting intellectual property in the global marketplace' Harvard Business School, Case Study N9-392-072 (Cambridge, MA.: Harvard Business School).

Scherer, F. M. (1993) 'Pricing, profits and technological progress in the pharmaceutical industry' *The Journal of Economic Perspectives* 7(3): 97–115.

Scherer, F. M. (2000) *The Pharmaceutical Industry* (Amsterdam: Elsevier).

Scherer, F. M. (2001) 'The Innovation Lottery' in R. C. Dreyfuss, D. L. Zimmerman and H. First (eds) *Expanding the Boundaries of Intellectual Property: Innovation Policy for the Knowledge Society* (Oxford: Oxford University Press).

Scherer, F.M. and J. Watal (2001) 'Post-Trips Options for Access to Patented Medicines in Developing Countries' Commission on Macroeconomics and Health Working Paper Series, Paper No. WG4:1.

Schultz, M. and D. Walker (2005) 'How intellectual property became controversial: NGOs and the new international IP agenda' *Engage* 6(2): 82–98.

SCRIPT (2009) 'SCRIPT's Pharmaceutical Company League Tables', SCRIPT Reports, UK, www.scripnews.com (home page) date accessed 10 March 2010.

Sell, S. (1995) 'Intellectual property protection and antitrust in the developing world: crisis, coercion and choice' *International Organization* 49(2): 315–349.

Sell, S. (1999) 'Multinational Corporations as Agents of Change: the Globalization of Intellectual Property Rights' in A. C. Cutler, V. Haufler and T. Porter (eds) *Private Authority and International Affairs* (Albany: State University of New York Press).

Sell, S. (2002) 'TRIPs and the access to medicines campaign' *Wisconsin International Law Journal* 20 (Summer): 481–523.

Sell, S. (2003) *Private Power, Public Law: the Globalization of Intellectual Property Rights* (Cambridge: Cambridge University Press).

Sell, S. (2005) 'The Doha Development Agenda: Intellectual Property' Paper presented at Conference 'Endgame at the WTO: reflections on the Doha Development Agenda', 1–2 September 2005, University of Birmingham, UK.

Sell, S. (2006) 'Books, Drugs and Seeds: the Politics of Access', Paper presented at the Transatlantic Consumer Dialogue Conference, 'The Politics and Ideology of Intellectual Property', March 20–21, Brussels, Belgium.

Sell, S. (2007) 'TRIPs-plus free trade agreements and access to medicines' *Liverpool Law Review* 28: 41–75.

Sell, S. and A. Prakash (2004) 'Using ideas strategically: the contest between business and NGO networks in intellectual property rights' *International Studies Quarterly* 48: 143–175.

Shaffer, G. (2004) 'Recognising public goods in WTO dispute settlement: who participates? who decides? the case of TRIPs and pharmaceutical patent protection' *Journal of International Economic Law* 7(2): 459–482.

Shanker, D. (2002) 'Brazil, the pharmaceutical industry and the WTO' *Journal of World Intellectual Property* 5(1): 53–104.

Sidley, P. (2001) 'South African Court Battle Damages Drug Industry's Image' *British Medical Journal* 322(1287): 635.

Smith, E. (1996) Testimony of Eric Smith, President of the US International Intellectual Property Alliance, Committee on Ways and Means, US House of Representatives, Washington DC, USA.

Srinivasan, T. N. (1999) 'Developing Countries in the World Trading System: From GATT, 1947 to the Third Ministerial Meeting of WTO' High-level Symposium on Trade and Development, WTO, Geneva, Switzerland, Geneva Blackwell Publishers.

Strange, S. (1993) 'Big Business and the State' in L. Eden and E. Potter (eds) *Multinationals in the Global Political Economy* (London: MacMillan Press).

t'Hoen, E. (2002) 'TRIPS, pharmaceutical patents, and access to essential medicines: a long way from Seattle to Doha' *Chicago Journal of International Law* 3(1): 27–46.

TABD (1998) 'Charlotte statement of conclusions', Transatlantic Business Dialogue, 5–7 November, Charlotte, North Carolina, USA.

Tarabusi, C. C. and G. Vickery (1998) 'Globalisation in the pharmaceutical industry' *International Journal of Health Services* 28(1): 67–105.

Trebilcock, M. J. and R. Howse (eds) (2005) *The Regulation of International Trade* 3rd ed. (London: Routledge).

Türmen T and Clift C. (2006) 'Public health, innovation and intellectual property rights: unfinished business' *Bulletin of the World Health Organization* 84(5).

Tussie, D. and M. Lengyel (2002) 'Developing Country Participation versus Influence. Development' in Hoekman, B., A. Mattoo and P. English (eds) *Trade and the WTO: A Handbook* (Washington DC:, World Bank).

Tweedy, B. and M. Lesney (2000) 'Prescriptions and Polio: Postwar Progress' American Chemical Society Publications, http://pubsacsorg/journals/pharmcent/indexhtml date accessed 12 August 2007.

UK IPR Commission (2002) *Integrating Intellectual Property Rights and Development Policy* Final Report (London: UK Government Commission on Intellectual Property Rights).

UNAIDS (2008) Report on the Global AIDS Epidemic, available at http://www.unaids.org/en/KnowledgeCentre/HIVData/GlobalReport/2008/, date accessed 10 March 2010.

UNICE (1999) 'UNICE and the WTO Millennium Round', Union of Industrial and Employers' Confederations of Europe (UNICE), September 1999, Brussels, Belgium.

UNICE (2000) 'UNICE Comments on TRIPs in the Context of the Millennium Round, in Intellectual Property Rights', Compendium of UNICE Position Papers, Union of Industrial and Employers' Confederations of Europe (UNICE), January 2000, Brussels, Belgium.

US ITA (2004) 'Pharmaceutical Price Controls in OECD Countries: Implications for US Consumers, Pricing, Research and Development, and Innovation' US Department of Commerce, International Trade Administration, Washington DC. USA.

USTR (1998) 'Trade Policy Agenda and 1997 Annual Report of the President of the United States on the Trade Agreements Program', The United States Office of the Trade Representative, Washington DC, USA.

USTR (2001a) 'United States and Brazil agree to use newly created Consultative Mechanism to promote cooperation on HIV/AIDS and address WTO patent dispute', http://www.ustr.gov, (home page) date accessed 27 August 2007.

USTR (2001b) USTR Fact Sheet Summarising Results from WTO Doha Meeting, 14th November, Washington DC, http://www.ustr.gov, (home page) date accessed 27 August 2007.

Vandoren, P. (1999) 'The implementation of the TRIPs agreement' *Journal of World Intellectual Property* 2(1): 25–34.

Vandoren, P. (2001) 'The TRIPs agreement: a rising star?' *Journal of World Intellectual Property* 4(3): 307–322.

Vandoren, P. (2002) 'Medicaments sans frontiers? clarification of the relationship between TRIPs and public health resulting from the WTO Doha Ministerial Declaration' *Journal of World Intellectual Property* 5(1): 5–14.

Vandoren, P. and J. C. van Eeckhaute (2003) 'The WTO decision on Paragraph 6 of the Doha Declaration on the TRIPs agreement and public health' *Journal of World Intellectual Property* 6(6): 779–793.

Vandoren, P. and P. V. Martins (2006) 'The Enforcement of Intellectual Property Rights: an EU perspective of a Global Question' in M. P. Pugatch (ed.) *The Intellectual Property Debate: Perspectives from Law, Economics and Political Economy* (Cheltenham, UK: Edward Elgar).

Vaver, D. and S. Basheer (2006) 'Popping Patented Pills: Europe and a Decade's Dose of TRIPs', Legal Studies Research Paper Series: Working Paper No 25/2006, University of Oxford, Faculty of Law, Oxford, UK.

von Braun, J. and M. P. Pugatch (2005) 'The changing face of the pharmaceutical industry and intellectual property rights' *Journal of World Intellectual Property* 8(5): 599–623.

Watal, J. (2000) 'TRIPs and the 1999 WTO millennium round' *Journal of World Intellectual Property* 3(1): 3–29.

Watal, J. (2001) *Intellectual Property Rights in the WTO and Developing Countries* (The Hague: Kluwer Law International).

Weiss, T. G. and R. Thakur (2010) *Global Governance and the UN: an Unfinished Journey* (Bloomington: Indiana University Press).

Weissman, R. (1996) 'A long, strange TRIPS: the pharmaceutical industry drive to harmonize global intellectual property rules, and the remaining WTO legal alternatives available to Third World Countries' *University of Pennsylvania Journal of International Economic Law* 17: 1069–1124.

WHO (2004) *The World Medicines Situation*, available at http://apps.who.int/medicinedocs/en/d/Js6160e/7.html, accessed on 10 February 2009.

WHO (2005) 'Intellectual property protection: impact on public health' *WHO Drug Information* Vol. 19, No. 3, available at http://www.who.int/medicines/areas/policy/AccesstoMedicinesIPP.pdf, date accessed 10 February 2009.

WHO (2005) Essential Medicines List, http://www.who.int/medicines/services/essmedicines_def/en/ date accessed 13 November 2007.

Williams, D. (2002) 'Developing TRIPs jurisprudence: the first six years and beyond' *Journal of World Intellectual Property* 4(2): 177–209.

Winham, G. R. (1986) *International Trade and the Tokyo Round* (Princeton: Princeton University Press).

WIPO (2001) 'WIPO's Legal and Technical Assistance to Developing Countries for the Implementation of the TRIPs Agreement from 1 January 1996 to 31 December 2000' The World Intellectual Property Organisation (WIPO), Geneva, Switzerland.

Wogart, J. P. (2006) 'Multiple Interfaces of Big Pharma and the Changes of Global Health Governance in the Face of HIV/AIDS Transformation in the Process of Globalization', Paper no 24, German Institute of Global and Area Studies (GIGA), Hamburg, Germany.

World Bank (2002) 'Global Economic Prospects and the Developing Countries: Making Trade Work for the World's Poor', The World Bank, Washington DC, USA.

World Bank (2008) *World Bank Updates Poverty Estimates for the Developing World*, available at http://econ.worldbank.org/WBSITE/EXTERNAL/EXTDEC/EXTRESEARCH/0,,contentMDK:21882162~pagePK:64165401~piPK:64165026~theSitePK:469382,00.html, date accessed 10 February 2009.

WTO (2001) Doha Declaration on TRIPs and Public Health, WT/MTN(01)/DEC/W/2, WTO, Geneva, Switzerland.

WTO (2005) Hong Kong Ministerial Declaration, WT/MIN (05)/W/3/Rev2, Geneva, Switzerland.

WTO (2007) 'Dispute Settlement: Dispute DS 196, Argentina – Certain Measures on the Protection of Patents and Test Data', http://www.wto.org (home page) date accessed 28 August 2007.

Young, O. (1991) 'Political leadership and regime formation: on the development of institutions in international society' *International Organization* 45(3): 281–308.

Zoellick R. (2002) 'The Reigning Champions of Free Trade' *Financial Times*, 13th March 2002.

Index

access
  knowledge, to 12, 22, 23, 38, 61,
    122, 126, 137
  medicines, to *see* Intellectual
    property rights
Access Campaign *see* non-
  governmental organisations
Access to Knowledge Treaty 126
African Group, the 81–83, 91–95,
  103–107

Berne Convention on the Protection
  of Literary and Artistic Work
  (1886), the 43, 127

commons, the 2, 18, 19, 122
  see also public domain
compulsory licensing 81, 82, 91
  Doha Declaration, and 83, 86–88
  FTAs, in 113–116
  negotiations 44, 52, 56–57
  TRIPs amendment, and 13, 91–98,
    101, 126, 133–134
Consumer Project on Technology
  (CPTech) 76–78, 81–82, 90, 107
Convention on Biodiversity (CBD) 4,
  74, 119, 121
  see also Intellectual Property
    Rights (IPR); Trade-related
    Aspects of Intellectual Property
    Rights (TRIPs) Agreement
copyright(s) 3, 20, 43, 44–49, 51,
  53, 56
creativity 2, 17, 21–23, 39, 116, 137
  see also innovation

data exclusivity 69–71, 78, 113–117
disease(s)
  coverage in the TRIPs
    amendment 88–101, 134
  infectious 79, 95
  neglected 28–29, 98, 120

Doha Declaration on the TRIPs
  Agreement and Public Health,
  the 13, 84, 88, 109, 126,
  135–137
  adoption, of 81–84
  interpretation 84, 116
  paragraph 1, of 94–96
  paragraph 6, of 87, 97
  reactions, to 85–86, 89
  relation to FTAs 115–116
  relation to WTO August 2003
    Decision 103, 107
  text 84, 86, 87, 100
drug(s)
  access, to 4–5, 31–36, 76, 78–79,
    82–83, 85–87, 95, 116, 119, 130
  development cost 26–28, 81
  discovery 24–26
  generic 30, 33, 35–36, 69–70, 83,
    88–89, 99, 114–118
  'me-too' 29–30
  prices 4, 30–33, 76, 80, 85, 119,
    130, 135
  reverse engineering 24, 35, 43, 88
  see also pharmaceuticals

EC Trade Commissioner 77, 118
education 2, 4–5, 39, 44, 62, 120,
  126, 128
European Federation of
  Pharmaceutical Industries and
  Associations (EFPIA) 69, 74, 78

food security 4, 13, 75, 125
'forum-shifting' 75, 119, 123, 128,
  132, 135–136
Free Trade Agreements (FTAs) 4, 65,
  71–72, 110–119, 123, 133

GATT
  Counterfeiting Code 44, 46
  Uruguay Round 38, 48–58, 62